WITHDRAWN

PLAIN TRUTH:

OR,

SERIOUS CONSIDERATIONS

On the PRESENT STATE of the

CITY of PHILADELPHIA,

AND

PROVINCE of PENNSYLVANIA.

By a TRADESMAN of *Philadelphia.*

---

*Capta urbe, nihil fit reliqui victis. Sed, per Deos immortales, vos
ego appello, qui semper domos, villas, signa, tabulas vestras, tan-
tæ æstimationis fecistis ; si ista, cujuscunque modi sint, quæ am-
plexamini; retinere, si voluptatibus vestris otium præbere vultis ;
expergiscimini aliquando, & capessite rempublicam. Non agitur
nunc de sociorum injuriis ; LIBERTAS & ANIMA nostra in du-
bio est. Dux hostium cum exercitu supra caput est. Vos cunctamini
etiam nunc, & dubitatis quid faciatis ? Scilicet, res ipsa asperu
est, sed vos non timetis eam. Imo vero maxume ; sed inertia &
mollitia animi, alius alium exspectantes, cunctamini ; videlicet,
Diis immortalibus confisi, qui hanc rempublicam in maximis peri-
culis servavere. NON VOTIS, NEQUE SUPPLICIIS MULIE-
BRIBUS, AUXILIA DEORUM PARANTUR : vigilando, agen-
do, bene consulendo, prospere omnia cedunt. Ubi socordiæ tete at-
que ignaviæ tradideris, nequicquam Deos implores ; irati, infesti-
que sunt.* M. POR. CAT. in SALUST.

Printed in the YEAR MDCCXLVII.

A Sweet Instruction

Franklin's Journalism as a Literary Apprenticeship

On every Thorn delightful Wisdom grows,
In every Rill a sweet Instruction flows.
Poor Richard, November 1747

By

James A. Sappenfield

Foreword by

Howard Rusk Long

SOUTHERN ILLINOIS UNIVERSITY PRESS
Carbondale and Edwardsville
Feffer & Simons, Inc.
London and Amsterdam

Library of Congress Cataloging in Publication Data

Sappenfield, James A   1940–
    A sweet instruction.

    (New horizons in journalism)
    Includes bibliographical references.
    1. Franklin, Benjamin, 1706–1790. I. Title.
E302.6.F8S33   808   73–7808
ISBN 0–8093–0610–7

For Max and Elizabeth Sappenfield

206805

Contents

Foreword

Imagine, if you will, Benjamin Franklin, not as a product of the eighteenth century, but as one destined to live in our own times. Born in the first decade of our century (instead of in 1709) he would have been too young for World War I; old enough to share the frustrations of American youths held back by the economic sterility of the Great Depression; virile enough to respond to the belated challenges of World War II; versatile enough to work his way into the vanguard of a dozen endeavors of the dynamic fifties and sixties, and flexible enough to adjust his stance to the changing demands of today and to the tomorrows yet to come.

Instead of the journey to London to polish his trade, young Franklin might have sought to improve himself by working his way through the University of Missouri. Here he would have been at home among the high school graduates of the Eastern Seaboard, attracted by the low fees and modest living costs in the state universities of the Middle West, and the bright young people from all the states drawn there by the golden image of Walter Williams and his school of journalism. Undoubtedly, Franklin would have felt at ease among the more creative of his peers and the less preoccupied of his professors. He would have scorned social fraternities, perhaps to the extent of leading a "barbarian" revolt to wrest student government from the control of the Greek letter caucus. Certainly

in the scramble for good assignments on the laboratory newspaper he would have emerged with the best. His honors would
have been many, including the supreme accolade, an invitation
to serve the great Walter Williams as student assistant in
charge of grading term reports and the examination papers
of other undergraduates. Moreover, unlike others of the class
of 1930, who survived on odd jobs until the birth of WPA,
he would have obtained a position of sorts on an important
newspaper.

Whether or not Franklin would have worked his way into
a dominant place in American journalism hardly is to be
doubted. Editorships, proprietorship of a publishing empire,
influence in business and political circles with a voice in Washington and a seat at the table when world leaders meet, is to be
assumed. The real question is whether or not Franklin's genius,
in our socioeconomic environment, could produce writings
worthy of literary analysis two hundred years after their publication.

Professor Sappenfield, at some time, may or may not have
given his attention to this question. Certainly he has not addressed himself to such speculation in this volume. Nevertheless, in this examination of the development of a style that
reached its perfection in the *Autobiography,* Franklin, a child
of adversity, is shown as utilizing every opportunity in a long
and busy life to perfect his skills of authorship. Consciously,
even self-consciously, the youthful Franklin, who created Silence Dogood as the spokesman for a boy reckoned unfit to
address his elders, borrowed the gifts and the mannerisms of
great men who used the printed page to discuss the issues confronted by them in London. But even at this stage, Franklin's
own creativity is evident. At other times, under the pressure of
his work and the need to adapt effectively to a new audience,
he seemed to depend upon intuition, or at least insights in the
process of developing his art.

For one who identifies with the world of journalism, Franklin's way of projecting himself through the development of such roles as Silence Dogood, Richard Saunders and the many other personalities of his pages, synthetic or real, suggests a rare ability to recognize what social scientists of a later century have defined as the "communication process." Franklin as the communicator felt the need to find the means by which to gain the confidence of his reader. What better device could he use than the creation of a universe of discourse, the common ground of shared interest?

Compared with two other important propagandists of the Revolution, Samuel Adams and Thomas Paine, Franklin, for the long haul, was much more effective. Adams the great organizer, controlled the mobs in Boston and sustained a running attack throughout the colonies against the British by means of his letters to the newspapers. But he was destroyed by his own contentious personality long before the need for his services was ended. Paine, who wrote so effectively the emotional appeals in behalf of the Revolution, remained an unrevealed shadow rather than a popular personality. Franklin, on the other hand, hid his youth, when necessary, behind the skirts of a fictional widow, assumed the identity of a humble tradesman in order to establish and hold credibility with the people who made up the popular audience for his *Almanac,* then as the editor of his own newspaper shifted roles rapidly and skillfully as he sought rapport with the diverse groups who make up the readership of a newspaper of general circulation. Once established as a public figure in his own right, Franklin, as Professor Sappenfield relates, then further perfected his skills as a communicator by adapting his personality to the stereotyped image built up by his reputation. Franklin the editor certainly was ahead of his times for these are skills infrequently understood and seldom mastered even in today's manipulated society.

Professor Sappenfield's analysis also underlines Benjamin Franklin's contributions to the development of humor and satire as important tools of the newspaper editor. The printers of his time, at least in print, were a humorless lot and the people who wrote tracts about the issues of the day took themselves too seriously to employ whatever wit they had. Yet Franklin never feared to turn a joke upon himself, never hesitated to employ innuendo, or even to resort to slapstick if it served his purpose. By no means alone as a progenitor of the newspaper humor so popular in the later history of American journalism, Franklin's contribution, nevertheless, persisted almost to the end of the next century and still is identifiable by those willing to make the effort.

Benjamin Franklin of the *Autobiography* may have been as capable of adjusting to our century as he was to his own. His literary style is relevant. The manner and the circumstances under which he perfected his art tells us that for a genius there are no obstacles too great to be surmounted. In fact, for all the frustrated artists covering the banquet circuit, and those writing singing commercials, his message is that nothing destroys genius except lack of genius. And for the men in public life, the lesson to be learned from Benjamin Franklin is that the work of their ghost writers will not keep them alive two hundred years from now.

HOWARD RUSK LONG

Southern Illinois University
January 17, 1973

Acknowledgments

I am grateful to the Research Committee of the Graduate School, the University of Wisconsin—Milwaukee, for summer grants in 1968 and 1970, which support enabled me to write this book. The Wisconsin Council of Teachers of English has allowed me to reprint portions of Chapter 5 from *Wisconsin Studies in Literature*. Professors Ralph M. Aderman and Thomas J. Bontly read the manuscript and offered warm encouragement and valuable advice. Mrs. Linda Ripple was an accurate and cheerful typist.

I am deeply indebted to Professor David Levin, Stanford University, who has tried to instill in his students the appreciation of historical literature and respect for the historian's art. His influence will be found wherever this book succeeds. To Professor Howard Rusk Long and to my wife—whose task it was to keep me in front of the typewriter—my thanks for their confidence in the book and the author.

A Sweet Instruction

Franklin's Journalism as a Literary Apprenticeship

ONE

Franklin's Journalism

If you would not be forgotten
As soon as you are dead and rotten,
Either write things worth reading,
Or do things worth the writing.
Poor Richard, 1738

ERNEST HEMINGWAY, as the critical cliché goes, learned his lean, muscular prose style as a reporter on the Kansas City *Star.* That other founder of literary modernism, Walt Whitman, is said to have developed his feeling for music and his heightened sensitivity to the American panorama from covering opera and politics for the Brooklyn *Eagle,* the *Freeman,* the New Orleans *Crescent.* Among America's writers of the first and second ranks, a striking number were onetime, part-time, or full-time journalists: Philip Freneau, William Cullen Bryant, E. A. Poe, Mark Twain, William Dean Howells, Stephen Crane, as well as Whitman and Hemingway. The first and certainly most celebrated of America's journalist-authors was Benjamin Franklin. Franklin was, of course, a multifaceted genius; history remembers him principally for his service to his country and his achievements in science. Yet his impact on history has been greater for his writings than for either his diplomacy or his physics. Other philosophers would soon have derived a workable "single fluid" theory of electricity, explained the condenser, "snatched lightning from the heavens," if Franklin had not. Other diplomats could have served ably, if less colorfully, at the court of Louis XVI. But only Franklin could have written his memoirs (we call them his *Autobiography*) and "The Way to Wealth" —the latter a piece of humble journalism. And in his own mind Franklin was first and last a journalist—or more precisely a "printer." In eighteenth-century America a printer was also customarily the editor of a newspaper, publisher of almanacs, tracts, and sermons, pirate publisher of British books, stationer, job printer, bookseller, and often postmaster. Benjamin Franklin was a printer who knew how to write; in his mind, writing was part of the printing trade—fundamentally neither more nor less important than composing or presswork. That the special demands of Franklin's journalistic career were the foundations of his masterpiece, is the thesis of this book.

This masterpiece, Franklin's memoirs, is generally acknowledged to have been the first classic of American literature. But the book is more than simply a classic. It is a seminal document in American cultural history. It is not merely the life story of an American; somehow it has seemed an account of the essential American life. Americans and Europeans alike have taken Franklin's memoirs as the definitive statement of the nature and quality of the American experience. Commentators who have sought to glorify the American spirit have found the warrant for so doing in Franklin's *Autobiography*. So too have critics of the American character taken their text from Benjamin Franklin. D. H. Lawrence, in a vitriolic attack, styled Franklin "the pattern American" and "the first down-right American." [1] Herman Melville, a writer deeply troubled about American ideals and American reality, found Benjamin Franklin to be "the type and genius of his land." [2] Nor was this remarkable quality of his memoirs lost upon the first readers of the manuscript. The vicissitudes of the American Revolution had placed some of Franklin's papers in the hands of a

Quaker merchant, Abel James, who wrote to Franklin at Paris in about 1782. He sent Franklin his outline, which accompanied the manuscript, urging him to finish his biography without delay, for "Life is uncertain as the Preacher tells us, and what will the World say if kind, humane and benevolent Ben Franklin should leave his Friends and the World deprived of so pleasing and profitable a Work, a Work which would be useful and entertaining not only to a few, but to millions." [3] James went on,

> The Influence of Writings under that Class have on the Minds of Youth is very great, and has no where appeared so plain as in our public Friend's Journal. It almost insensibly leads the Youth into the Resolution of endeavouring to become as good and as eminent as the Journalist. . . . I know of no Character living nor many of them put together, who has so much in his Power as Thyself to promote a greater Spirit of Industry and early Attention to Business, Frugality and Temperance with the American Youth. Not that I think the Work would have no other Merit and Use in the World, far from it, but the first is of such vast Importance, that I know nothing that can equal it.

Franklin solicited the advice of his friend, the British publisher Benjamin Vaughan, who wrote at greater length, but to the same purpose. "All that has happened to you is also connected with the detail of the manners and situation of *a rising* people; and in this respect I do not think that the writings of Caesar and Tacitus can be more interesting to a true judge of human nature and society."

Franklin has loomed large among the legendary figures in American history, and his *Autobiography* has seemed central to American mythology. Though himself a product of the Puritan ethos of Christian calling and stewardship, Franklin has been taken as the inventor and principal tomtom-beater of American self-education and self-help. At least one of the great American fortunes was founded upon his principles. Andrew Mellon regarded "the reading of Franklin's 'Autobiography' as the turning point in my life." [4] Mellon added, "For so poor and friendless a boy to be able to become a merchant or a professional man had before seemed an impossibility; but here was Franklin, poorer than myself, who by industry, thrift and frugality had become learned and wise, and elevated to wealth and fame." We have Mellon's testimony of the direct influence of Benjamin Franklin, but we have no way of knowing how many other millionaires (not to speak of spectacular failures) answered the clarion call of his *Autobiography*. Throughout the nineteenth century, the cult of self-help spawned an entire genre of tracts, manuals, and storybooks. Horatio Alger's books were only the most famous. But the widely disseminated formula was Franklin's, and Franklin's *Autobiography* seemed to provide the "living" proof of its magical properties.[5]

Among the doubters of this magic was Mark Twain, a speculator singed in the Great Barbecue. In a "memoir" of 1870, Twain sought to put Franklin in his proper place:

> Benjamin Franklin did a great many notable things for his country, and made her young name to be honored in many lands as the mother of such a son. It is not the idea of this memoir to ignore that or cover it up. No; the simple idea of it is to snub those pretentious maxims of his, which he worked up with a great show of originality out of truisms that had become wearisome platitudes as early as the dispersion from Babel; and also to snub his stove, and his military inspirations, his unseemly endeavor to make himself conspicuous when he entered Philadelphia, and his flying his kite and fooling away his time in all sorts of such ways when he ought to have been foraging for soap-fat, or constructing candles. I merely desired to do away with somewhat of the prevalent calamitous idea among heads of families that Franklin *acquired* his great genius by working for nothing, studying by moonlight, and getting up in the night instead of waiting till morning like a Christian; and that this program, rigidly inflicted, will make a Franklin of every father's fool. It is time these gentlemen were finding out that these execrable eccentricities of instinct and conduct are only the *evidences* of

genius, not the *creators* of it. I wish I had been the father of my parents long enough to make them comprehend this truth, and thus prepare them to let their son have an easier time of it. When I was a child I had to boil soap, notwithstanding my father was wealthy, and I had to get up early and study geometry at breakfast, and peddle my own poetry, and do everything just as Franklin did, in the solemn hope that I would be a Franklin some day. And here I am.[6]

Twain's little essay is interesting in several ways. Though he treats Franklin satirically, as a person "of a vicious disposition" and "full of animosity toward boys," Twain does arrive at the essential fact of Franklin's life and experience: that he succeeded more because he was a genius than because he studied "algebra by a smoldering fire." Twain also showed himself entirely typical of commentators on Franklin, in that he has read —or seems to have read—only two of Franklin's works, the *Autobiography* and "The Way to Wealth." And he read neither with sympathy nor enthusiasm; although of course he had his reasons to be resentful. D. H. Lawrence appears to have based his analysis entirely upon the same two works, and probably Melville his.

F. Scott Fitzgerald's greatest fictional creation, Jay Gatsby, was another embodiment of Franklinian failure. Gatsby was a self-made man, one indeed who "sprang from his Platonic conception of himself." [7] Juxtaposing two great figures of the American myth, the self-made man and the cowboy, Fitzgerald makes the young boy, who became the Great Gatsby, inscribe schedules of his day's activity and tables of Franklinian resolves ("Study electricity, etc. . . . Study needed inventions") on the flyleaf of a novel entitled *Hopalong Cassidy* (p. 174). Yet for Fitzgerald's narrator, "Gatsby turned out all right at the end"; for Fitzgerald admired his hero's Franklinian "heightened sensitivity to the promises of life" (p. 2), "an extraordinary gift for hope" which Fitzgerald associated with the American continent itself. He concluded the novel with a revery on Long Island, seeing it as it had "flowered once for Dutch sailors' eyes—a fresh green breast of the new world. Its vanished trees, the trees that had made way for Gatsby's house, had once pandered to the last and greatest of all human dreams; for a transitory enchanted moment man must have held his breath in the presence of this continent, compelled into an aesthetic contemplation he neither understood nor desired, face to face for the last time in history with something commensurate to his capacity for wonder" (p. 182).

Scott Fitzgerald was perhaps the first serious, and critical, commentator of the Franklinian strain in American life to identify it with hope or wonder, or indeed with any emotion at all. To D. H. Lawrence, Franklin seemed soulless and mechanical; Lawrence compared Franklin's scheme for the perfectibility of man to "the perfectibility of the Ford car." Melville had the same flaw in mind when he surveyed Benjamin Franklin's manifold accomplishments and concluded, "Franklin was everything but a poet." Literary historian Charles Angoff, in another memorable denunciation of Franklin, has written that the popularity of Franklin and particularly of *Poor Richard's Almanac* "was probably a colossal misfortune to the United States, for despite his good fellowship and occasional good sense, Franklin represented the least praiseworthy qualities of the inhabitants of the New World: miserliness, fanatical practicality, and lack of interest in what are usually known as spiritual things." [8] Paul Elmer More put the same objection less splenetically: "In the end, one feels that both in Franklin's strength and his limitations, in the versatility and efficiency of his intellect as in the lack of the deeper qualities of the imagination, he was the typical American." [9] Franklin, then, embodies the spirit that made America great, while at the same time personifying the nation's fundamental mediocrity of spirit. This is perhaps not paradoxical, though it may seem so. It is certainly testimony to the complexity and richness of Franklin's character as he transmitted it to his posterity.

For Franklin's character is largely self-created. Benjamin Vaughan advised Franklin to finish his memoirs, because "Your history is so remarkable, that if you do not give it, somebody else will certainly give it; and perhaps so as nearly to do as much harm, as your own management of the thing might do good." Unlike George Washington, for example, who was turned to marble under the reverent hands of his biographers, Franklin remains alive in his own words. Nor has this been lost on thoughtful commentators. Visiting the Louvre on an inclement day in January 1858, Nathaniel Hawthorne chanced upon two miniatures of Benjamin Franklin—"both good and picturesque," he wrote in his notebook. Pondering one of the tiny images with its "cloud-like white hair," Hawthorne reflected, "I do not think we have produced a man so interesting to contemplate, in many points of view, as he. Most of our great men are of a character that I find it impossible to warm into life by thought, or by lavishing any amount of sympathy upon them. Not so Franklin, who had a great deal of common and uncommon nature in him." [10]

Franklin's literary achievement is perhaps unique in American letters. As William B. Cairns, a literary historian typical of the early twentieth century, wrote of Franklin's *Autobiography,* "It is the first book written in America which an American to day need hesitate to say he has not read." [11] In this book we shall examine the evolution of Franklin's skill as a writer —his apprenticeship for the masterpiece that would shape America's concept of itself. Like the apprenticeship of John Milton before him, Franklin's was a long period of preparation stretching from the second to the sixth decade of the eighteenth century. Like Milton, Franklin served much of his apprenticeship in the heat of controversy. And though Franklin was almost invariably an occasional writer, he was a self-conscious, careful, and methodical one. We shall discuss his theory of the nature and function of writing later on in this chapter.

Virtually everything Benjamin Franklin wrote during the forty or so years of his journalistic career is somehow relevant to the *Autobiography*. As everyone knows, Franklin was a prudent man. "Dost thou love Life," he wrote, "then do not squander Time, for that's the Stuff Life is made of." And as everyone knows, Franklin was an experimenter: "This is the Age of Experiments," he observed in his memoirs. Franklin did not waste the time he spent with a pen in his hand, nor did he squander the results of his experiments in writing. As we shall see, he was fundamentally a rhetorician; he studied the art of persuasion. When he happened upon a method, a technique, a device, that worked to disarm his reader's skepticism or tricked his reader into acquiescence or humored him into agreement—that device was installed in Franklin's workshop to be used over and over and never lost. For as Poor Richard said, "the used Key is always bright." Likewise, Franklin seems to have noted and subsequently avoided techniques of suasion that did not work. Franklin taught himself to write creditably before he was twenty, but he did not put the capstone on his skill until the 1750s. Only then did he find the voice that would do—more than a decade later—to narrate the events of his own life.

Franklin put no great emphasis upon originality. His times did not; it was for artists of a later generation to concern themselves with imagination. Benjamin Franklin had it, of course, but he took no special pride in it. As the work of earlier scholars has amply proven, he borrowed from Addison and Defoe, especially from Swift, and from countless others. His imagination, his own special gift—we may suppose—enabled him to transform everything he borrowed into something of his own. Often he improved what he borrowed, as for example, many of Poor Richard's proverbs. Always he adapted it so cleverly to his own purposes, situation, or readership that he enhanced its effectiveness.

The *Autobiography* was the only book Franklin ever wrote, though he evidently planned others he was too busy to write. In fact, his memoirs remain unfinished, carrying the narrative of his life only into the late 1750s. It may seem curious that he learned how to write a book by writing essays, sketches, and pamphlets of a few lines to a few pages in length. Particularly curious when we discover that the success of the *Autobiography* as rhetoric depends largely upon its structure as a whole. Critics and scholars puzzled over this for a long time. So brilliant are Franklin's sentences that it was assumed the work's excellence resided there. Historian William B. Cairns wrote, "The qualities which have made the *Autobiography* one of the few American classics are its simplicity of style and the frankness and openness with which the author reveals his personality. Few books can charm readers of all ages and all temperaments; Franklin's *Autobiography* comes very near doing this." Richard E. Amacher surveyed the "many strained efforts" of critics to describe Franklin's style, and he offered this collection:

> One calls it "bold and joyous"; another, "almost matter-of-fact." One thinks it "simple and charming"; one characterizes it as "inimitable." It is above all a *clear* style, Nye insists; but he uses many other epithets to describe it—vivid, economical, uncluttered, plain, easy, graceful, forceful, flexible, charming, sensible, honest, witty, and orderly. Finally he quotes Franklin's own statement to the effect that the norm of style in writing should be that of informed and intelligent conversation. Another critic states that the style is clear and vigorous and "moves forward easily and rapidly." Yet another calls it limpid and racy.[12]

Amacher held to last the chef d'oeuvre of stylistic criticism, a description by Franklin's nineteenth-century biographer, John Bigelow. The *Autobiography,* said Bigelow, is a "limpid narrative, gemmed all over, like a cloudless firmament at night, with anecdotes, curious observations, and sage reflections." It to avoid a morass in which so many have been lost, ..c in fact, prose style is not the key to the *Autobiography*'s rhetorical success. Like the fine shell carving on a stout Chippendale desk, Franklin's prose adds only ornament to structural soundness. The persuasiveness of the book is owing to the structure of the fable itself. Franklin had never before attempted to erect a large rhetorical structure, but confronted with the problem he selected voices, modes of characterization, and episodic patterns which had succeeded in the past. The structure he devised for his memoirs is a masterpiece of deceptive simplicity and economy. The final chapter of this book presents a detailed account of that structure.

2

Franklin's practice as a journalist was a sort of amalgam of eighteenth-century journalism in the English-speaking world. The makeup of his own Philadelphia paper, the *Pennsylvania Gazette* was not significantly different from that of other colonial newspapers. It contained old foreign news, state papers, commercial intelligence, and some advertisements. Like some other colonial editors, Franklin made an attempt to cover local stories: fires, drownings, murders, and suicides. It was in the choice and presentation of local news that colonial journalists typically displayed such flair and wit as they could command. But to his wry accounts of bizarre accidents and domestic tragedies, Franklin occasionally added pieces of entertainment and instruction; and it is for this reason that students of American letters remember the *Gazette*. Franklin himself devised the formula for spicing his weekly with hoaxes and moral essays, but the formula owed much to James Franklin's journalistic experiment, the *New-England Courant,* and to Benjamin's experience as apprentice in James's Boston shop. The *Courant* and Benjamin Franklin's writings for it are the subject of Chapter 2 of this book; it is enough to say here

that the *Courant* was the first self-consciously literary periodical in America, and that its failure was partially owing to a
lack of wit and partially to the lack of a market. The English
colonies were not ready for an American *Spectator,* but James
Franklin had proved that there were readers who appreciated
wit and sense. And his younger brother was not the only
printer in the colonies to realize that literary materials might
be introduced into the conventional colonial newspaper to enhance its commercial appeal. In 1727, shortly after the demise
of James Franklin's *Courant,* another Boston printer by the
name of Samuel Kneeland began the publication of the *New-
England Weekly Journal.* Quite independently of each other
Kneeland and Benjamin Franklin had derived the same lesson
from the unlucky *New-England Courant.* Kneeland enlisted
the pens of Cotton Mather's nephew, the Reverend Mather
Byles, the Reverend Thomas Prince of the Old South Church,
and even of Governor Burnet.[13] Some of Kneeland's contributors may have been the very same Harvard wits (James
Franklin called them "young, scribbling collegians") who defended the Massachusetts establishment against Silence Dogood and the *Courant,* and who wrote exultant elegies on the
death of Franklin's paper. The *New-England Weekly Journal*
blended news and features and survived until 1741 when its
publishers bought the old *Boston Gazette* and combined the
two papers into the *Boston Gazette and Weekly Journal.*
Kneeland apparently could not write himself, and when his
contributors' stocks of wit were exhausted after two or three
years, he turned to reprinting English materials.

Benjamin Franklin was more fortunate. He was already a
good writer and he loved writing. Philadelphia was deficient
in learned divines, and did not have even the equivalent of
James Franklin's Hell-Fire Club of irreverent modern wits.
Franklin himself was obliged to supply most of the pieces of
entertainment and instruction for his publications, but he was
equal to the task. The sort of writing that Franklin enjoyed

most, that which he did for his own amusement, was the sort found in the *Spectator* and the other British literary periodicals. These publications were James Franklin's inspiration for the *Courant* as well, and Benjamin had cut his teeth on the *Spectator*-style letters of Silence Dogood written for his brother's paper.

The elegant and successful *Spectator* was, of course, the work principally of two hands: Joseph Addison and Richard Steele. Its immediate predecessor, the *Tatler*, was Steele's project, though like the *Spectator* it had many and distinguished contributors. In the planning of the *Tatler* Steele was evidently conscious of several and varied antecedents to the periodical essay. Walter Graham writes,

> Steele was a good journalist. He gave his readers what he knew they liked to read. It is reasonable to believe that before entering upon this new enterprise he made himself intimately acquainted with all the methods and devices of Motteux, Dunton, Defoe, and others of his more successful predecessors. Moreover, there could have been no uncertainty in his mind as to the tone of his publication or the kind of matter that should fill his columns. La Crose, Dunton, and Defoe had popularized reform. Manners and morals, matters of human conduct and social relations, had long been the subjects of discussion by writers of periodicals. For example, the genial observations of Steele regarding the worth of family ties and the delights of conjugal felicity find certain anticipation in the *Ladies Mercury* of 1694 and the *Memoirs for the Curious* of 1701. In its subject matter, the *Tatler* shows constantly the influence of Ned Ward's wit and comment on London life, the reforming urge of Dunton, Defoe, and Tutchin, Motteux's miscellaneous entertainment, and the increasing tendency to comment on books and writers illustrated in the *History of Learning,* 1691, the *Compleat Library,* 1692, and the *Monthly Miscellany* of 1707–8. In short, it may be said that everything in the evolution of the literary periodical in England leads up to the *Tatler*.[14]

John Dunton's *Athenian Mercury* (originally the *Athenian Gazette, or Casuistical Mercury*), which first appeared in

1691, offered to answer queries from its readers. The work of three or four men, it pretended to be a publication of a populous club, the "Athenian Society"; and its writers addressed themselves to a range of questions, scientific and moral: "Whether or no fishes think? Which is greater, the hurt or profit that cometh of love? Whether negroes shall rise at the last day?" Steele frequently used letters from his readers in his issues of the *Spectator,* and he was not the first of the journalists accused "of first Writing Letters to themselves, and then answering them in Print." [15] It is generally assumed that Benjamin Franklin wrote most of the letters addressed to the editor of the *Pennsylvania Gazette,* but this may not be true. In 1725, Charles Lillie issued, with Steele's permission, two volumes of unused letters to the *Spectator.* In any event, Dunton's *Athenian Mercury* provided two devices which survived to the heyday of the literary periodicals: authorship by an imaginary club and correspondence between the editor and his readers. Edward Ward's *London Spy* (1698–1700) introduced the motif of a peripatetic observer of manners and morals. Steele used it and passed it to Franklin, who employed it in the Busy-Body, and combined it with the device of the imaginary correspondent in the Dogood Papers and on numerous other occasions. The *Weekly Comedy* ("as it is dayly acted at most coffee-houses in London") ran ten numbers between May and July of 1699. It may have been written by Ward also, and is memorable for the tag-names of its dramatis personae: "Squabble, a lawyer; Whim, a projector; Prim, a beau," among others. Ward's stock in trade was "filth and ribaldry" [16] and the several variations of the *Weekly Comedy* which appeared between 1699 and 1708 were all short lived. Daniel Defoe's *Weekly Review,* begun in February 1704, drew upon Dunton's device of answers from a group of writers: "Advice from the Scandal Club."

Steele invented a club of five men for the *Tatler.* Besides the author and an anonymous bencher at the Trumpet in

Sheer-Lane, the group included Sir Geoffrey Notch, Major Matchlock, and Dick Reptile. This circle of "heavy, honest men" anticipated the circle of characters in the *Spectator* which included Sir Roger de Coverley, Captain Sentry, Sir Andrew Freeport, and Will Honeycomb. Benjamin Franklin never employed the device of an imaginary coterie of characters, but he formed a real-life club for mutual entertainment and improvement, that is, the Junto of Philadelphia.

This is not to say that Franklin naïvely transferred fiction into real life, as the lad who grew up to be the Great Gatsby tried to do. But it is interesting that the creation of imaginary characters and correspondents was so congenial to Franklin's imagination. It was a mode of writing ideally suited to prepare him for the composition of his materpiece, but for Franklin it was more than that. Something in Benjamin Franklin's nature embraced the device he found in the *Spectator* of inventing fanciful masks and voices. It was a clever technique invented by journalists long before Steele, and Franklin used it with great skill and sensitivity. But this device he did not confine to his journalism, nor even to his memoirs—the climax of his journalistic career. Franklin transferred the device to real life. His greatest achievement in real-life masquerade was the image of fur-hatted American rusticity which he projected in the glittering French court during the American Revolution. Franklin's name was virtually a household word in France before he arrived. He was famous as the physicist whose lightning experiment had first been performed by French philosophers and as the author of *La Science du Bonhomme Richard*. The French expected to find him the embodiment of natural reason, a kind of white noble savage, a homely "Quackeur" sage. Franklin was neither a Quaker nor a rustic, but he altered his cosmopolitan manners and dress to match French expectations, and they lionized him. Unquestionably the role that Franklin played in France was useful to him and to the American cause, but its utility was scarcely all that recommended it to him. It is clear that he played the role with great relish. As he himself observed, "So convenient a thing it is to be a *reasonable Creature,* since it enables one to find or make a Reason for every thing one has a mind to do." [17] In the *Autobiography* Franklin did rationalize his habit of public masquerade. The difficulty he encountered in soliciting funds for his first public project, the Philadelphia subscription library, made him "soon feel the Impropriety of presenting one's self as the Proposer of any useful Project that might be suppos'd to raise one's Reputation in the smallest degree above that of one's Neighbours, when one has need of their Assistance to accomplish that Project. I therefore put my self as much as I could out of sight, and stated it as a Scheme of a *Number of Friends,* who had requested me to go about and propose it to such as they thought Lovers of Reading. In this way my Affair went on more smoothly, and I ever after practis'd it on such Occasions; and from my frequent Successes, can heartily recommend it" (*Autobiography,* p. 143). Again, describing his campaign to establish the Pennsylvania Academy, Franklin presented his proposals "not as an Act of mine, but of some *publick-spirited Gentlemen;* avoiding as much as I could, according to my usual Rule, the presenting myself as the Author of any Scheme for [the public's] Benefit" (*Autobiography,* p. 193). Franklin's "usual Rule" made him seem sinister and devious to those inclined to oppose his beneficent projects. In 1740, an attacker writing in a rival newspaper complained that Franklin was "never at a Loss for something to say, nor for some Body to say it for you, when you don't care to appear yourself." [18] We need not arrive at a final moral judgment of Benjamin Franklin, nor for that matter a judgment about his psychic health. We need, however, to note this impulse of his to play roles—in his writings and in real life. The canny Melville recognized this tendency and in the novel *Israel Potter,* in which Franklin appears, Melville made his Franklin a character of several guises, protean in his shifts of voice and manner. For Franklin then, the popular journalistic device of employing masks or personae was a form which allowed him to indulge his natural bent. As we survey his career we shall find him using his journalistic masks sometimes for his own amusement and that of his readers, sometimes to engage rivals in mock-serious controversies, sometimes in quarrels of deadly seriousness, sometimes to inform or persuade his readers of the utility or importance of one of his projects.

Whatever the particular application of a journalistic mask, the habitual use of them by Benjamin Franklin was the key to his development as a writer. We know that, whether consciously or not, every writer adopts a mask or pose or attitude when he begins to write. But Franklin was acutely conscious of the process. His impulse in writing, like his impulse in projecting, was to get his job of persuading done. As in the case of his projects, he usually decided to invent someone to speak for him rather than appearing himself. Franklin rationalized this journalistic device as well, writing an essay "On Literary Style" in 1729: "When the Writer conceals himself, he has the Advantage of hearing the Censure both of Friends and Enemies with more Impartiality." [19] Doubtless he based this observation on his own experience in Boston with the anonymous Silence Dogood Papers. But unlike the strategy of projecting, the purpose of adopting a journalistic or literary mask was not always concealment. The use of the journalistic mask was, after all, conventional; readers recognized that letters signed Alice Addertongue or Anthony Afterwit were likely to be the work of Benjamin Franklin, editor of the *Gazette,* just as they knew that Poor Richard Saunders was really the proprietor of the New Printing-Office. Yet, as a comic device, the journalistic mask functions to separate the actual author from his message. More often than not, Franklin's little sketches carried a serious message. Employing a persona accomplished precisely what hiding behind *"a Number of Friends"* did; that is, it relieved the reader of the unpleasant experience of taking advice from Benjamin Franklin. In addition, the persona might be tailored to the occasion and the circumstances. The mask could be male or female, old or young, poor or rich. We shall find Franklin using all of these with great skill and sensitivity. He was indeed a man with "a great deal of common and uncommon nature in him."

Girding Franklin's sense of the human commonplaces was a stout theory of the nature and function of writing that he had inherited from his Puritan forebears. It was scarcely an aesthetic. When Franklin expressed himself on style he always spoke in terms of the effects of writing not upon the heart but upon the rational faculties of the reader. This he offered in the form of a maxim in his essay, "On Literary Style": *"That no Piece can properly be called good, and well written, which is void of any Tendency to benefit the Reader, either by improving his Virtue or his knowledge."* To be good, literature had either to educate the reader or provide him moral instruction. Good writing served a social function. Some of Franklin's most arresting pieces might fall outside his definition, but relatively few of his writings may be said to be totally devoid of at least a pretended social or moral purpose. And this principle, laid down before the first appearance of *Poor Richard's Almanac,* stayed with Franklin throughout his life, becoming, it seems, almost instinctive with him. When he came to write his life story, a work he knew to be of the greatest importance, he could hardly have framed it on other principles.

Franklin knew, of course, that in order to be beneficial, writing had first to be palatable. To that end, a young man "extreamly ambitious" as he was "to be a tolerable English Writer," must study style. Writing, as we have seen, was related to "informed and intelligent conversation," of which Franklin wrote in the *Autobiography*: "And as the chief Ends of Conversation are to *inform,* or to be *informed,* to *please* or to *persuade,* I wish wellmeaning sensible Men would not lessen their Power of doing Good by a Positive assuming Manner that seldom fails to disgust, tends to create Opposition, and to defeat every one of those Purposes for which Speech was given us, to wit, giving or receiving Information, or Pleasure: For if you would *inform,* a positive dogmatical Manner in advancing your Sentiments, may provoke Contradiction and prevent candid Attention." Franklin quoted with approbation a line from Alexander Pope's *Essay on Criticism*: "Men should be taught as if you taught them not." [20] To be effective, writing should first "be *smooth, clear,* and *short:* For the contrary Qualities are apt to offend, either the Ear, the Understanding, or the Patience." For the sake of clarity, the writer should choose plain words. "If a Man would that his Writings have an Effect on the Generality of Readers, he had better imitate that Gentleman, who would use no Word in his Works that was not well understood by his Cook-maid." Finally, the writer must consider order or method in his compositions. "If a Writer would *persuade,* he should proceed gradually from Things already allow'd, to those from which Assent is yet withheld, and make their Connection manifest. If he would *inform,* he must advance regularly from Things known to things unknown." "Perhaps," he concluded, "a Habit of using good Method, cannot be better acquired, than by learning a little Geometry or Algebra." [21]

The examples of algebra and geometry are instructive. It was Franklin's assumption, and the assumption of his neoclassic age, that art, like mathematics, was subject to rules. Writing well meant writing correctly, according to the rules. In practice, Augustan writers and critics (including Franklin himself) struggled with the rules, bent them, and often finally abandoned them to the eighteenth century's growing awareness and relish of the emotions or "sensibilities." But they clung to the notion that young men should begin by studying the rudiments of language, the rules of grammar and orthography. In Franklin's view, pupils should be instructed early and strenuously in their own language. In his anonymous *Proposals Re-*

lating to the Education of Youth in Pensilvania (1749), he recommended that the youngsters be *enticed* to study the classical languages in order to appreciate the original elegance of the Ancients. For "it would be well if they could be taught *every Thing* that is useful, and *every Thing* that is ornamental: But Art is long, and their Time is short." [22]

English must come first. Franklin was only one of a number of distinguished theorists in education who shared this view, and he marshaled authority behind him, quoting at length from John Locke, Obadiah Walker, M. Charles Rollin, George Turnbull, M. Jean-Francois Simon. A fair example of their opinions is Locke's recommendation for the training of those "whose Business in this World is to be done with their Tongues, and with their Pens." Locke wrote, "He ought to study *Grammar,* among the other Helps of Speaking well, but it *must be* THE GRAMMAR OF HIS OWN TONGUE, of the Language he uses." In teaching students their own language, modern educators would in fact be imitating the Ancients. The Greeks studied no language but their own, considering all others barbarous; and the Romans studied Greek only after mastering Latin. M. Simon applauded Roman education for the results it produced—the same results Franklin desired. "Masters of Rhetoric taught them early the Principles, the Difficulties, the Beauties, the Subtleties, the Depths, the Riches of their own Language. When they went from these Schools, they were perfect Masters of it, they were never at a Loss for proper Expressions; and I am much deceived if it was not owing to this, that they produced such excellent Works with so *marvellous Facility.*" It was a "marvellous Facility," a readiness of words and quickness of expression, on which Franklin's journalistic practice chiefly depended.

For Benjamin Franklin writing was functional; so then was education: functional and practical. The pattern of the Latin school was firmly established in European education, but because the English school was an innovation Franklin laid out a plan for one in 1751. His sample curriculum proceeded from class to class, beginning with the grammar and spelling. The second class should learn to read aloud "with Attention, and with proper Modulations of the Voice according to the Sentiments and Subject." [23] The third class should be taught public speaking and the elements of rhetoric. The last three classes would then be devoted to English composition. The scholars must learn to form their letters and point properly, then be given exercises in writing personal letters of various types. These "Letters to each other" might include brief narratives of "any common Occurrences, and on various Subjects, imaginary Business, &c. containing little Stories, Accounts of their late Reading, what Parts of Authors please them, and why." The regimen of the Fifth Class is of particular interest, as it recalls Franklin's own program of self-education. "To improve the Youth in *Composition,* they may now . . . begin to write little Essays in Prose; and sometimes in Verse, not to make them Poets, but for this Reason, that nothing acquaints a Lad so speedily with Variety of Expression, as the Necessity of finding such Words and Phrases as will suit with the Measure, Sound and Rhime of Verse, and at the same time well express the Sentiment." Next Franklin proposed an exercise in imitation: "let the Sentiments of a *Spectator* be given, and requir'd to be cloath'd in a Scholar's own Words."

Franklin's plan for an English education was orderly and methodical, advancing "regularly from Things known to things unknown." He assumed, as for better or worse we no longer assume, that there was a correct way to write and that the way to achieve correctness was to imitate the most elegant authors—but this only after the fundamentals of language were mastered. Good writing reflected the author's attention to a serious moral or social purpose. It must be graceful without seeming artificial. It must teach without seeming didactic or pedantic. It must not "offend, either the Ear, the Understanding, or the Patience" of the reader.

Franklin himself went without the benefits of an English school education, though elements of his improvised course in composition self-taught survived in his plans for the Pennsylvania Academy. The apparently bizarre program he describes in the *Autobiography* was capable of being expanded into a full-blown English curriculum, though Franklin himself started in the Fifth Class. As a boy, Franklin made the acquaintance of another "bookish lad," John Collins. Both youngsters were of a "disputacious Turn," and they engaged one another in debates, sometimes writing down their arguments. Franklin's father came upon transcripts of their speeches and "took occasion to talk to me about the Manner of my Writing, observ'd that tho' I had the Advantage of my Antagonist in correct Spelling and pointing (which I ow'd to the Printing House) I fell far short in elegance of Expression, in Method and in Perspicuity, of which he convinc'd me by several Instances." Having been made aware of his deficiencies, the young boy set about to improve the *"Manner"* of his writing.

About this time I met with an odd Volume of the Spectator. It was the third. I had never before seen any of them. I bought it, read it over and over, and was much delighted with it. I thought the Writing excellent, and wish'd if possible to imitate it. With that View, I took some of the Papers, and making short Hints of the Sentiment in each Sentence, laid them by a few Days, and then without looking at the Book, try'd to compleat the Papers again, by expressing each hinted Sentiment at length and as fully as it had been express'd before, in any suitable Words, that should come to hand.

Then I compar'd my Spectator with the Original, discover'd some of my Faults and corrected them. But I found I wanted a Stock of Words or a Readiness in recollecting and using them, which I thought I should have acquir'd before that time, if I had gone on making Verses, since the continual Occasions for Words of the same Import but of different Length, to suit the Measure, or of different Sound for the Rhyme, would have laid me under a constant Necessity of searching for Variety, and also have tended to fix that

Variety in my Mind, and make me Master of it. Therefore I took
some of the Tales and turn'd them into Verse: And after a time,
when I had pretty well forgotten the Prose, turn'd them back again.
I also sometimes jumbled my Collections of Hints into Confusion,
and after some Weeks, endeavour'd to reduce them into the best
Order, before I began to form the full Sentences, and compleat the
Paper. This was to teach me Method in the Arrangement of
Thoughts. By comparing my work afterwards with the original, I
discover'd many faults and amended them; but I sometimes had the
Pleasure of Fancying that in certain Particulars of small Import,
I had been lucky enough to improve the Method or the Language
and this encourag'd me to think I might possibly in time come to
be a tolerable English Writer, of which I was extreamly ambitious.
(*Autobiography*, pp. 61–62)

By youthful experimentation Franklin happened upon a workable method of training writers, which included the imitation
of elegant authors, development of vocabulary, and attention
to the problems of organization and order. In essence he followed precisely the course he described in his *Proposals Relating to the Education of Youth*, having absorbed the rudiments
of orthography and punctuation as a printer's apprentice.

The attitude toward poetry that he expresses here and elsewhere in his memoirs has put many of his posterity out of countenance. We recall Melville's sad comment, "Franklin was
everything but a poet." After some local success with a pair
of broadside ballads, young Benjamin's vanity was flattered
and he thought of becoming a poet. But his father thought no
more of this than of Benjamin's plan of becoming a sailor.
Josiah Franklin ridiculed his son's verses and told him "Verse-
makers were generally Beggars." He seems to have been persuaded only of the utility of poetry. "I approv'd the amusing
one's self with Poetry now and then," he says later, "so far
as to improve one's Language, but no farther" (*Autobiography*, p. 90). Yet in the *Autobiography* Franklin is concerned
to demonstrate the importance of learning to write correct

prose; he is not concerned to display his appreciation of good poetry. He says that thanks to his father's objections he "escap'd being a Poet, most probably a very bad one." And when he says that he approved of poetry only to improve one's language, he is speaking of another bad poet of his acquaintance, James Ralph, who continued to write poems until Pope ridiculed him in the *Dunciad*. On the other hand, Franklin reveals his respect for serious verse when he makes fun of the slovenly manner in which his sometime employer, Samuel Keimer, composed it. "He could not be said to write [verses], for his Manner was to compose them in the Types directly out of his Head; so there being no Copy, but one Pair of Cases, and the Elegy likely to require all the Letter, no one could help him" (*Autobiography*, p. 78). To infer from Franklin's passing remarks in his memoirs that he was hostile to poetry and hence otherwise deficient in "the deeper qualities of the imagination," is brutally to simplify a very complex personality. If Franklin was cold to emotion and sensibility, how may we account for the benevolent phase of *Poor Richard's Almanac*? Or how account for his letter of appreciation upon reading James Thomson's *The Seasons*? "That charming Poet has brought more Tears of Pleasure into my Eyes than all I ever read before." [24] Franklin was by no means unresponsive to the beauties of expression; obviously he could even give way, from time to time, to a delicious emotion.

It is true, however, that Franklin never attempted to emulate Thomson or Richardson (though he pirated the first American edition of *Pamela* in 1744), nor did he offer advice to "imaginative" writers. As this brief survey of his writings about writing has shown, the literature which principally concerned him was that in which the teaching function was primary rather than secondary. Franklin wrote about writing only infrequently and then briefly, yet he retained essentially the same views on the subject from 1729 to 1771 and beyond. These few short statements are fundamental to an understanding of Franklin's writing because he took them seriously. To a degree, Franklin's theories ran counter to his inclinations, as Mark Twain hinted when he accused Franklin of using the key on his kite as an excuse for flying it on Sunday. Actually Twain was wrong about the kite and wrong about Franklin's playing "mumble-peg" after the age of sixty and catching flies and sliding on a cellar door. Twain was right only about the essence of Franklin: that he was a man who loved to play and believed in working, who loved to entertain and believed in teaching. Franklin himself cited this tension when he made Poor Richard observe that it was inconsistent in a man who had enough sense to write satire that he be foolish enough to publish it.[25] Nowhere may this tension in Franklin be so readily observed than in his career as a writer, particularly in the evolution of his use of literary or journalistic masks. I have spoken of the efficacy of the persona as a rhetorical or pedagogic device, but this was for Franklin to learn. Or perhaps more accurately, the development of the literary mask as a rhetorical device was for Franklin the operation of a reasonable creature's mind, enabling him "to find or make a Reason for everything one has a mind to do."

3

Franklin's writings as a journalist are important. They are apprentice pieces for a masterwork. We shall examine this body of material with greater attention and in greater detail than it has ever been examined before. A surprising amount of it is both demanding and entertaining, worthy of examination and admiration. Yet these ephemeral works are of much greater importance as they chronicle and punctuate the growth of a mind. We have been speaking here in terms of development, evolution, progression; and this process must be the focus of our attention. It is not only the development of Franklin's rhetorical skill, his control of his reader, though this is an important element. It is a gathering of forces; it is the seasoning and maturing of a mind. Franklin learned not only the control of his language, but also the control of himself. He developed the ability not to subdue his inclinations like St. Augustine—Franklin was too skeptically human for that— but to manage them. As other writers have pointed out, this made him not only an effective writer but an extremely effective human being. His retirement from "journalism" in 1748 launched his career as the servant of his province and later of his country. His success in that greater career depended upon his control of his public image. "For," as John William Ward has written, in "this world, what others think of you is what is important. If Franklin, viewed from the perspective of Max Weber and students of the Protestant ethic, can seem to be the representative, par excellence, of the character who internalizes the imperatives of his society and steers his own course unaided through the world, from a slightly different perspective he also turns out to be the other-directed character David Riesman has described, constantly attuned to the expectations of those around him, responding swiftly to the changing situations that demand he play different roles." [26]

There is, in short, a significant biographical dimension in all of this, although this book is neither a biography nor even a partial biography. We shall not be concerned with everything that Franklin did during the more than thirty years spanned by this investigation. We shall, in fact, focus attention upon only a part of what he wrote. But the assumption must be that Franklin meant what he wrote, that he wrote about what was on his mind. Taken altogether, Franklin's journalism is more revealing than has generally been supposed.

Because Franklin's years of active journalism were the years he narrated in his memoirs, this investigation must have a double focus. The *Autobiography* is a work of rhetoric, compressing and ordering the events of Franklin's first fifty years into a moral fable. We shall be seeing those years from a different vantage point, but always with attention focused upon the *Autobiography*. It is not the purpose of this survey to prove that Franklin's own account of his life was incomplete, false, or misleading—for in fact it was really none of these things. Rather we would see the period of Franklin's narrative in something of its fullness. That is not to say *all* of its fullness, but the richness and variety of Franklin's voices and ideas as a journalist sharply contrast with the lean unity of the *Autobiography*. There is perhaps no better means of demonstrating the literary art of Franklin's *Autobiography* than by such a survey as this.

Benjamin Franklin, printer and journalist, literary apprentice, was a dynamic, growing human being. Too many of his posterity have reduced him to a cipher. It may be, as John William Ward suggests, that in his very complexity Franklin symbolizes America; that the tensions manifest in Franklin's character are those of all his countrymen in their search for identity as Americans. But in any event, something like the real Franklin must be seen through the masks which simplify and grossly distort him. The essence of any man is elusive while he lives and certainly irretrievable after centuries. The canny Poor Richard Saunders observed, "Historians relate, not so much what is done, as what they would have believed." [27] Yet with their preconceptions, historians have responsibilities. Benjamin Franklin has been used irresponsibly. Commentators have written with assurance that one of his fictional creations, Poor Richard Saunders, was none other than Franklin himself—commonly basing the assertion on their reading of only one of the *Almanac*'s prefaces. Finding the memoirs a story of success through industry and frugality told in accents similar to Poor Richard's, these writers have rejoiced at discovering so easily the truth about Ben Franklin. He emerges as a heartless automaton, unsusceptible to the tender influences of poetry, the priggish model for generations of prigs. Even when this was an honest mistake (too often it was not), it was bad historiography. Moreover, bad things have a way of getting worse. The distorted caricature of Benjamin Franklin has been used to exalt and contemn the American national character. Bad enough that it served to define the national character. And, in one form or other, the tendency has persisted beyond the cynicism of Fitzgerald and the liberalism of Angoff, so that as late as 1965 we find Paul W. Conner marring a serious scholarly work with the title *Poor Richard's Politicks*. No matter if the Benjamin Franklin caricature was a self-portrait; it must be recognized and treated as a caricature. If we can never retrieve the artist as he was, we must be content to understand, as thoroughly as possible, the processes of his art.

Chapter 2 is an examination of the Silence Dogood Papers, written anonymously to the *New-England Courant* when Benjamin Franklin was sixteen. Classics in American journalism, the letters show Franklin's remarkable aptitude for creating lively and flexible personae. Mrs. Dogood offered her opinions on a variety of subjects, from elegiac poetry to Harvard College to the clergy in politics. On several occasions she reflected opinions Franklin never abandoned. Major chapters are devoted to the publications of Franklin's New Printing-Office in Phildelphia. A chapter on the *Pennsylvania Gazette* and miscellaneous pamphlets and writings for other papers during the 1730s and 1740s chronicles the growth of Franklin's talent and the gradual maturing of his public face. The phenomenon of *Poor Richard's Almanac* is the subject of the fourth chapter. Poor Richard Saunders was Franklin's most durable and convincing literary mask. His almanac was an annual reflector of Franklin's ideas and attitudes for twenty-five years. In addition the demands of *Poor Richard's Almanac* whetted Franklin's talent as a didactic writer to its final sharpness. The success of the *Autobiography* depends heavily upon the teaching voice Franklin evolved for Poor Richard. The final chapter is an extended analysis of the *Autobiography* itself.

In line with Franklin's own dicta, this book is short, and I hope smooth, clear, and orderly. Franklin's works are quoted very liberally, so as to place my evidence before the reader. Thus, he may formulate conclusions different from mine. Franklin himself was not always victorious when he argued an issue in print, but he never failed to be provocative. Perhaps no man of sense can expect or hope for more from his writing. The great need, in the study of Benjamin Franklin and his work, is to reintroduce the fullness and complexity of the man. The method of this book derives from that premise. In 1968 historian Cecil B. Currey closed his book, *Road to Revolution,* with the hope that "as the bicentennial of the American Revolution nears, the sum of books about Benjamin Franklin will continue to increase." That sounds like a scholar's wish. But Currey must have envisioned not merely library shelves groaning under the weight of many slender scholarly volumes as a dusty memorial to Franklin. He must have been echoing the belief of so many of the signal interpreters of the American experience—Hawthorne, Melville, Twain, More, Lawrence, Fitzgerald—that to know about Benjamin Franklin is to know something important. The nature and development of Franklin as a writer may be among the most important things to understand about him.

Silence Dogood of Boston

He makes a Foe who makes a Jest.
Poor Richard, 1740

J AMES FRANKLIN was eleven years older than Benjamin. He had served an apprenticeship to printing in London and returned to Boston in 1717 with the equipment to set up for himself. In about 1718 he took his twelve-year-old brother as his apprentice; he also secured the printing of the *Boston Gazette,* the city's second newspaper compiled by postmaster William Brooker. Two years later, however, another postmaster took the *Gazette* from James Franklin, leaving him to eke out his living with job printing. In the summer of 1721 he took a bold and historic step: he issued the first biweekly edition of the *New-England Courant.* If only because its run contained the first published writings of Benjamin Franklin, the *Courant* would have a place in the history of American journalism and American letters. But it has a place of its own aside from that fact. James Franklin was a young cosmopolitan. He had seen the coffeehouses where the London wits read and wrote sheets like the *Review,* the *Tatler,* and the *Spectator*; he may possibly have seen the insides of some of those coffeehouses. Even the London newspapers were lively, printing moral essays and pieces of entertainment along with the news. James Franklin was not interested in duplicating the

Gazette or its older rival the *Boston News-Letter*. They were nothing more than compilations of the stale dispatches received by the postmaster. He reasoned that a city with a college and a waterfront, slums and prostitutes as well as divines, must contain wits enough to write and read a paper with literary pretensions; that, as Perry Miller puts it, Boston "might be amused by something more topical than a jeremiad." [1] The *New-England Courant* was the first self-consciously literary periodical in America. It was presumptuous. It failed to live up to James Franklin's ambition, and his brother Benjamin never attempted anything like it. But although no one may have been aware of it at the time, James Franklin was fighting a little battle in the long struggle for the freedom of the American press. And he was at least dimly conscious that he was striking a blow for intellectual freedom in New England. In the perspective of New England history, writes Perry Miller, "the *Courant,* pitiful as it was and failure though it became, is momentous; something over a century would still be needed before Dr. Holmes of Beacon Street could say that the worst affliction to fall upon a land is boredom, but the *Courant* had glimmerings of his perception. It grew out of disruptive forces that had long been gathering momentum; it was the first open effort to defy the norm, and though it did not succeed, it foretold a time when increasing complexity would of itself engender intellectual rebellion." [2]

James Franklin had a circle of about a dozen "ingenious Men"—some of them Anglicans—to contribute essays to the *Courant,* and he had an issue on which to lash the Massachusetts clerical establishment. Boston was that summer in the grip of its worst smallpox epidemic. Cotton Mather, who had been trained as a physician before studying theology, had introduced the new and controversial method of inoculation. The best medical opinion in Boston opposed the practice and the populace was terrified of it. It is ironic that Benjamin Franklin, the great American scientist, should have striven against scientific progress: particularly so when the innovation was being led by Cotton Mather, notorious witch-hunter of Salem and symbol of superstition and credulity. In fact, of course, we know too little about Franklin and even less about Cotton Mather when we assign them symbolic value. In any event, the first number of the *Courant,* dated August 7, 1721, contained two essays which made the position of the paper perfectly clear. The Oxford scholar and Anglican John Checkley sounded the keynote of wit for the paper: *"It's an hard Case, that a Man can't appear in Print now a Days, unless he'll undergo the Mortification of Answering to ten thousand senseless and Impertinent Questions like these,* Pray Sir, from whence came you: And what Age may you be of, may I be so bold? Was you bred at Colledge Sir?" [3] Checkley provided only a sketchy character of the Couranteer, promising to give an account of the outward as well as the inner man in his next. But he marked his prime target as *"a certain Set of men, of whom I hope to give a very good Account,*

> Who like faithful Shepherds take care of their *Flocks,*
> By teaching and practising what's Orthodox,
> Pray hard against Sickness, yet preach up the *P O X!*"

Dr. William Douglass's essay, presented under the banner of what amounted to the Boston medical society, was a history of inoculation written for the purpose of warning against the practice.

Cotton Mather had a not very illustrious nephew, Thomas Walter, who had been set up as a pastor at Roxbury. He had already "done penance," as Perry Miller says, for his earlier association with Checkley, by writing an answer in 1720 to an attack by Checkley on New England theology. Now he felt called upon to respond to Checkley's wit as well. His animadversion was an excruciating little broadside titled "The Little-Compton Scourge: Or, The Anti-Courant." James Franklin, as it happens, had learned something of the art of publicity in

England along with his appreciation of wit, and he published the "Little-Compton Scourge" himself at three pennies per copy. A fair sample of Walter's prose is the paragraph devoted to Checkley's promise that he would reveal his outer and inner self. "But," brayed Walter, "to be sure get your self *Dissected* (according to your Promise) that the World may have a full View of your *Outward Man,* for you are a Misterious Piece of Skin, that cannot disclose your *Exteriors* without the help of Anatomy. And, Sir, as for the Dissection for the Discovery of the *inward Man,* the World thinks it needless, for that your Works declare, your *Guts are in your Brains.*" The battle continued on a plane not very much higher than this. Perry Miller contends that James Franklin's greatest affront to the clergy was not in attacking them on the inoculation issue, but first in making fun of them and later in presuming to infringe on the clerical prerogative of castigating public morals. Cotton Mather's father Increase, no longer the power he had been in the 1690s, longed for those days again: "I can well remember when the Civil Government would have taken an effectual Course to suppress such a Cursed Libel!" He had in the 1720s only the rhetoric of the jeremiad to call down providential ruin upon the land and the *Courant*: "I cannot but pity poor Franklin, who tho' but a Young Man, it may be Speedily he must appear before the Judgment Seat of God." [4]

These must have been hard days for Josiah Franklin, a professing member of Cotton Mather's congregation. But they were days of heady excitement for his youngest son, Benjamin. "Hearing [the Couranteers'] Conversations, and their Accounts of the Approbation their Papers were receiv'd with, I was excited to try my Hand among them. But being still a Boy, and suspecting that my Brother would object to printing any Thing of mine in his Paper if he knew it to be mine, I contriv'd to disguise my Hand, and writing an anonymous Paper I put it in at night under the Door of the Printing House. It was found in the Morning and communicated to his Writing

Friends when they call'd in as usual. They read it, commented on it in my Hearing, and I had the exquisite Pleasure, of finding it met with their Approbation, and that in their different Guesses at the Author none were named but Men of some Character among us for Learning and Ingenuity" (*Autobiography*, pp. 67–68).

The letter from a correspondent who signed herself Silence Dogood appeared in the *Courant* of April 2, 1722. It followed the essay by Philanthropos on the definition of an honorable man. Mrs. Dogood's subsequent offerings occupied the featured position at the head of the *New-England Courant*. The fourteen letters, though sophomoric enough, are extraordinary performances for a boy of sixteen. But they are more than remarkable juvenilia. In their spirit and in the techniques the young Franklin employed, they are adumbrations of his entire journalistic career. In the first place, Franklin clearly conceived of the Dogood Papers as a series. "It may not be improper . . . to inform your Readers," Mrs. Dogood began, "that I intend once a Fortnight to present them, by the Help of this Paper, with a short Epistle, which I presume will add somewhat to their Entertainment." [5] From the outset Franklin thought of Mrs. Dogood as more than simply a tag-name to be signed to a letter; she was to be a role he could assume, a literary or journalistic mask. Silence Dogood did not really have much to say. In his memoirs Franklin admitted that his "Fund of Sense for such Performances" was small. She devoted her first three letters to her own character and circumstances, taking a cue, perhaps, from John Checkley's introduction of the Couranteer. And three of her remaining letters were substantially reprints from the *London Journal,* the *Spectator,* the *Guardian,* and Defoe's *Essay on Projects.* Critics of the Dogood Papers have typically found them faithful to the prevailing mode of the *Courant* essays. In a general way Franklin imitated the *Spectator,* according to George F. Horner, but his "more immediate models were his fellow

Couranteers, who had already domesticated the *Spectator*-type essay." [6] That is, they avoided the elegant Addisonian language and adopted what Horner terms the *Spectator*'s "middle style." Horner attributes this attempt to write in the vernacular in Franklin's *Courant* as a bid for popular support, a move to establish a sense of identity and worth in the lower classes of Massachusetts society. It was, in other words, an attack on the intellectual elitism of the theocrats. Engaged in dialogue with an imaginary clergyman, one of the Couranteers wrote on January 22, 1722, "I know you cannot endure that Laymen should write and Know anything: You would have them know but just enough to get to Heaven." The Widow Dogood's homely prose was indeed in this spirit, but she was created in a different spirit from Zechariah Hearwell, Ephraim Rotewell, Christopher Pottash, or Anthony de Potsherd from Cuckold's Point. They were conceived to write a single letter, then disappear, whereas Mrs. Dogood was a mask to be worn over and over again. Most of the imaginary correspondents were convenient spokesmen for particular pieces of wit or instruction; Silence Dogood was the very opposite. The content of her letters was incidental to her character. The fun Franklin derived from her was in becoming the person he had created. To write from the point of view of a middle-aged widow required something of an imaginative leap for a sixteen-year-old boy. She was a more elaborate characterization than James Franklin's Timothy Turnstone or Couranteer Matthew Adams's Harry Meanwell. She had to seem consistently feminine and middle aged, as well as being clever and satirical. Franklin managed this illusion of reality with great success; although on occasions Mrs. Dogood's femininity may seem to give way to a spoof of her sex, it is possible to attribute this to her broadly human sensibilities. She can see the follies of her sex and herself as well as those of the men. Other Couranteers were not so skillful as the young Franklin in sustaining the illusion of their journalislic masks. Elisha Trueman appears twice, on April 30 and May 14, 1722. In his first letter he manifests a rather broad country dialect, but when next he writes his style has been elevated to that typical of the *Courant,* something akin to the style Richard Steele usually employed in his essays for the *Spectator.*

It is significant too that Franklin preferred the challenge of a believable and fully realized New England character, rather than employing the common device of a biblical or pseudoclassical *nom de plume:* Aminadab, Hypercriticus, Philander, or simply initials: A.B. or Z.Y. These latter devices were common in the *Courant.* But again these were not masks; they were merely conveniences. They served the writers as a graceful and self-consciously literary alternative to leaving their essays unsigned altogether, as many *Courant* pieces were. Franklin's choice of a female persona for his journalistic debut may seem surprising, but it was to be a favorite device of his. His most arresting creations, in fact, are female: from the Widow Dogood to Bridget Saunders and Miss Polly Baker. He relished the imaginative leap, but perhaps more than that he found the shrill, scolding feminine voice a splendid comic scourge of vice and folly. In her second letter Mrs. Dogood observed of herself, "I have . . . a natural Inclination to observe and reprove the Faults of others, at which I have an excellent Faculty. I speak this by Way of Warning to all such whose Offences shall come under by Cognizance, for I never intend to wrap my Talent in a Napkin." Franklin shared Dr. Johnson's amusement at the spectacle of a woman preaching. Johnson told Boswell that that was "like a dog's walking on his hinder legs. It is not done well; but you are surprized to find it done at all." Then too, the invention of a female preacher for his letters might serve to blunt the accusation that the Couranteer's apprentice was arrogating the responsibilities of the clergy. No one could hope to silence the likes of a Mrs. Dogood.

In the *Autobiography* Silence Dogood's creator says that a short while before writing her letters, he had been endeavoring to improve his writing by performing various exercises with the papers in the third volume of the *Spectator*. If he did as he says he did, he was literally steeped in that volume. It is a matter of speculation how many scholars have set out to trace the influence of those papers on Silence Dogood. The negative results of some of these investigations have found their way into print; it is impossible to know how many other students have simply given it up as a bad job. George F. Horner's important paper states the case in a straightforward fashion: "The surface resemblance of Benjamin Franklin's *Dogood Papers* to the *Spectator* has led to the belief that the *Papers* are little more than imitation. But this conclusion becomes untenable when the *Papers* are examined in their contemporary controversial setting." [7] Mrs. Dogood is genuinely a New England lady with local interests and a provincial style. None of her letters is derivative in any obvious respect of anything in the *Spectator*, Volume 3. However, Mrs. Dogood quotes two of the *Spectator* papers directly—numbers 185 and 247—both of which appeared in the third volume.[8] And throughout the fourteen Dogood Papers there are motifs and devices possibly reminiscent of the *Spectator*. These are little more than echoes; they fade under close scrutiny and warrant only passing notice. Horner was exactly right that the Dogood Papers are shaped by the prevailing mode of the *Courant* and the local "controversial setting" much more than by Joseph Addison and Richard Steele. The *Spectator* papers were ten years old when the young Franklin invented the Widow Dogood, but reading the two collections today, one is struck by the fact that they were separated by much more than an ocean and a decade. The issues which concerned Mr. Spectator and his correspondents were those of a metropolitan society whose politics, economics, and amusements gave the writers and their readers an outlook totally foreign to provincial New England. The American Revolution was more than a half century away, but the Empire was already sharply divided; Englishmen and their American cousins already spoke subtly different languages. When they would come seriously to discuss their differences, they would find that they no longer understood each other.

Silence Dogood opened her correspondence as Checkley had introduced the Couranteer. "And since it is observed," she wrote, "that the Generality of People now a days, are unwilling either to commend or dispraise what they read until they are in some measure informed who or what the Author of it is, whether he be *poor* or *rich*, *old* or *young*, a *Schollar* or a *Leather Apron Man*, &c. and give their Opinion of the Performance, according to the Knowledge which they have of the Author's Circumstances, it may not be amiss to begin with a short Account of my past Life and present Condition." Mrs. Dogood was the widow of a country pastor, who had also been the benefactor of her youth. Their marriage, when Silence came of age, "was very astonishing to all the Country round about, and served to furnish them with Discourse for a long Time after." But the Reverend Mr. Dogood had, after all, "brought [her] up cleverly to his Hand." In his household she had learned to read and love books, as well as to write a polished, though previously unpublished style. In her widowhood she kept house for the minister who succeeded her husband, enjoying his conversation and that of her neighbor, Rusticus, and his family. "I shall conclude this with my own Character," she wrote, at the end of her second letter. "*Know then*, That I am an Enemy to Vice, and a Friend to Vertue. I am one of an extensive Charity, and a great Forgiver of *private* Injuries: A hearty Lover of the Clergy and all good Men, and a mortal Enemy to arbitrary Government & unlimited Power. I am naturally very jealous for the Rights and

Liberties of my Country; & the least appearance of an In-
croachment on those invaluable Priviledges, is apt to make my
Blood boil exceedingly." Mrs. Dogood went on to promise
ceaseless vigilance and the vigorous exercise of her "excellent
Faculty" for observing and reproving her neighbors' faults.
Neither she nor her arrogant young creator intented to wrap
their talents "in a Napkin." This is among the seminal passages in Franklin's writing, for Silence Dogood voiced principles and reflected attitudes that Franklin never abandoned.
He followed the lead of his older brother in protesting a
"hearty" love of the clergy; the question was whether love of
the clergy and hatred of arbitrary power were not mutually
exclusive in Massachusetts. Both James and Benjamin Franklin eventually left home to find atmospheres of greater tolera-
tion. Benjamin ended up in Quaker Pennsylvania; James found
refuge in Rhode Island, the haven of outcasts from Massachusetts since the days of Roger Williams and Ann Hutchin-
son. The journalistic writings of the young Benjamin Franklin
are typically colored by Mrs. Dogood's tone of bellicosity.
Franklin was a good man in a fight, and it would be twenty
years before his temperament would allow him to pass one up.

Mrs. Dogood's third letter "finish'd the Foundation" of
her correspondence with a reflection upon the difficulty of
writing for a varied readership.

I AM very sensible that it is impossible for me, or indeed any
one Writer to please *all* Readers at once. Various Persons have
different Sentiments; and that which is pleasant and delightful to
one, gives another a Disgust. He that would (in this Way of Writing) please all, is under a Necessity to make his Themes almost as
numerous as his Letters. He must one while be merry and divert-
ing, then more solid and serious; one while sharp and satyrical,
then (to mollify that) be sober and religious; at one Time let the
Subject be Politicks, then let the next Theme be Love: Thus will
every one, one Time or other find some thing agreeable to his own
Fancy, and in his Turn be delighted.

Here the young Franklin may consciously have been rewriting a passage from the *Spectator*, No. 179, by Addison. "Were I always Grave," Addison observed,

> one half of my Readers would fall off from me: Were I always Merry I should lose the other. I make it therefore my endeavour to find out Entertainment of both kinds, and by that means perhaps consult the good of both more than I should do, did I always write to the particular Taste of either. As they neither of them know what I proceed upon, the sprightly Reader, who takes up my Paper in order to be diverted, very often finds himself engaged unawares in a serious and profitable Course of Thinking; as on the contrary the Thoughtful Man, who perhaps may hope to find something Solid, and full of deep Reflection, is very often insensibly betrayed into a Fit of Mirth. In a word, the Reader sits down to my Entertainment without knowing his Bill of Fare and has therefore at least the Pleasure of hoping there may be a Dish to his Palate.[9]

The sentiment of the two passages is the same, and they are organized in roughly the same pattern. Both are, of course, conventional set pieces. Franklin could have modeled Mrs. Dogood's apologia after any number of similar statements by other writers. But Addison's *Spectator*, No. 179, was probably his original, for the metaphor of food and palate emerged in a similar statement of purpose by Poor Richard Saunders in his almanac for 1739. And Addison's "sprightly Reader" who may be surprised into serious thought turns up in Poor Richard's preface for 1747 as "light airy Minds" who read the almanac for the jokes but may be "struck by somewhat of more Weight and Moment."

In her fourth letter Silence Dogood reported a dream vision of an institution of higher learning. Scholars have noted the resemblance of this letter to the *Spectator*, No. 3, a paper not, of course, included in the third volume. Gaining admittance to a great hall, Mrs. Dogood saw a magnificent throne on which sat LEARNING:

she was apparelled wholly in Black, and surrounded almost on every Side with innumerable Volumes in all Languages. She seem'd very busily employ'd in writing something on a half Sheet of Paper, and upon Enquiry, I understood she was preparing a Paper, call'd *The New-England Courant*. On her Right Hand sat *English,* with a pleasant smiling Countenance, and handsomely attir'd; and on her left were seated several *Antique Figures,* with their Faces vail'd. I was considerably puzzl'd to guess who they were until one informed me, (who stood beside me) that those Figures on her left Hand were *Latin, Greek, Hebrew,* &c. and that they were very much reserv'd, and seldom or never unvail'd their Faces here, and then to few or none, tho' most of those who have in this Place acquir'd so much Learning as to distinguish them from English, pretended to an intimate Acquaintance with them.

Mrs. Dogood then followed the greatest crowd of students to the Temple of Theology, where she saw Pecunia beckoning the young men to orders and Plagius "diligently transcribing some eloquent Paragraphs out of *Tillotson's* Works, *&c.* to embellish his own." Aroused from her dream by her lodger, she was informed by him "*That it was a lively Representation of* HARVARD COLLEGE." Two weeks later (May 28, 1722) the young wits of Harvard struck back in the *Boston Gazette*. Perry Miller identifies the author of this reply as Samuel Mather, Cotton's son and Benjamin Franklin's exact contemporary. Signing himself "John Harvard," Mather stung the young Couranteer by dissecting an embarrassingly mixed metaphor in his dream-allegory. "Well done Rustic Couranto!" crowed John Harvard.[10]

Silence Dogood's fifth and sixth letters were essays on manners and morals somewhat in the vein of the *Spectator*. In her fifth, she reprinted a letter to herself from Ephraim Censorious (presumably another invention of Franklin's but possibly not, since the *Courant* had invited readers to engage the widow in correspondence). Ephraim urged Mrs. Dogood to reprove the follies of her sex before turning to those of the men. She replied that men were actually the cause of any faults women might have. But she did return in her sixth letter to a castigation of the "Pride of Apparel" and specifically the hoop-petticoat. The *Spectator,* No. 127, had treated of the same garment—the fashion in London eleven years before—however, Silence Dogood's letter owes little or nothing to Addison.

Perhaps Mrs. Dogood's most entertaining performance was her seventh, which was a kind of parody of Addison's elegant literary essays for the *Spectator.* Her subject was "a most Excellent Piece of Poetry" of native New England composition. She reflected upon the common notion that good verse was not to be expected of New England writers, but she professed to doubt this, and "I have determined, when I meet with a Good Piece of *New-England* Poetry, to give it a suitable Encomium." The verses she had currently in hand were entitled "*An Elegy upon the Much Lamented Death of Mrs.* Mehitebell Kitel, *Wife of Mr.* John Kitel *of Salem, &c.*" Mrs. Dogood praised the poem in the best Addisonian manner: "The Language is so soft and Easy, the Expression so moving and pathetick, but above all, the Verse and Numbers so Charming and Natural, that it is almost beyond Comparison." Addison had written the *Spectator,* No. 223, on Ambrose Philips's translation of Sappho: "The Reader will find in it that Pathetick Simplicity which is so peculiar to him, and so suitable to the Ode he was here Translated. . . . I must further add, that the Translation has preserved every Image and Sentiment of *Sappho,* notwithstanding it has all the Ease and Spirit of an Original. In a Word, if the Ladies have a mind to know the manner of Writing practised by the so much celebrated *Sappho,* they may here see it in its genuine and natural Beauty, without any foreign or affected Ornaments." [11] Franklin did not lift his language bodily from Addison, but he had absorbed all of the critical clichés. Silence Dogood proceeded to a detailed explication of the *Elegy.*

BUT the Threefold Appellation in the first Line

———— *a Wife, a Daughter, and a Sister,*
must not pass unobserved. The Line in the celebrated Watts,

GUNSTAN *the Just, the Generous, and the Young,*

is nothing Comparable to it. The latter only mentions three Qualifications of *one* Person who was deceased, which therefore could
raise Grief and Compassion but for *One.* Whereas the former, (*our
most excellent Poet*) gives his Reader a Sort of an Idea of the
Death of *Three Persons, viz.*

———— *a Wife, a Daughter, and a Sister,*

which is *Three Times* as great a Loss as the Death of *One,* and
consequently must raise *Three Times* as much Grief and Compassion in the Reader.

Mrs. Dogood ventured to say that this poem had inaugurated
an entirely new form. It was neither Epic, Sapphic, Lyric, nor
Pindaric. Thus she presumed to call it the Kitelic, and she
offered "A RECEIPT *to make a New-England Funeral*
ELEGY": "For the Title of your Elegy. *Of these you may
have enough ready made to your Hands; but if you should
chuse to make it your self, you must be sure not to omit the
Words* Aetatis Suae, *which will Beautify it exceedingly.* For
the Subject of your Elegy. *Take one of your Neighbours who
has lately departed this Life; it is no great matter at what
Age the Party dy'd, but it will be best if he went away sud-
denly, being* Kill'd, Drown'd, *or* Froze to Death." Mrs. Dogood recommended certain "Melancholly Expressions," such
as "Dreadful, Deadly, cruel cold Death, unhappy Fate, weep-
ing Eyes, *&c.*" The motif of a recipe for writing occurs twice
in the third volume of the *Spectator,* and Franklin's prescrip-
tion for Kitelic verse may have found its inspiration there. A
correspondent writing in the *Spectator,* No. 220, told of a projector of his acquaintance: "This Virtuoso being a Mathematician, has, according to his Taste, thrown the Art of Poetry

into a short Problem, and contriv'd Tables by which any one, without knowing a Word of Grammar or Sense, may, to his great Comfort, be able to compose or rather to erect Latin Verses. His Tables are a kind of poetical Logarithms, which being divided into several Squares, and all inscribed with so many incoherent Words, appear to the Eye somewhat like a Fortune-telling Screen. What a Joy it must be to the unlearned Operator, to find that these Words, being carefully collected and writ down in order according to the Problem, start of themselves into Hexameter and Pentameter Verses." Addison proposed a similar device in the *Spectator,* No. 241, a mechanical contrivance for sending love letters by telepathy. "I would propose," he wrote, "that upon the Lover's Dial-plate there should be written not only the four and twenty Letters, but several entire Words, which have always a place in passionate Epistles, as Flames, Darts, Die, Languish, Absence, Cupid, Heart, Eyes, Hang, Drown, and the like." [12]

In the summer of 1722, Silence Dogood found serious topics to occupy her papers. On June 11 the *Courant* had implied that the government was negligent in its efforts to apprehend a pirate vessel reported to be prowling off the coast. The General Court of Massachusetts was at the end of its patience with James Franklin. The Mather faction had denounced the Couranteers as a Hell-Fire Club, and Increase Mather had applied pressure on the Court by recalling the days when the civil authorities would not have countenanced a paper objectionable to the clergy. Now it was ordered that James Franklin be confined in jail until the end of the legislative session. For about two weeks Benjamin was left to run the paper, "and I made bold to give our Rulers some Rubs in it, which my Brother took very kindly, while others began to consider me in an unfavourable Light" (*Autobiography,* p. 69). Two of these rubs were Silence Dogood's eighth and ninth letters. The eighth was a long quotation from the *London Journal* hastily introduced by Mrs. Dogood. The subject of the essay was freedom of speech. Number 9 was Mrs. Dogood's own essay on what she called "State Hypocrites." " 'Tis not inconsistent with Charity," she announced, "to distrust a Religious Man in Power, tho' he may be a good Man; he has many Temptations 'to propagate *publick Destruction* for *Personal Advantages* and Security:' And if his Natural Temper be covetous, and his Actions often contradict his pious Discourse, we may with great Reason conclude, that he has some other Design in his Religion besides barely getting to Heaven." Silence Dogood had reservations about her hearty love of the clergy. If such remarks were not pointed enough, she went on to cite as the most dangerous hypocrite in a commonwealth *"one who leaves the Gospel for the sake of the Law."* The reference was evidently to the widely hated Governor Joseph Dudley, who had graduated from Harvard in 1665 with the intention of studying for the ministry, but had instead turned to politics.[13] This was the most barbed of the Dogood letters.

The next four papers were noncontroversial reflections upon human nature. Mrs. Dogood devoted two papers to the subject of widows' and spinsters' relief. In her tenth she quoted at length from one of Franklin's favorite books, Daniel Defoe's *Essay on Projects.* Defoe had proposed a kind of Friendly Society or insurance plan for widows, and it was a plan that might have merited serious consideration in Massachusetts. Silence Dogood had plenty of company in her widowhood; in 1718 Cotton Mather had remarked that one fifth of his congregation were widows. And widows had a hard time making a living, many of them being engaged in small businesses. Josiah Franklin's only competitor in vending soap and candles was a widow, Mary Hamilton; and another, a Mrs. Adams, advertised in the *Boston Gazette* that she had an African lion to exhibit for a small admission.[14] In her eleventh letter, Mrs. Dogood presented a project of her own, much like Defoe's in form, but intended for the relief of a class of females whose predicament was more comical than widow-

hood. She reprinted a letter from Margaret Aftercast, whom
Mrs. Dogood described as "a Virgin well stricken in Years
and Repentance." She had dismissed a succession of gallants
in better days, but now she was reduced to the annual consumption of "Fifty Pounds Worth of the most approved *Cos-
metics*. But all won't do." Mrs. Dogood proposed a Friendly
Society for old maids "whereby every single Woman, upon full
Proof given of her continuing a Virgin for the Space of Eighteen Years, (dating her Virginity from the Age of Twelve,)
should be entituled to *500 £.* in ready Cash." Among the con-
ditions to be observed, Silence Dogood offered that "NO
Woman, who after claiming and receiving, has had the good
Fortune to marry, shall entertain any Company with En-
comiums on her Husband, above the Space of one Hour at a
Time, upon Pain of returning one half the Money into the
Office for the first Offence; and upon the second Offence to
return the Remainder."

The twelfth Dogood letter was on the subject of drunkenness; the widow quoted briefly from a paper (No. 247) in
the third volume of the *Spectator*. She employed in her thir-
teenth paper a device Steele had used in the *Spectator*, No.
218: the writer being abroad incognito hears herself spoken
about. Poor Richard would report that experience more than
once. It was, in fact, the frame for Father Abraham's famous
address on industry and frugality. Mrs. Dogood went on to
anatomize the nightwalkers of Boston, a very common motif
in the *Spectator*, but also commonly employed by writers in
the *Courant*.

The fourteenth and last of Mrs. Dogood's essays took up
the topical subject of the Connecticut clergymen who had been
charged with introducing Anglican and Arminian views at
Yale.[15] Mrs. Dogood took most of her words from the *Spectator* (No. 185, from Franklin's third volume) and the
Guardian, but the burden of the message was characteristic of
Franklin. She wrote, "he that propagates the Gospel among

Rakes and *Beaus* without reforming them in their Morals, is every whit as ridiculous as a Statesman who makes Tools of Ideots and Tale-Bearers."

Silence Dogood vanished as unexpectedly as she had come. Her letters had appeared regularly in the *Courant* from April 2 to October 8, 1722. In December a correspondent to the *Courant* appealed to Mrs. Dogood—or challenged her—to resume. "Is your Common-Place Wit all Exhausted, your stock of matter all spent? We thought you were well stor'd with that." [16] Franklin's recollection of the affair in his memoirs suggests that this writer may have diagnosed the case correctly. It is not known whether Benjamin Franklin replenished his fund of sense sufficiently to write anything further for the *New-England Courant*. Scholars have nominated several essays and letters in later issues, but none of these has been firmly installed in the canon. Benjamin was not the only Couranteer who was weary from his labors of wit. The lightning which Increase Mather called down upon James Franklin never actually struck. But as if by glacial erosion, the enormous pressure exerted by the Mathers and their allies finally blunted and wore away the sharpness of the *Courant*. After Number 78 the paper no longer bore James Franklin's name, but proclaimed itself "Printed and sold by BENJAMIN FRANKLIN." This was but a subterfuge, "a very flimsy Scheme" as Franklin remembered it, to circumvent an order by the General Court that James Franklin no longer publish his newspaper. Before the *Courant*'s run ended, with No. 255, it had declined into a mere compilation like its rivals.

At the end of Number 113, on September 30, 1723, James printed a melancholy and historic advertisement: "James Franklin, Printer in Queen-Street, wants a likely lad for an Apprentice." His brother, Benjamin, had run away to Philadelphia.

THREE

The Philadelphia Years

At 20 years of age the Will reigns;
at 30 the Wit; at 40 the Judgment.
Poor Richard, 1741

Benjamin Franklin introduced himself to Philadelphia wearing the mask of the Busy-Body in Andrew Bradford's *American Weekly Mercury.* At least the Busy-Body was Franklin's literary introduction to the city; he had been a journeyman printer for Samuel Keimer off and on from the fall of 1723 until 1729, having sojourned in England for almost two years (1724–26). In the summer or early fall of 1728, Franklin and his partner, Hugh Meredith, had opened the New Printing-Office on Market Street a few doors below Second. But until January, 1729, nothing written by Benjamin Franklin appears to have been published in Pennsylvania. Franklin would have preferred not to write for a rival's newspaper, one which he remembered in his memoirs as "a paltry thing, wretchedly manag'd, and no way entertaining" (*Autobiography,* p. 119). One of the first projects of the New Printing-Office was to begin a competing weekly paper, for though the *Mercury* was by no means as paltry as Franklin later described it, he was right that the city could support a second newspaper. Franklin divulged his plans to one George Webb, who had recently bought his release from Samuel

Keimer and was seeking employment as a journeyman with Franklin and Meredith. "I requested Webb not to mention it," Franklin wrote, "but he told it to Keimer, who immediately, to be beforehand with me, published Proposals for Printing one himself, on which Webb was to be employ'd" (*Autobiography*, p. 120). Franklin realized that there could be no profit in a third Philadelphia paper. "I resented this, and to counteract them, as I could not yet begin our Paper, I wrote several Pieces of Entertainment for Bradford's Paper, under the Title of the Busy-Body which Breintnal continu'd some Months." [1]

Actually, the campaign against Keimer's *Universal Instructor in all Arts and Sciences; and Pennsylvania Gazette* was joined by two irate female correspondents to the *Mercury*. Either of them might have been a sister of Mrs. Silence Dogood of Massachusetts. The instructional function of the *Universal Instructor* was to be performed by a serial reprinting of Chambers's *Cyclopaedia*, alphabetical and unabridged. Proceeding leadenly through the early entries in this first English encyclopedia, Keimer printed, in his fifth *Instructor,* the article on abortion. One week later, on January 28, two outraged letters appeared in the *Mercury*. The first writer, Martha Careful, was of a sanguinary disposition, objecting to the publication of the secrets of her sex to be read "in all *Taverns* and *Coffee-Houses,* and by the Vulgar: . . . I say, if he Publish any more of that kind, which ought only to be in the Repositary of the Learned; my Sister Molly and my Self, with some others, are Resolved to run the Hazard of taking him by the Beard, at the next Place we meet him, and make an Example of him for his Immodesty." [2] Caelia Shortface, the second writer, used the gentle language of a Quaker lady, but her message was substantially the same. She addresses a polite preface to "Friend Andrew Bradford" in which she begs that he print her letter, "for by doing it, Thou may perhaps save Keimer his Ears." In the letter to "Friend Samuel Keimer" Mrs. Shortface declares that she has been chosen spokesman by a group of her acquaintance who are of a mind to deprive him of his right ear the next time he prints "such Things . . . as would make all the Modest and Virtuous women in Pennsilvania ashamed." If he can make no better use of his "great Dictionary," she advises him to sell it, "and if Thou hath nothing else to put in Thy *Gazette,* lay it down."

This was to be the burden of the Busy-Body papers as well, though the Busy-Body went at Keimer by infuriating indirection. First, as Franklin remembered, the Busy-Body was "entertainment." It was in fact the first such feature in the ten-year history of the *Mercury,*[3] and so was bound to attract attention to that paper and away from the *Instructor.* The Busy-Body first appeared on February 4. Like Silence Dogood he came immediately to the purpose of his writing and announced his intention of contributing regularly. In the first place, he said, he had often been concerned that the *Mercury* was not constantly entertaining, notably when ships carrying dispatches were delayed or when the river froze.

> With more Concern have I continually observ'd the growing Vices and Follies of my Country-folk. And tho' Reformation is properly the concern of every Man; that is, *Every one ought to mend One;* yet 'tis too true in this Case, that *what is every Body's Business is no Body's Business,* and the Business is done accordingly. I, therefore, upon mature Deliberation, think fit to take *no Body's Business* wholly into my own Hands; and, out of Zeal for the Publick Good, design to erect my Self into a Kind of *Censor Morum;* proposing with your Allowance, to make Use of the *Weekly Mercury* as a Vehicle in which my Remonstrances shall be convey'd to the World.[4]

Andrew Bradford apparently realized immediately the commercial possibilities of the Busy-Body, for he not only made it his front-page feature but headed it with a by-line in large type. It was not until the third Busy-Body letter that the authors set upon their real adversary. This letter contrasted two "characters" named Cato and Cretico. Cato was advanced to demonstrate that *"Virtue alone is sufficient to make a Man Great, Glorious and Happy."* Cretico, on the other hand, was a cautionary character.

> O Cretico! Thou sowre Philosopher! Thou cunning States-man! Thou art crafty, but far from being Wise. When wilt thou be esteem'd, regarded and belov'd like Cato? When wilt thou, among thy Creatures meet with that unfeign'd Respect and warm Goodwill that all Men have for him? Wilt thou never understand that the cringing, mean, submissive Deportment of thy Dependants, is (like the Worship paid by Indians to the Devil) rather thro' Fear of Harm thou may'st do them, than out of Gratitude for the Favours they have receiv'd of thee? Thou art not wholly void of Virtue; there are many good Things in thee, and many good Actions reported of thee. Be advised by thy Friend: Neglect those musty Authors; let them be cover'd with Dust, and moulder on their proper Shelves; and do thou apply thy self to a Study much more profitable, The Knowledge of Mankind, and of thy Self.

This was a cruel and telling portrait of the clumsy and churlish Keimer, as Franklin saw him. The account of Keimer in Franlin's memoirs is consistent with the Busy-Body's references to Cretico's "Dependants." Franklin tells of Keimer's mistreating of his apprentices, some of whom ran away and all of whom had greater respect for the skilled Franklin than for their incompetent master. And according to Franklin, Keimer had craftily hired him, only so that the apprentices could be properly trained; "then, they being all articled to him, he should be able to do without me" (*Autobiography*, p. 108). The remark about "musty Authors" echoes Caelia Shortface's advice on the use of Keimer's "great Dictionary." The Busy-Body added a footnote, thinly veiled as a disclaimer.

> *This is to give Notice that the* BUSY-BODY *strictly forbids all Persons, from this Time forward, of what Age, Sex, Rank, Quality, Degree or Denomination soever, on any Pretence to enquire who is the Author of this Paper, on Pain of his Displeasure, (his own near and Dear Relations only excepted).*

'Tis to be observ'd that if any bad Characters happen to be drawn in the Course of these Papers, they mean no particular Person, if they are not particularly apply'd.

Likewise that the Author is no Partyman, but a general Meddler.

N. B. Cretico lives in a neighbouring Province.[5]

The irascible Keimer recognized the caricature. The *Instructor* for the next week, February 18, printed an essay by "The Casuist" inveighing against the "Desire of gaining popular Applause." Immediately beneath, Keimer addressed the Busy-Body in admonitory tones: "We have now three Papers published in *Bradford's* Mercury, under the Title of the BUSY-BODY: Many of the Customers of that Paper were pleas'd at the coming out of the first, in Expectation they would now have some Entertainment for their Money: But I must confess, there appear'd to me broad Signs that it would be at the Cost of their Neighbours in the Process." The pathetic Keimer warned the Busy-Body against defamation, which, though it may at first be favorably received by the public, will eventually arouse in them "a secret Grief to see the Reputation of their Neighbours blasted." Keimer closed his remarks with an appeal to the Busy-Body to avoid applying his "characters" by "gross Descriptions" and to keep his papers within the bounds of decency.

The Busy-Body, Number 4, printed in the *Mercury* of the same day, was given over to the sadly funny letter of a lady petitioning for the writer's advice. The body of the paper was therefore innocuous, but Franklin continued to needle Keimer in a lofty introductory statement. To begin, he promised (or threatened) that the Busy-Body had a sufficient stock of wit to continue weekly "at least for a Twelvemonth." He then went on to defend his occasionally satiric characters.

> For my own Part, I have already profess'd that I have the Good of my Country wholly at Heart in this Design, without the least sinister View; my chief Purpose being to inculcate the noble Principles of Virtue, and depreciate Vice of every kind. But as I know

the Mob hate Instruction, and the Generality would never read beyond the first Line of my Lectures, if they were usually fill'd with nothing but wholesome Precepts and Advice; I must therefore sometimes humour them in their own Way. There are a Set of Great Names in the Province, who are the common Objects of Popular Dislike. If I can now and then overcome my Reluctance, and prevail with my self to Satyrize a little, one of these Gentlemen, the Expectation of meeting with such a Gratification, will induce many to read me through, who would otherwise proceed immediately to the Foreign News.[6]

After that inflated apologia, Keimer could surely take little comfort in the fact that he was not the butt of the present paper. The Busy-Body's supposed correspondent was a single woman, Patience, who depended for her livelihood on a small shop. She was plagued by a prying and persistent neighbor. While not wishing to offend the woman for fear of losing her custom, Patience was at her wit's end.

But, alas, Sir, I have not yet told you half my Afflictions. She has two Children that are just big enough to run about and do pretty Mischief: These are continually along with Mamma, either in my Room or Shop. . . . Sometimes they pull the Goods off my low Shelves down to the Ground, and perhaps where one of them has just been making water; My Friend takes up the Stuff, and cries, *Eh! thou little wicked mischievous Rogue!—But however, it has done no great Damage; 'tis only wet a little;* and so puts it upon the Shelf again.

Patience is another of Franklin's memorable female sketches. In her dilemma he captured one of the commonplaces of the tradesman's life; in her appeal he created the vivid illusion of the woman herself, proving that he was capable of presenting a range of female emotions, not merely the shrewish accents of Silence Dogood and Martha Careful. Distracted by the children, Patience nevertheless hints at her desire to have children of her own. She is tormented by the conviction that "a handsome Gentleman" who wants to pay her court is being prevented from doing so by the constant intrusion of her neighbor. The implied poignance of her story lends force and substance to Franklin's comic intent.

The fifth Busy-Body was the work of both Franklin and Breintnall. Franklin's part was a particular vindication of the paper containing the Cretico caricature. Breintnall, who opened the paper, assailed Keimer specifically and savagely, though without mentioning him by name. He began by congratulating himself on the general approbation the papers had received, adding "that few are against me but those who have Reason to fear me." [7] He goes on magnanimously to declare a general amnesty; that all the world may judge him humane in his office of *Censor Morum,* "and that even my Enemies may be convinc'd I take no Delight to rake into the Dunghill Lives of vicious Men; and to the End that certain Persons may be a little eas'd of their Fears, and reliev'd from the terrible Palpitations they have lately felt and suffer'd, and do still suffer; I hereby graciously pass an Act of general Oblivion, for all Offences, Crimes and Misdemeanors of what Kind soever, committed from the Beginning of Year sixteen hundred and eighty one, until the Day of the Date of my first Paper." Samuel Keimer was born in 1688; the date appears to have been Breintnall's fairly accurate guess. The Busy-Body went on to detail the crimes he would thereafter ignore: "I shall take no Notice who has, (heretofore) rais'd a Fortune by Fraud and Oppression, nor who by Deceit and Hypocrisy: What Woman has been false to her good Husband's Bed; nor what Man has, by barbarous Usage or Neglect, broke the Heart of a faithful Wife, and wasted his Health and Substance in Debauchery: What base Wretch has betray'd his Friend, and sold his Honesty for Gold, nor what yet baser Wretch, first corrupted him and then bought the Bargain." The only apparent red herring in the list was the unfaithful wife. All the rest of these crimes might have applied directly to Samuel Keimer. Keimer had left a wife in England, from whom Franklin "heard a bad Character of him" while in London (*Autobiography*, p. 108). The last two wretches on the list are certainly Webb and Keimer.

This was too much for the irritable publisher of the *Universal Instructor*. On March 13, he loosed a barrage of acid verse and prose against the Busy-Body. "An Answer to the BUSY-BODY" opened the attack in spirited doggerel couplets.

> Tho' 'tis against the Grain to do it;
> Yet Point of Honour prompts me to it.
> You think there's no one can be smarter,
> But now you'll find you've caught a *Tartar*.
> What a confounded Noise and Racket,
> There is about your Weekly *Pacquet*?
> Some Parts good, and some Parts bad,
> Shew it has different Authors had.
> The Author of the *Good's* unknown;
> But all the *bad ones* are your own,
> And thus your own Stuff does infest,
> And bastardizes all the rest.
> Thus *Indian* Men on Modern Whores
> Beget a Tribe of Tawny-Moors:
> Thus Horses breaking Nature's Rules,
> On slow-pac'd Asses beget Mules:
> But prithee tell me, art thou mad,
> To mix good Writing with the bad?
> Fie, Sir, let all be of a Piece,
> *Spectators, Swans,* or *Joseph's Geese:*
> You hinted at me in your Paper,
> Which now has made me draw my Rapier.
> With scornful Eye, I see your Hate,
> And pity your unhappy Fate:
> For all those Vices you have shewn,
> Are but faint copies of your own.[8]

The conventional inference of plagiarism was clearly the burden of this piece. There seems to be no specific reference to

Franklin in the verses; the reference to *Joseph's Geese* may have been directed at Joseph Breintnall. It is irresistible to imagine the hysterical Keimer standing at his case composing these verses "in the Types directly out of his Head." Elsewhere in the same paper, Keimer offered a megalomaniac beast fable addressed to the authors of the Busy-Body, who "have feebly attack'd" his piece on vanity and ill nature. In the fable the owls, bats, and other night birds are discussing their neighbors and happen to turn their criticism on the sun. The latter replies that he could incinerate all of them in an instant, but instead, "the only Answer I shall give you, or the Revenge I shall take of you, is *to shine on.*"

But the most personal attack came in the prose dialogue, "*Hue and Cry* after the Busy-Body." It was headed by a quatrain from *Hudibras*.

> *For Mastiffs only have the Knack*
> *To cast the Bear upon his Back,*
> *But when the unwieldy Beast is thrown,*
> *Mongrels may serve to keep him down.*

The persons of the dialogue were Eucrates, Philander, and Puribolus.[9] Puribolus brings up the subject of the Busy-Body. "*Is it not a Shame,*" he remarks, "*this Fellow should swagger at this Rate without any Restraint. I vow I'd give 40s. I knew who he was.*" Soon a fourth character, Pandexius, arrives. He seems to know the identity of the Busy-Body but protests that he has been sworn to secrecy. However, he has a magic mirror in which the company sees a figure with two heads joined to one trunk. Pandexius explains that when separate these are two distinct creatures, to whom he assigns the "feign'd Names of *Lantnirbio* and *Bebegio.*" Here is the most knavish of Keimer's assaults—a caricature of the authors. Breintnall received the more cruel personal abuse, being described as "a Free-Thinker of the Peripatetick Sect," who "is commonly observed, at the Fagg-end of a Market, exercising himself with

Pride and Pleasure." He is pictured as grinning "an Hour at the busy Concourse (a Trick he learn'd of his Monkey)" and then strutting off "with some Refuse-Joint thro' *Elbow-Lane,* &c. to the venerable Tubb his Mansion: For it's remarkable in the whole Breed of his dear Doltobesa[?], that tho' none are greater Lovers of Flesh, yet they always expect it brought to them." This portrait of Lantnirbio may have been recognizable to Keimer's readers, though the references are now obscure. The picture of Bebegio is as clear today as in 1729.

> As for *Bebegeo* [*sic*],
>   *He seems to be*
>   *Not one but every A pe's Epitome.*

A Fellow whose Person's as obscure as the Sham *Cato's* Habitation; Merit's as threadbare as his Great Coat, and Scull as thick as his Shoe-Soles.

At first his Employment was to tag Mottoes; but is since admitted a Partner in the Tinsel Performance, on Account of his impenetrable brazen Shield.

The highest Sphere he ever yet acted in, was that of an Understrapper to a Press, till his Advancement, by that Prodigy of Wit, *Mr. B——d.*

It's true, I have heard, he has seen the Inside of a College, and that in a very famous one he chopt Bread for the Scholars, But this seems to want Confirmation.

The reference to "tagging Mottoes" might refer to Keimer and Franklin's last job together, the printing of an issue of paper currency in New Jersey. Franklin's account of that episode (*Autobiography,* pp. 112–13) would suggest that Keimer had grounds for resentment. And Franklin had lived near a famous college, as a boy in Boston.

Keimer's *Instructor* for March 13, 1729, is an interesting document. It is a scurrilous footnote to Benjamin Franklin's biography: a remarkably early dissenting opinion. One could wish that Keimer had been more gifted as a satirist, so that

he might have rendered a more particular and telling picture
of Franklin. Perhaps his most provocative phrase is that about
Bebegio's "impenetrable brazen Shield." The young Franklin
was obviously a brash and aggressive personality, and his combination of ambition and intellectual superiority often served
to humiliate Keimer. But Keimer's counterattack is perhaps
most interesting as a sample of the quality of Franklin's opposition. Poor Keimer—and most of Franklin's competition in
journalistic controversies—were hopelessly overmatched. The
"Hue and Cry after the Busy-Body" is a impossibly unwieldy
tangle of characters and magic mirrors. Having hacked
through to the point, the reader finds only an ugly smear of
the Busy-Body's two authors, scurrilous references to their
appearance and backgrounds. Keimer never hit upon a persuasive accusation to level at Franklin and Breintnall. He accused them lamely of plagiarism and poor prose style—in his
own execrable Hudibrastic couplets. He whined that the community would rise up against the Busy-Body for defamation of
their neighbor's good character. Yet probably the Cretico
character would have passed unrecognized had not Keimer
taken umbrage. Had he ignored the Busy-Body entirely Keimer
might have forced Franklin and Breintnall into overt and un-
seemly references to his person and his newspaper. Instead he
bolted the first tiny fragment of bait and then provided the
Busy-Body a running advertisement in the *Instructor*.

It is difficult to determine how much the Busy-Body contributed to Keimer's downfall. The serial publication of the
Chambers's *Cyclopaedia* and Defoe's *Religious Courtship* (begun on April 24) may, in themselves, have provided sufficient
weight to sink the *Instructor*. In any case, Keimer was seldom
out of the clutches of his creditors. On July 3 he roasted them
for having confined him to jail the previous week, thereby pre-
venting the publication of the newspaper. On the seventeenth
he appealed to those indebted to him to pay, but things
worsened rapidly. On September 18 he announced his decision

to leave Pennsylvania, and on September 25 he printed his last number of the *Instructor,* announcing its sale to "B. Franklin and H. Meredith, at the New Printing Office." The Busy-Body abruptly ceased publication the same day, and on October 2 Franklin issued the *Pennsylvania Gazette* for the first time.

In some respects the letters of the Busy-Body are a less compelling performance than those of Mrs. Dogood. In Silence Dogood, Franklin created a vibrant and living presence. The reader has the vivid sense of her personality and situation. There is no such illusion in the Busy-Body papers. The Busy-Body is patterned after the elegant faceless "Mr. Spectator" of Addison and Steele. Nonetheless, the Busy-Body represents a significant advancement over Franklin's juvenilia. The featureless voice was ideally suited to the purpose; Keimer could not respond to the Busy-Body himself, for the Busy-Body eluded him. He had to heap his abuse upon the authors personally. The letters of the Busy-Body were stylistically correct and economical. Except to Keimer, the characters drawn in the letters seemed blandly instructive. The Busy-Body papers were a masterpiece of a cruel genre. For finally they were cruel and vicious. Their cruelty was not the sophomoric taunting of Silence Dogood's "Temple of Theology." It was a delicate and exquisite thing. Never again did Franklin subject a rival or enemy to such abuse, and never could he have found so pathetic a victim. Everything that we know of Samuel Keimer suggests that he was a rascal, but he was a rascal so puny that despite his own analogies to sun and mastiff, his fall was paltry and soundless.

If the public subscribed to the new and streamlined *Pennsylvania Gazette* expecting to read weekly brilliant essays and letters in the manner of the Busy-Body, they were doomed to disappointment. The *Gazette,* taken as a whole, was not very much more lively than the *Mercury.* It was not another *New-England Courant*—the forum of ready and prolific wits. Indeed, on January 6, 1730, Franklin printed an announcement of "a Course of Papers of Speculation and Amusement," which was actually an appeal. "Those Gentlemen and others, who may be inclined to divert themselves or their Friends by trying their Hands in some little Performance of that Nature, are hereby invited to make use of this Opportunity." [10] There was almost no response to the invitation. But Franklin's "characters" and essays frequently did enliven the paper, particularly during the early years. As "The Casuist" he advanced solutions to knotty, if esoteric, legal problems, usually revolving around lost or stolen livestock. On January 18, 1732, for example, a writer signing himself "T.P." posed a problem:

> A Man bargained with another, for the Keeping of his Horse six Months, while he made a Voyage to Barbadoes. At his Return, he demands the Horse. The Man who had him to keep, assures the Owner, that his Horse stray'd away, or was stolen, within a few Days after he receiv'd him, and that he has not heard of him since. The Owner then demands the Value of his Horse in Money. *Query,* Whether the Man who took the Horse to keep, may not justly demand a Deduction of so much as the Keeping of the Horse would have amounted to for Six Months, according to the Agreement? [11]

The next week's *Gazette* contained three solutions, all evidently by Franklin, though nominally by three writers. "The Keeper," wrote one, "being accountable for the Value of the Horse, at the end of Six Months, to his Owner, should then ask him if he's willing to sell the Horse, and for what Price. The Owner setting a reasonable Price, may thereout deduct his Charge for Keeping (according to Agreement) and pay the remaining Sum to the Owner in Money." This correspondent went on to raise such problems as the owner's possible refusal to sell the missing horse or his setting an unreasonable price. Yet his is the simplest of the three proposed solutions.

As a sort of disembodied voice or as the "Gazetteer" Franklin wrote "On Conversation," and his opinions recall a passage on the subject in the *Autobiography*. "The common Mistake is that People think to please by setting themselves to View, and shewing their own Perfections, whereas the easier and more effectual Way lies quite the contrary." [12] The famous hoax now called "A Witch Trial at Mount Holly" appeared in 1730, as did "Printers' Errors." Franklin's authorship of the former, however, seems dubious.[13]

In 1732 Franklin published a series of letters purporting to be from Anthony Afterwit, Celia Single, and Alice Addertongue. Anthony Afterwit's story of courtship is unmistakably drawn from life, as it recounts an unlucky episode of Franklin's own. Anthony had been enamored of a girl whose father had promised to give her £200 on the day of her marriage. He had seemed welcome enough in the house, and he had formed several schemes for improving his business with the money. "But," he lamented, "unluckily it came to pass, that when the old Gentleman saw I was pretty well engag'd, and that the Match was too far gone to be easily broke off; he, without any Reason given, grew very angry, forbid me the House, and told his Daughter that if she married me he would not give her a Farthing." [14] Two years earlier Franklin's tenant, Mrs. Thomas Godfrey, had essayed to make a match for Franklin with a young lady whose name is lost to history. The affair had proceeded normally, though the girl's father hedged on the subject of a dowry. At length, like Anthony, Franklin was dismissed by the parents "and the Daughter shut up." Franklin suspected this to have been an artifice, "on a Supposition of our being too far engag'd in Affection to retract, and therefore that we should steal a Marriage, which would leave them at Liberty to give or withold what they pleas'd." Unlike the indignant and rational Franklin, Anthony and the girl "stole a Wedding," and were accordingly very poor. Anthony went on at length, and the burden of his letter was not to castigate his father-in-law, but in fact to complain of his wife's extravagance. It is a conventional but amusing performance:

I soon saw that with Care and Industry we might live tolerably easy, and in Credit with our Neighbours: But my Wife had a strong Inclination to be a *Gentlewoman*. In Consequence of this, my old-fashioned Looking-Glass was one Day broke, as she said, *No Mortal could tell which way*. However, since we could not be without a Glass in the Room, *My Dear,* says she, *we may as well buy a large fashionable One that Mr. Such-a-one has to sell; it will cost a little more than a common Glass, and will be much handsomer and more creditable*. Accordingly the Glass was bought, and hung against the Wall: But in a Week's time, I was made sensible by little and little, *that the Table was by no Means suitable to such a Glass. . . .* And thus, by Degrees, I found all my old Furniture stow'd up into the Garret, and every thing below alter'd for the better.

For any other husbands similarly afflicted, Anthony had a solution. While his wife was visiting friends at the River "because *she could not bear the Heat of the Town,*" he had affected reversals in their style of living. "I have dispos'd of the Tea-Table, and put a Spinning Wheel in its Place, which methinks *looks very pretty:* Nine empty Cannisters I have stuff'd with Flax; and with some of the Money of the Tea-Furniture, I have bought a Set of Knitting-Needles."

The first paragraphs of the Afterwit letter are inconsistent with the temper of the rest. The reader is not prepared to learn that Anthony's wife, so dearly bought, turned into a poor bargain. The effect is to make the letter seem broken-backed, but like the concealed parodies of Samuel Keimer in the Busy-Body, the account of Anthony's courtship is a curious footnote —a measure of Franklin's resentment—and a jibe intended to be painful to the real people who had thought to wrong Benjamin Franklin. He made Anthony underscore this application: "And I have since learn'd that there are old Curmudgeons (*so called*) besides him, who have this Trick, to marry their Daughters, and yet keep what they might well spare, till they can keep it no longer: But this is by way of

Digression; *A Word to the Wise is enough*." Suffering in silence was not the young Franklin's style.

Celia Single answered the Afterwit letter two weeks later. She maintained that it provoked strife in many families, and that while she had "several times in your Paper seen severe Reflections upon us Women," she could not "remember to have once seen any such Animadversions upon the Men." This was a common complaint of female correspondents to the *Spectator,* as well as an inversion of Ephriam Censorious's letter to Silence Dogood (No. 5). Mistress Single presented a dialogue she had heard in a home disrupted by Afterwit's letter.

> If I had married Capt. ———, he would have scorn'd even to mention Knitting of Stockins. Prithee, says he, (a little nettled) what do you tell me of your Captains? If you could have had him, I suppose you would; or perhaps you did not very well like him; If I did promise to maintain you like a Gentlewoman, I suppose 'tis time enough for that when you know how to behave like one; mean while 'tis your Duty to help make me able. How long d'ye think I can maintain you at your present Rate of Living? *Pray,* says she, (somewhat fiercely, and dashing the Puff into the Powder-Box) *don't use me after this Manner, for I assure you I won't bear it. This is the Fruit of your poison News-papers; there shall come no more here, I promise you.*[15]

Then Celia turned on the printer to remind him that "those that are affronted by the Satyrs you may publish, will not consider so much who *wrote* as who *printed.*" Evidently Franklin was unwilling to take the chance that his readers might not recognize himself behind his various journalistic masks. He often played this game with the readers of *Poor Richard's Almanac.*

Alice Addertongue, who spoke up two weeks later, bore another curious resemblance to her creator: she kept an account book of her moral transgressions. In her case, however, the purpose was not self-improvement. "A young Girl of about thirty-five," Alice found it her "Duty as well as Inclination, to exercise my Talent at CENSURE, for the Good of my Country folks." A *Censor Morum* like the Busy-Body and Mrs. Dogood, Alice added a wrinkle of her own. "In my *Daybook*," she explained, "I enter every Article of Defamation as it is transacted; for Scandals *receiv'd in,* I give Credit; and when I pay them out again, I make the Persons to whom they respectively relate *Debtor.* In my *Journal,* I add to each Story by Way of Improvement, such probable Circumstances as I think it will bear, and in my *Ledger* the whole is regularly posted." [16] Mistress Addertongue is the ancestor of Sheridan's Lady Sneerwell.

Three years later, in November 1735, Franklin printed another imaginary exchange of letters. The first was apparently from a young man.

> Mr. Franklin:
> Pray let the prettiest Creature in this Place know, (by publishing this) That if it was not for her Affectation, she would be absolutely irresistible.

Six of Franklin's feminine subscribers felt called upon to respond, of whom the following are representative:

> Sir,
> Since your last Week's Paper I have look'd in my Glass a thousand Times, I believe, in one Day; and if it was not for the Charge of Affectation I might, without Partiality, believe myself the Person meant.

> Mr. Franklin,
> They that call me affected are greatly mistaken; for I don't know that I ever refus'd a Kiss to any Body but a Fool.[17]

In January 1737, the *Gazette* inveighed against drunkenness in the famous Drinker's Dictionary. But these humorous sketches gradually disappeared from the pages of the *Pennsylvania Gazette*. In the last decade of Franklin's active publication of the paper the Yale editors cannot confirm his authorship of a single such piece. He had not entirely stopped writing them, though we may reasonably suppose that his deepening involvement in business and civic affairs during the late 1730s and 1740s left him less time for composing ephemera. Nevertheless, three sensational pieces survive from this period. Two of them, "Advice to a Young Man on the Choice of a Mistress," and "The Antediluvians Were All Very Sober," were never published during his lifetime, leading us to wonder if there were not other pieces of this kind either lost completely or no longer ascribable to Franklin. The third, "The Speech of Miss Polly Baker," seems first to have appeared in the *General Advertiser* of London on April 15, 1747. This hoax was a resounding success, being reprinted in a number of provincial papers and then in the monthly magazines, including the prestigious *Gentleman's*. When the monthlies arrived in America that summer, the "Speech" began to appear in the New York, Boston, and Annapolis papers. It was widely circulated in French. Inevitably it began to be taken seriously, as a factual defense "before a Court of Judicature, at Connecticut near Boston in New-England; where [Polly Baker] was prosecuted the Fifth Time, for having a Bastard Child: Which influenced the Court to dispense with her Punishment, and induced one of her Judges to marry her the next Day." [18] But Franklin kept the secret of its origin until 1777 or 1778. He revealed the truth to the Abbé Raynal, who had included Polly's address in his *Histoire Philosophique et Politique* (1770). Franklin was present one evening when his colleague Silas Deane argued with the Abbé that the piece was a joke. The Abbé persisted that his account had been authentic. "Dr. Franklin after having enjoyed listening to the debate for some time, broke his silence and addressing the Abbé Raynal, said, 'M. l'Abbé, I am going to set you straight. When I was young and printed a newspaper, it sometimes happened, when I was short of material to fill my sheet, that I amused myself by making up stories, and that of Polly Baker is one of the number.' " The gracious and clever Abbé responded, "My word, I would rather have included your tales in my book than many other men's truths." This is one of the most charming accounts preserved of Franklin in France, but the history of the Polly Baker hoax reveals the change in Franklin's attitude toward his frivolous and ribald writings. By the 1740s he had begun habitually to suppress these pieces or to publish them anonymously. It is not known how "Polly Baker" got to London (or in fact if the *Advertiser* was its first publisher), but the speech never entertained the subscribers to the *Pennsylvania Gazette*.

As Franklin admitted to the Abbé Raynal, he wrote these "stories" to amuse himself, and he wrote them to amuse his readers. They were all basically imitative. They treated—or purported to treat—of the conventional moral subjects: vanity, infidelity, scandal. None of them was devoid of its moral application, though none was written primarily to instruct. Franklin was imaginatively at his best when speaking in a feminine voice, though, of course, he did not range widely in his presentation of female psychology. The character of Patience in the Busy-Body gives some indication of his ability to capture a variety of female characters. He specialized in shrews. His ear for dialogue was extremely keen for his times, as revealed in the admonitions of Patience's neighbor to her mischievous children or Celia Single's snatch of a domestic quarrel.

All of these pieces were written to enliven and sell the *Pennsylvania Gazette*. Sometimes Franklin invented a correspondent to puff the *Gazette* by ridiculing the rival *Mercury*, as in the case of MEMORY's letter, of November 9, 1732.

To the Printer of the Gazette.

As you sometimes take upon you to correct the Publick, you ought in your Turn patiently to receive publick Correction. My Quarrel against you is, your Practice of publishing under the Notion of News, old Transactions which I suppose you hope we have forgot. For Instance, in your Numb. 669, you tell us from London of July 20. That the Losses of our Merchants are laid before the

Congress of Soissons, by Mr. Stanhope, &c. and that Admiral Hopson died the 8th of May last. Whereas 'tis certain, there has been no Congress at Soissons nor anywhere else these three Years at least; nor could Admiral Hopson possibly die in May last, unless he has made a Resurrection since his Death in 1728.[19]

The printer of the *Gazette* was only too happy to offer his justification. "I need not say more in Vindication of my self against the Charge," wrote Franklin, "than that the Letter is evidently wrong directed, and should have been *To the Publisher of the Mercury*: Inasmuch as the Numb. of my Paper is not yet amounted to 699, nor are those old Articles any where to be found in the *Gazette,* but in the *Mercury* of the two last Weeks."

On occasion, Franklin invented a character to remind his subscribers of their civic duties or to promote a project for public improvement. On two such occasions he chose for his spokesmen wise old gentlemen. A writer who signed himself "N.N." addressed the Gazetteer in January 1733. "Walking the Street on one of these late slippery Mornings," he related, "I caught two terrible Falls, which made me, by way of Precaution for the future, get my Shoes frosted before I went home: for I am a stiff old Fellow, and my Joints none of the most pliant." [20] What irked this correspondent was the way in which some of his neighbors "made themselves wonderful merry with my Misfortune." Having now prepared himself for walking safely on the slippery sidewalks, the writer proposed to tour the town on the next icy morning, making a survey of the housekeepers and dividing them into three classes. "The humane, kind, compassionate, benevolent Class, I shall easily distinguish by the Ashes at their Doors, as God's people were distinguish'd in Ægypt by the sprinkling of their Door-posts." Such folk should receive some kind of award, he said, "They shall, however, be sure of my Respect and Friendship. With regard to those of my two latter Classes, I am resolved, I will not so much as civilly salute one of them, I will not give one of them the Wall, I will not make Room for any of them at a Fire, nor hand them any Thing at a Table, I will not direct a Customer to one of them, if any of my first Class deal in the same Things: In short, I will be as cross-grain'd towards them as 'tis possible for a good-natur'd old Man to be." The heart of this letter is a very practical suggestion to Franklin's townspeople that they spread cinders on their icy walks. Yet it is a beautifully managed piece of instruction. Franklin begins with a predicament, realizing that for narrative to be compelling it must present conflict. He employed this formula frequently: in the letters of Martha Careful and Caelia Shortface, Patience, Anthony Afterwit, Celia Single, and in *Poor Richard's Almanac*. He adapted the formula for the *Autobiography*. The old man must have fallen on the ice (all the better that he fell twice), and he must have been laughed to scorn by "a Gentleman-like Looby, with a couple of Damsels." He pretends to be angry with people who "delight in the Mishaps which befal People who have no way disoblig'd" them, but then he subtly associates that class of rascals with all those of his neighbors who do not put ashes on their walks. Finally he returns to the comic mode in his plan for retribution, sugaring both sides of his instructive pill. His phrase about refusing to make room for such villains at a fire would have delighted Mark Twain; it is in the best tradition of what we call American humor—a tradition we often associate with writers a generation or two later than Benjamin Franklin.

A writer very much like N.N. wrote to the *Gazette* on February 4, 1735, to alert his townsmen of a more pressing civic problem, the lack of adequate fire protection. From the beginning of his newspaper career Franklin had been an ardent publicist for better fire defenses in Philadelphia. For example, on April 30, 1730, the *Gazette* ran an account of a fire near Fishbourne's wharf, including the comment, "It is thought that if the People had been provided with good Engines and other suitable Instruments, the Fire might easily have been prevented

spreading, as there was but little Wind." [21] In 1735 Franklin
wrote a paper for the Junto on this subject, and he revised it
for publication in the *Gazette*. The real issue in Philadelphia
was the protection of homes and business buildings owned by
members of Franklin's class of tradesmen, but Franklin did
not present his case as a middle-class problem. Rather, he chose
as his spokesman an apparently disinterested and benevolent
old man "old and lame of my Hands, and thereby uncapable of
assisting my Fellow Citizens, when their Houses are on
Fire." [22] The writer, A.A., offered a variety of suggestions,
beginning with a Franklinian maxim: "In the first Place, as
an Ounce of Prevention is worth a Pound of Cure, I would
advise 'em to take Care how they suffer living Brands-ends, or
Coals in a full Shovel, to be carried out of One Room into
another . . . for Scraps of Fire may fall into Chinks, and
make no Appearance till Midnight; when your Stairs being in
Flames, you may be forced, (as I once was) to leap out of
your Windows, and hazard your Necks to avoid being over-
roasted." A.A. could write more vividly than could Franklin
of the horrors of a house on fire, because it had happened to
the old man himself. He went on to propose licensing of chimney sweeps and regulating of bakeries and cooperages as well
as building codes for hearths in private dwellings. His principal suggestion, however, was a well-organized company of
fire fighters. Franklin used as his model the Boston Fire Society founded in 1717, and he recalled in his memoirs, his essay
"was much spoken of as a useful Piece, and gave rise to a Project, which soon followed it." The articles of the Union Fire
Company of Philadelphia were adopted December 7, 1736.
A.A. was capable of turning a witty phrase, but he presented
his argument without the humor of the letter on slippery sidewalks. This writer was solemn and modest, leaving some of
his suggestions "to better Judgments" and concluding his paper, "Let others communicate their Thoughts as freely as I

have done mine, and perhaps something useful may be drawn from the Whole."

Franklin's correspondents wrote on a range of subjects and in a variety of tones. Like the early years of *Poor Richard,* the early years of the *Gazette* are marked by Franklin's racy youthful spirit. The more substantial Benjamin Franklin of the later years toned down this robust spirit in his own publications, while occasionally composing pieces of entertainment for himself or for anonymous publication elsewhere. In the Busy-Body and in that little jibe at Andrew Bradford's habit of reprinting old news, we have seen that Franklin was a young man always ready for a fight; but to understand how really ready he was for controversy we need to survey his writings on more serious subjects.

2

Franklin's memoirs testify to his deep personal religious convictions, and his lack of interest in sectarian matters. He regretted that his father's library had "consisted chiefly of Books in polemic Divinity," for he spent his boyhood reading them, when he might have been reading "more proper Books" (*Autobiography,* p. 58). He seems to have believed in the social utility of religious institutions, and so he supported the Presbyterian congregation of Philadelphia of which he was nominally a member, and regularly contributed to other denominations when their solicitors came to him. But he avoided attending services, finding the clerical preoccupation with doctrine irrelevant, the aim of the sermons "seeming to be rather to make us Presbyterians than good Citizens" (*Autobiography,* p. 147). His Philadelphia career was marked by only one direct assault upon the church and church authority, but his attitude toward the religious institution found expression, during the early years, in a strain of robust irreverence that frequently made him the object of criticism. Silence Dogood had described herself as "A hearty Lover of the Clergy," but she had gone on to accuse them of plagiarism and profiteering. And one of the reasons Franklin gave for leaving Boston was that his "indiscrete Disputations about Religion began to make me pointed at with Horror by good People, as an Infidel or Atheist" (*Autobiography,* p. 71). He was more discrete in Philadelphia, but he occasionally inspired horror in good people there with his barbs leveled at the clergy. For though all of these were intended to be humorous, not all of them were in impeccable taste.

Surely the best example of the censure Franklin brought upon himself by his irreverence was the case of the "sea-hens and black gowns" advertisement which prompted his "Apology for Printers." Franklin published the essay in the *Gazette* for June 10, 1731. He implied in the opening paragraph that his press was often the object of criticism. "Being frequently censur'd and condemn'd by different Persons for printing Things which they say ought not to be printed," Franklin began, "I have sometimes thought it might be necessary to make a standing Apology for my self, and publish it once á Year, to be read upon all Occasions of that Nature." [23] Remarking that he had recently "given extraordinary Offence," he asked that "all who are angry with me on the Account of printing things they don't like" consider several particulars. The argument of the "Apology" is generally that printers deal in opinions, that there are as many opinions as there are men, that some opinions will necessarily be opposed to others, and that printers must remain generally indifferent to the various opinions they print. He concluded his argument by declaring that "Printers do continually discourage the Printing of great Numbers of bad things, and stifle them in the Birth." Franklin then undertook to defend himself on the issue of the moment.

I come now to the particular Case of the *N.B.* above-mention'd, about which there has been more Clamour against me, than ever

before on any other Account. In the Hurry of other Business an
Advertisement was brought to me to be printed; it signified that
such a Ship lying at such a Wharff, would sail for Barbadoes in
such a Time, and that Freighters and Passengers might agree with
the Captain at such a Place; so far is what's common: But at the
Bottom this odd Thing was added, N.B. *No Sea Hens nor Black
Gowns will be admitted on any Terms.* I printed it, and receiv'd
my Money; and the Advertisement was stuck up round the Town
as usual. I had not so much Curiosity at that time as to enquire
the Meaning of it, nor did I in the least imagine it would give so
much Offence. Several good Men are very angry with me on this
Occasion; they are pleas'd to say I have too much Sense to do such
things ignorantly; that if they were Printers they would not have
done such a thing on any Consideration; that it could proceed from
nothing but my abundant Malice against Religion and the Clergy:
They therefore declare they will not take any more of my Papers,
nor have any farther Dealings with me; but will hinder me of all
the Custom they can. All this is very hard!

I believe it had been better if I had refused to print the said
Advertisement. However, 'tis done and cannot be revok'd. I have
only the following few Particulars to offer, some of them in my
Behalf, by way of Mitigation, and some not much to the Purpose;
but I desire none of them may be read when the Reader is not in a
very good Humour.

In fact, most of the twelve particulars were decidedly "not
much to the Purpose" of mitigation. Franklin claimed that he
had never before encountered the word *sea-hen*—the common name of a garrulous and quarrelsome species of auk—
and that, though he knew that "black gowns" in the context
referred to the clergy, he relied upon their "generous good
Temper" at "such a trifling mention of their Habit." Acknowledging "the Rashness and Inexperience of Youth, which
is most likely to be prevail'd with to do things that ought not
to be done," he nevertheless insisted that he had consciously
avoided printing things offensive to the church. The clergy of
Pennsylvania and the neighboring colonies were his customers

and friends, he said; and he wondered "That if I have much Malice against the Clergy, and withal much Sense; 'tis strange I never write or talk against the Clergy my self."

Three of Franklin's points were particularly inappropriate to be read "when the Reader is not in a very good Humour."

> 6. That I got Five Shillings by printing the advertizement.
>
> 7. That none who are angry with me would have given me so much to let it alone. . . .
>
> 12. And lastly, That I have printed above a Thousand Advertisements which made not the least mention of *Sea-Hens* or *Black Gowns;* and this being the first Offence, I have the more Reason to expect Forgiveness.

Franklin's "Apology" was not the outpouring of a contrite heart. Nor was it uniformly ironic throughout. The statement of the dilemma of a printer faced with a variety of opposing opinions demanding vent through his press is a standard one. It remains valid to this day. And Franklin seems to have been serious in his denial of the imputation of malice against the clergy, if for no other reason, than that it is bad business to alienate one's influential customers. But mixed with serious considerations of the printer's plight and the disclaimer of the charge of malice are the playful items which undercut the defense. The "Apology" leaves the impression that Franklin saw the whole affair as a tempest in a teapot at which any good-natured reader should be amused. Readers who found the advertisement in poor taste must have felt that the "Apology" only compounded it, though good-natured readers—Franklin was probably right in believing them the majority—doubtless agreed that the offense was slight and forgivable.

Nevertheless, Franklin's supposed infidelity was a weapon which his opponents in the early years liked to use against him. During a controversy of 1735 Andrew Bradford printed a letter from "A. Truman," who objected to Franklin's "running violently on the side of the Populace," and referred slurringly to "pious F——" and "religious Mr. F——." In the same year, on at least two occasions, Bradford pointed selections from Addison in the direction of his young rival. On October 9 he printed the *Spectator*, No. 441, on trust in divine goodness and including Addison's version of Psalm 23. The letter "To Mr. Bradford" that introduced the selection strikes a dignified Addisonian tone: " 'Tis an Observation of my Lord Bacon, that a little Natural Philosophy inclines Men to Atheism; but depth in Philosophy always brings them about to Religion." [24] The correspondent went on to deplore the loss of reverence among Americans, especially young Americans. Franklin was twenty-nine at the time, and though he was not the only irreverent young Pennsylvanian, Bradford's biographer, Anna Janney DeArmond, believes that he was a prime target of this letter. The writer then recalled that Addison "was not ashamed to own himself a Religious man; tho' in natural and acquired Knowledge was as much Superior to our Modern Skeptical Refiners, as were Socrates or Plato to a Toland or a Woolston."

Nor had the *Pennsylvania Gazette* always been innocent of levity on the subject of public infidelity. The topic was common enough for essayists in the eighteenth century, and on March 23, 1732, the *Gazette* had printed a letter from "Marcus," which appeared to be typical of the genre. Upon closer scrutiny, however, the good people among Franklin's subscribers discovered that Marcus was satirizing the ordinary treatise on infidelity, and more particularly a specimen of the sort that had appeared in the *Mercury* the previous week.

> How unaccountable is this strange Race of Unbelievers! Often have they been attack'd with great Strength and Judgment . . . but never so effectually as in the last week's *Mercury:* Portius has afforded a Blow that staggers even the stoutest of 'em. . . . I therefore add my Force to his, and, to their utter Confusion, I design in the following Discourse, to advance Five Hundred Several Propositions, Doctrines, or Matters of Belief, each of which shall be clear to the Understanding.[25]

There is no evidence that Franklin himself wrote the Marcus letter. Presumably he remained true to the letter of his assertion that he had never written nor spoken against the clergy; clearly, however, he sometimes violated its spirit.

He was content to offer his press to the mild ridicule of the clergy until they raised for him the specter of arbitrary and unlimited power. Then, in 1735, he plunged into the controversy surrounding the Reverend Samuel Hemphill, even going so far as to adopt the style of the polemical divines in his writings on the affair. Ordained in Ireland and recommended by the Presbytery of Strabane, Hemphill was received by the Synod of Philadelphia in the autumn of 1734. Though dogged by a charge of heterodoxy brought against him in Ireland, Hemphill was invited to assist the aged Reverend Jedediah Andrews of the Philadelphia congregation by preaching there each Sunday. It was Andrews who had once persuaded Franklin to attend church five Sundays in a row, only to lose him again by preaching "very dry, uninteresting, and unedifying" doctrinal sermons. Hemphill's preaching was of a different sort. His apparently extemporaneous sermons, wrote Franklin in the *Autobiography*, "drew together considerable Numbers of different Persuasions, who join'd in admiring them. Among the rest I became one of his constant Hearers, his Sermons pleasing me, as they had little of the dogmatical kind, but inculcated strongly the Practice of Virtue, or what in the religious Stile are called Good Works" (*Autobiography*, p. 167). The Reverend Mr. Andrews saw the affair in a different light: "Some desiring that I should have assistance,—and some leading men not disaffected to that way of Deism, as they should be,—that man was imposed on me and the congregation. Most of the best of the people were soon so dissatisfied that they would not come to meeting. Freethinkers, deists, and nothings, getting a scout of him flocked to hear." [26] At length Andrews denounced Hemphill from the pulpit and brought charges against him in the Synod. As the holder of a pew in the Presbyterian congregation, Franklin had every right to speak out on the affairs of that church. On the other hand, he was clearly to be recognized as one of the "Freethinkers, deists, and nothings" of the city, to whom questions of heterodoxy and orthodoxy were irrelevant and distasteful. Nor did he manage his published writings in defense of Hemphill in such a way as to be of much help in the hearings of a doctrinal commission. In the "Dialogue Between Two Presbyterians," published in the *Gazette* April 10, 1735, Franklin argued the deist position. Socrates spoke for Franklin.

> *S.* I do not conceive . . . how you can dislike the Preaching of Morality, when you consider, that Morality made the principal Part of [Christ's and His Apostles'] Preaching as well as of Mr. H's. What is Christ's Sermon on the Mount but an excellent moral Discourse, towards the End of which, (as foreseeing that People might in time come to depend more upon their *Faith* in him, than upon *Good Works,* for their Salvation) he tells the Hearers plainly, that their saying to him, *Lord, Lord* (that is, professing themselves his Disciples or *Christians*) should give them no Title to Salvation, but their *Doing* the Will of his Father; and that tho' they have prophesied in his Name, yet he will declare to them, as Neglecters of Morality, that he never knew them.[27]

Socrates' foil in the dialogue protests that faith is also recommended in the New Testament, but Socrates asserts that faith is recommended only as a means of producing morality. Only morality could lead to salvation; to say that faith in Christ would make a man a Christian is tantamount to saying "that my bare Believing Mr. Grew to be an excellent Teacher of the Mathematicks, would make me a Mathematician."[28] Furthermore, he thinks it ironic "That," as local wits had been heard to reflect, "the Presbyterians are going to persecute, silence and condemn a good Preacher, for exhorting them to be honest and charitable to one another and the rest of Mankind."

Orthodox Presbyterians did not regard their actions against

Samuel Hemphill as persecution, nor were they persuaded by the reasoning of the "Dialogue." [29] It was another case of the failure of the Socratic method, which Franklin discussed in his memoirs. He discovered it as a boy and "delighted in it" as the safest mode of argumentation for himself "and very embarassing to those against whom I used it" (*Autobiography*, p. 64). But though it allowed him to ensnare his enemies "in Difficulties out of which they could not extricate themselves," it produced only logical or technical victories. It exasperated his adversaries without winning them. The fact that he opened the Hemphill controversy with a Socratic dialogue may be a measure of the desperation with which he viewed the chances of a victory. If so, his fears were well grounded. The Commission met on April 17, and ten days later Hemphill was unanimously censured and suspended from his ministerial office for doctrines "Unsound and Dangerous, contrary to the sacred Scriptures and our excellent Confession and Catechisms." [30] The discussion provoked by the Commission's action forced it to print extracts from its minutes. These extracts appeared in May, and about the middle of July, Franklin published *Some Observations on the Proceedings against the Rev. Mr. Hemphill; with a Vindication of his Sermons.*

The major objection Franklin made against the Commission in this pamphlet and in his subsequent ones was to what he found to be injustice in procedural matters during the hearing. In *Some Observations* he accused the Commission of putting false glosses and willful misinterpretations on Hemphill's sermons. Franklin argued, in effect, that Hemphill *was* orthodox and differed from his accusers in minor points of nonessential doctrine. Moreover, Franklin introduced evidence that two members of the tribunal had prejudged Hemphill's case without meeting him or hearing him preach, and that witnesses who could have supported Hemphill's disclaimers to certain obviously heretical statements were not allowed to take the stand.

In September the New Printing-Office issued *A Letter to a Friend in the Country,* containing the substance of a sermon by Mr. Hemphill, in the form of a letter. Franklin wrote the preface, which sounded his old objection to the clergy in power.

> My Brethren of the Laity, as it is to you that this Letter is address'd, and chiefly for your Sakes that I take the Liberty of Publishing it, it is hop'd you'll seriously consider the Contents of it. The Generality of the Clergy were always too fond of Power to quit their Pretensions to it, by any thing that was ever yet said by particular Persons; but my Brethren, how soon should WE humble their Pride, did we all heartily and unanimously join in asserting our own natural Rights and Liberties in Opposition to their righteous claims. . . . Truth manag'd by the Laity in Opposition to them and their temporal Interests, would do much.[31]

Franklin may as well have signed his name to this bellicose preface; he headed it, "THE PUBLISHER TO HIS LAY-READERS." This was a crude and artless incitement to rebellion, and what was more unusual, offered by Benjamin Franklin unmasked. He was not in fighting trim, but it was to get worse.

At about the time Franklin issued *A Letter to a Friend,* his *Some Observations* was answered by *A Vindication of the Reverend Commission of the Synod.* The writer, who has been identified as Jonathan Dickinson, defended the Commission on the grounds that the Synod had the right to judge its own members. Franklin wrote one more rejoinder to the Commission and its proponents. *A Defense of the Rev. Mr. Hemphill's Observations, etc.* appeared about the end of October. In this pamphlet Franklin angrily denied that the Synod had the rights its defender had claimed.

> If, by judging of their Members Qualifications, they mean, that they have a Right to censure them, as they have done him, and expel 'em their Society; I think it is clear they have no such Right; for, according to this way of Reasoning, the Spanish Inquisitors may say to a Person they imagine heretical, You, 'tis true, have a Right to judge for your self, to quit our Communion, and declare your-

self Protestant; but we have likewise the common and natural Right
of Societies, to expel you our civil and ecclesiastical Society, destroy
your Reputation, deprive you of your Estate, nay your Life, or in
other Words do you all the Mischief we please, notwithstanding
your Right of declaring Non-Communion with us. How so? Because we have the Power, and Inclination to do it.[32]

He described the Presbyterian clergy in a syllogism:

> *Asses are grave and dull Animals,*
> *Our Authors are grave and dull Animals; therefore*
> *Our Authors are grave, dull,* or if you will, *Rev. Asses*

And he closed on a note of unrestrained fury: "For all these
Things have been so strongly charg'd and fairly prov'd upon
'em, that they must of Necessity confess their Guilt in Silence,
or by endeavouring a Refutation of the plain Truth, plunge
themselves deeper into the Dirt and Filth of Hypocrisy, False-
hood and Impiety, 'till at length they carry their quibbling
Absurdities far enough to open the Eyes of the weakest and
most unthinking Part of the Laity, from whom alone they
can expect Support and Proselytes."

Even before the *Defense* was published, however, the case
was irretrievably lost by what Franklin was to call the "unlucky Occurrence" of the discovery that the minister's eloquent
sermons were plagiarized—and worse, that they were borrowed from such notorious Arians as Foster, Ibbots, and
Clarke. The public was losing interest in the controversy; the
Synod ignored Hemphill's defiant demand that they excom-
municate him and instead merely voted to make his suspen-
sion permanent. Utterly ruined, Hemphill left Philadelphia;
or as one Presbyterian historian related it, "he slunk away into
deserved obscurity." [33]

Franklin's writings during the Hemphill controversy are at
once the dullest and most fascinating of the Philadelphia years.
They are all tedious; they are works in the mode of eighteenth-
century polemical divinity, which Franklin himself considered

a waste of time. He essayed to write in the fashion appropriate to the controversy at hand. His failure to write well in that mode was not altogether owing to his lack of interest and experience in it, nor was it because he was sparing of his energy and commitment to the quarrel. He lavished more printed words on this controversy than on any other of his Philadelphia career. Indeed, it is the vehemence with which he prosecuted the affair and the quality of his failure that renders the controversy so fascinating. His failure here was not the failure to save Samuel Hemphill. The Presbyterian historian was probably right that Hemphill's obscurity was deserved. Franklin's failure was journalistic or literary. He prosecuted the controversy clumsily, and clumsiness is a weakness rarely to be found in Franklin's mature work. He began the controversy with a desperate Socratic dialogue and ended it by calling the ministers and their friends, asses. If he thought to arouse the laity against the clerical establishment—as he pretended to be doing—he sadly misjudged his readers. Franklin made substantially the same mistakes in his defense of Hemphill that Samuel Keimer had made in his own defense against the Busy-Body. As Keimer had done, Franklin failed to find an issue on which he could win. He dropped his masks and he lost his temper.

Had Franklin been confronted with a like situation again, he might have taken up the cudgels of polemical divinity once more—in spite of the drubbing he took over Hemphill. Fortunately he was soon to find an indirect but rather more effective means of attacking the established religious institutions of Pennsylvania. The arrival in America of the itinerant evangelists, especially George Whitefield, afforded him the opportunity of listening to sermons of which he approved. The Grand Itinerants were men of more substance than Hemphill had been, and they caused a revolution in American Protestantism. Franklin worked silently in support of their ministry, as he relates in the *Autobiography* (pp. 176–80); but he contributed nothing to the tidal wave of pamphlets which followed the shock of the Great Awakening. The *Gazette,* however, was embroiled in the fight between the pro- and anti-Whitefield factions; a squabble in which Benjamin Franklin served as referee. In fact, both Franklin and Bradford were accused of partiality to Whitefield and his proponents. Franklin printed a piece which he considered "Invective" on May 8, 1740, with apologies to his subscribers: "Yet, as the publishing of this, will obviate a groundless Report (injurious to that Gentleman) that Mr. Whitefield had engag'd all the Printers not to print any Thing against him . . . I shall print it as I received it." [34] Two months later, the *Gazette* printed another such letter, this time accompanied by Franklin's "Statement of Editorial Policy." Again Franklin alluded to the rumor that the printers "were under some undue Influence, and guilty of great Partiality in favour of the Preaching lately admir'd among us, so as to refuse Printing any Thing in Opposition to it." He went on to recapitulate his argument of the "Apology for Printers"—this time in all seriousness. He reminded the reader that "Englishmen thought it an intolerable Hardship" when Parliament established the office of *"Licenser of the Press."* The result of that decision was that the nation might read "but the Opinions, or what was agreeable to the Opinions of ONE Man." Yet the situation would be no better if each "petty Printer" erected himself into a licenser of his press. " 'Tis true," Franklin concluded, "where Invectives are contain'd in any Piece, there is no good-natur'd Printer but had much rather be employ'd in Work of another kind: However, tho' many personal Reflections be interwoven in the following Performance, yet as the Author (*who has subscrib'd his Name*) thought them necessary . . . the Reader will excuse the Printer in publishing them." [35]

Benjamin Franklin's alleged "abundant Malice against Religion and the Clergy" was hotly denied but not wholly unfounded. Only once, during the Hemphill imbroglio, did it boil up into furious prose; but it simmered constantly. For the most part it showed itself in the form of conventional sophomoric irreverence. Its most characteristic expression is to be found in the earlier issues of *Poor Richard's Almanac,* where ministers are lumped for abuse with lawyers and doctors. Like the sea-hens and black gowns handbill, these are gentle "Rubs." Franklin wrote most frequently and skilfully in quarrels with his competitors and on provincial affairs. Printing and journalism were the meat on his table, and as the years wore on politics overtook and passed business as the area of his prime concern.

As a printer, Franklin was a "leather-apron" man, but as Carl and Jessica Bridenbaugh have demonstrated, the demands of their business placed printers intellectually and economically at the head of the middle class. It was this milieu that encouraged Franklin's rise to influence. His prosperity and intellectual superiority led him to associations outside the "mechanicks" class—notably, in the early years, the members of the Masonic lodge and his private club, the Junto. Among the first members of the Junto was Nicolas Scull, "a Surveyer, afterwards Surveyer-General, Who lov'd Books, and sometimes made a few Verses" (*Autobiography,* p. 117).

Among Scull's verses is perhaps the first description of Benjamin Franklin. Presumably in the spring of 1731, Scull composed an account of a Junto meeting. Cast in heroic couplets the poem presents a dream vision:

> But restless fancy with a mem'rous train
> Of P[l]easing Ideas soon Possest my brain
> The Junto room did first to View appear
> And whilst I slept I saw the Junto there
> Three Queeries, in Philosophy were first
> Gravely considered & at length Discust.[36]

Scull went on to describe the various types of discourse common to a Junto meeting, and then he introduced Bargos, or Franklin, speaking on a favorite topic of his.

Bargos whos birth is by fair Boston claimd
And Justly is for a great Genius fam'd
Proceeded next to sing New Englands fate
Her case how Des'prate and her foes how great
How B[elche]r crost the seas to plead her cause
Secure her freedom and support her laws
How like a rock unmovd the Hero stod
Exposd to danger for his countrys good
And as the only means for her Reliefe
Wisely Procurd himself to be her Cheife
How cloth'd with Power how he Perceives his faults
Her Power and Granduer gives of strength of thought
He tells New England now, her cause is wrong
Thus with her sovreign to contend so long
Perswades her sons two thousand pounds is just
The King Commands it and obey they must
Yet they maintain what their forefathers held
Nor to their monarch will their freedom yeild.

As with Keimer's scurrilous picture of Bebegio, we could wish Scull had expanded his description of Franklin's person and mannerisms. He tells nothing directly of either, except for the conventionally hyperbolic claim of great genius for Franklin. In the context of Scull's poem, the description of Bargos occupied a prominent place and a disproportionate number of lines, reflecting Franklin's preeminence in the Junto. More significantly, however, the passage characterizes Bargos as the Junto member most concerned with politics—and intercolonial politics at that. In other words, a poet wanting to sketch a recognizable picture of Benjamin Franklin in the early 1730s, presented him talking earnestly and ironically about politics. To his friends and subscribers, Franklin was probably not so much the young tradesman who studied algebra by a smoldering fire or the young "satyrist" and preacher-baiter. He was not Poor Richard Saunders, because *Poor Richard's Almanac* was yet to appear. Benjamin Franklin was first of all, the bold, incisive antiroyalist, and antiproprietary newspaper editor.

Silence Dogood had first sounded the theme, lining up with the Couranteers as "a mortal Enemy of arbitrary Government and unlimited Power." Franklin's printing house issued the first of his political writings on April 3, 1729. This was a pamphlet *The Nature and Necessity of a Paper-Currency*. It was published anonymously, but signed with the initials "B.B." which may have suggested the Busy-Body. Relying heavily on Sir William Petty's *Treatise of Taxes and Contributions* (1662) Franklin argued the importance of a circulating medium in adequate supply to the conduct of a community's business, and then addressed the question of how much paper money was to be considered safe in a given economy and how it might be safeguarded against a damaging depreciation. The Pennsylvania Assembly was successful in negotiating a generally favorable compromise with Governor Patrick Gordon, who in May signed a bill providing for the emission of £30,000 in bills of credit. Franklin remembered in his memoirs that his pamphlet had had its impact on the deliberations, in that its opponents had no writers equipped to answer it. "My Friends [in the Assembly], who conceiv'd I had been of some Service," he wrote, "thought fit to reward me, by employing me in printing the Money, a very profitable Jobb, and a great Help to me." [37]

Franklin had no newspaper of his own during the paper money campaign; but no sooner had the *Pennsylvania Gazette* been acquired by the New Printing-Office than it fired a political broadside. Franklin recalled that "some spirited Remarks of my Writing on the Dispute then going on between Govr. Burnet and the Massachusetts Assembly, struck the principal People, occasion'd the Paper and the Manager of it to be much talk'd of, and in a few Weeks brought them all to be our Subscribers" (*Autobiography*, p. 121). This was the controversy to which Nicolas Scull alluded in his Junto verses. It was a Massachusetts problem. In 1728 the Assembly there had granted Governor William Burnet a salary only large enough "to enable him to manage the public affairs of the government" rather than the "fixed and honorable" amount recommended in the governor's instructions from the Crown. The question was whether the colonial Assembly had the right to determine a royal governor's salary. Constitutional arguments were raised on both sides, the case for Massachusetts being argued by Jonathan Belcher. The Board of Trade, unable to come to a decision, finally recommended that the Assembly's conduct be investigated by Parliament. In the meantime Governor Burnet died, and Belcher was himself named to the post. In the second number of the *Gazette* issued by Franklin, he reported the sudden death of Burnett and reviewed the controversy, hinting that the new governor seemed desirous of prosecuting the case further in his own behalf. The Assembly, wrote Franklin, objected to the fixed salary demanded in the governor's instructions because "they thought it an Imposition, contrary to their own Charter, and to *Magna Charta*; and they judg'd that by the Dictates of Reason there should be a mutual Dependence between the *Governor* and the *Governed,* and that to make any Governour independent on his People, would be dangerous, and destructive of their Liberties, and the ready way to establish Tyranny." [38] The article's conclusion was ironic but fervid: "Their happy Mother Country will perhaps observe with Pleasure, that tho' her gallant Cocks and matchless Dogs abate their native Fire and Intrepidity when transported to a Foreign Clime (as the common Notion is) yet her SONS in the remotest Part of the Earth, and even to the third and fourth Descent, still retain that ardent Spirit of Liberty, and that undaunted Courage in the Defense of it, which has in every Age so gloriously distinguished BRITONS and ENGLISHMEN from all the Rest of Mankind."

The Masschusetts dispute did not admit of easy solutions. When the new governor arrived in Massachusetts, Franklin continued his discussion of the affair by printing periodically extracts from Belcher's speeches and the Assembly's resolutions. On September 24, 1730, the *Gazette* promised to publish, the next week, Belcher's speech to the House, and Franklin observed sardonically that "he has brought with him those very Instructions that occasion'd the Difference between Governor Burnet and that People, which were what he went home commission'd as Agent for the Country, to get withdrawn, as an intolerable Grievance. But by being at Court, it seems, he has had the *advantage* of seeing Things in another Light, and those Instructions do now appear to him highly consistent with the Privileges and Interest of the People, which before, as a *Patriot,* he had very different Notions of." [39]

Franklin's boldness and his control of irony were new elements in Philadelphia journalism. A Pennsylvania paper could perhaps afford to be bold on a Massachusetts issue, but Franklin's pen had already made its contribution to a popular cause in Pennsylvania, and the Proprietary party was mistaken if it anticipated that the *Gazette* would be more temperate on local issues. Bradford's *Mercury* was generally conservative in politics, leaning toward the Proprietary faction—often called "the Gentlemen" by Franklin—but Bradford and Franklin agreed on the paper money question. The *Gazette* and the *Mercury* first took opposite sides of a major political question—Franklin began "running violently on the side of the populace"—during the election campaign of 1733, when the central figure in the controversy was Andrew Hamilton. Hamilton was one of the most powerful men in Pennsylvania from 1727 until his death in 1741. A lawyer by profession, he had entered public service in 1717 when he was appointed attorney general of the province under Governor Keith. He sojourned in England for three years, and upon his return in 1727, he was elected to the Assembly from Bucks County. Reelected the next year, he rose to the post of Speaker. He was also a trustee of the powerful Loan Office and recorder for Philadelphia.

In the Assembly of 1727 Hamilton had opposed former Governor Keith's bid for a political comeback, and therefore is presumed to have been a friend of Governor Patrick Gordon. As a close associate of James Logan, one of the most prominent and wealthy of the Quaker gentlemen, Hamilton ought to have been sympathetic to Proprietary interests.[40] However, a realignment somehow took place during 1732–33. There was a rumor of wide currency that the daughters of Hamilton and Gordon quarreled during this time, but it was presumably for better reasons that Hamilton and the Assembly balked at Gordon's reappointment as governor in 1733. The Assembly affected to doubt the governor's authority, and after angry words on both sides it adjourned permanently. In retaliation the governor sought to prevent Hamilton's reelection.[41]

We know nothing of the background of Andrew Bradford's stand on the Hamilton affair. Whether the *Mercury* was merely made the tool of the governor's party or if Bradford had some personal stake in the outcome are questions his biographer cannot answer. Whatever the reason, the *Mercury* became the forum for virulent attacks against Hamilton during the campaign. Four days before the election a correspondent signing himself "Cato, Junior," called for the election of a slate of candidates among whom Hamilton's name was notably absent. Immediately after the election Cato, Junior, reappeared with an essay in praise of the electorate, headed, "When the Wicked Perish there is Shouting." Next to this expression of exultation, Bradford printed the list of candidates elected to the Assembly. Such results were usually printed on the third or fourth page of the papers, but conspicuously placed next to Cato's victory letter, they were doubtless meant to celebrate the defeat of Andrew Hamilton.

The attacks on the still-potent Hamilton did not abate, however. An essay in the *Mercury*, "On Infidelity," was evidently pointed at both Hamilton and Franklin.[42] The attacks culminated on October 18 in an anonymous charge that Hamilton's control of the Assembly, the courts, and the Loan Office was dictatorial and sinister. At that point Franklin was moved to answer; and on November 16 he published a "Half-hour's Conversation with a Friend." Certainly the most artful political document of Franklin's Philadelphia career, the "Conversation" reported an interview with Hamilton. It was not a conventional dialogue, but rather an informal account of the interview, quoting liberally, as if from memory. The tone is one of subdued and dignified rationality in the face of the *Mercury*'s shrill attack. This was precisely the tone that Franklin needed and could not achieve in his defense of Samuel Hemphill less than two years later. The writer of the "Conversation" characterized the volley of charges leveled at Hamilton as Franklin loved to do it, by alluding to an "old Saying, *Throw Dirt enough, and some will stick.*" [43] He then recounted the beginning of his talk with his prominent "Friend." The Friend acknowledged that the attacks were obviously pointed at him, but he preferred not to answer charges by anonymous writers, "seeing it was commonly agreed to be wrote by nobody, he thought no body should regard it."

The interviewer had pressed him, however, pointing out that silence might be taken as an admission of his guilt. The Friend then answered, apparently in a quiet tone, that the people of Pennsylvania were wise enough to recognize that their liberties were guaranteed by the provincial charter, so that they could "laugh at the impotent Efforts of the Great and Powerful" to deprive them of those liberties. Here again the interviewer interrupted his Friend to observe that he had yet to answer the charges directly. The Friend replied, maintaining his restraint, but introducing a note of ridicule: "Sir, you know in Law a particular Answer to a general Charge is never required of any Man, and therefore it cannot be expected that I should make a particular Answer to a Number of general Charges, such as, *speaking contemptibly* (I suppose the polite Author means *contemptuously*) *of the Proprietor, abusing and displacing the Governor, endeavouring to put a Stop to the Proceedings of Government and to the Administration of*

*Justice, Partiality in Lending out Money at the Loan-Office,
&c.*" Nonetheless, he went on to answer several of the charges
directly, pointing to inconsistencies in some of the arguments
and demanding evidence and witnesses to support others. To
the charge of pride and other personal vices, the Friend could
only appeal, he said, for the mercy of a higher Power than the
American Weekly Mercury.

Having established Hamilton's reasonable and reverent
character, Franklin then allowed him to ridicule his tormenters
broadly and with incisive wit.

> And then taking up the Letter in his Hand, he merrily said, "Was
> this fine Letter but stript of all the affected simplicities and dis-
> guises the Author has been at the pains to dress it up in . . . and
> put into plain English, methinks it would read pretty much to the
> following purpose; '*Loving, Loving, Loving Friends,* hear and
> believe, and then you will see, there is risen up amongst us a
> dangerous, proud, wicked, witty Fellow, whose Life is inconsistent
> with your Lives and Liberties, as by the following Instances will
> to you my dearest Countrymen be most manifest. He speaks con-
> temptibly of the Pr——r, for I my self have heard him swear ter-
> ribly, that Gentleman was not tall enough to touch the Moon, nor
> strong enough to remove a Mountain: He abuses the Go——r, and
> has endeavoured to displace him, for it is commonly reported, that
> he should say in a certain Place, that his Honour don't see now so
> well as when he was but one and twenty. . . . He's proud and
> revengeful to the last Degree, for he will not be thankful to his
> Betters for abusing him; and upon a certain Time publickly exposed
> me for insinuating he had taken greater Fees in his Office than by
> Law he was entitled to.' "

The sentiments and even the wit may have been Hamilton's,
but unmistakable in the "Conversation" is Franklin's acute ear
for the rhythm and cadence of prose as well as his ability to
construct a sentence that held its telling point to the last, cli-
matic phrase.

Franklin had reason to be proud of this piece, but he did

not record anything of the episode in his memoirs. It was a relatively insignificant one, both to Franklin and to Hamilton. The *Mercury* answered the "Conversation" ironically, stating that part of the Friend's marks had been omitted, and offering to supply them in verse. Hamilton's vanity was to be demonstrated by the following lines:

> 'Tis I, 'tis I alone
> Can Mountains move, and reach the Moon,
> And see as well as Twenty-one.

The squabble dragged on until late in 1734. In the meantime, Hamilton was reelected Speaker of the Assembly, an office he held until 1739, two years before his death. As an attorney he distinguished himself in his defense of John Peter Zenger in 1735—a landmark decision in the history of the free American press, but a story which neither Bradford nor Franklin printed at the time.

The success of the "Half-hour's Conversation" is not to be measured by its impact on Pennsylvania history, anymore than Hemphill's disappearance was the index of Franklin's failure in that controversy. The "Conversation" is a superbly persuasive document. In form it is unusual if not plainly unique. Franklin eschewed the stiff formality of a conventional dialogue and so presented Hamilton as the rational gentleman at his leisure. The supposed informality creates a sense of immediacy, and Hamilton's elegant answers seem the more brilliant for being apparently impromptu. Hamilton's reticence to discuss the accusations against him and the reasons he gives for that reticence, combine to make his tormentors seem themselves contemptible. They write from the cowardly covert of anonymity and they insult the intelligence of their neighbors by suggesting that one man might destroy all of the liberties of Pennsylvanians. Moreover, they are at best semiliterate. Franklin manages to insert the *Mercury* writer's unlucky malapropism twice into the "Conversation." In Friend Andrew

Hamilton, Franklin created another mask—a speaking voice who characterizes himself in the style of his conversation. He is modeled upon Franklin's own conception of the ideal conversationalist, as described in the *Gazette* essay of 1730: "Let his Air, his Manner, and Behaviour, be easy, courteous and Affable, void of every Thing haughty or assuming; his Words few, express'd with Modesty, and a Respect for those he talks to. . . . Let him never trouble other People about his own Affairs, nor concern himself with theirs. Let him avoid Disputes; and when he dissents from others propose his Reasons with Calmness and Complaisance." [44]

Subjected to analysis, the Friend's remarks are clearly an ad hominem argument. He laughs the charges off rather than answering them; he assails the knavery and literacy of his adversaries, ignoring for the most part substantive matters. Yet the charges against Hamilton were evidently insubstantial. Franklin was probably right that at that stage of the protracted controversy plain ridicule of the accusers and their accusations was the indicated reaction.

The writer of journalistic hoaxes and characters in Franklin's time had little occasion to create a totally sympathetic figure: a character with dignity, wit, charm. The greatest demand was for Silence Dogoods and Anthony Afterwits. As autobiographer, Franklin would need to create several exemplary characters, his own included. In the portrait of his Friend, Andrew Hamilton, Franklin showed that he had mastered the technique.

Benjamin Franklin was chosen clerk of the Pennsylvania Assembly in October 1736. In October 1737, he succeeded his competitor, Andrew Bradford, as postmaster of Philadelphia. Those two "Promotions" made Franklin a public man, subject to criticism for his actions as well as the conduct of his press. Andrew Bradford was twenty years Franklin's senior, and as Franklin remembered "rich and easy." Yet he could not but be graveled by the success of his young competitor, and he proved an avid watchdog. In the fall and winter of 1737–38 the *Mercury* dragged Franklin's name into a bizarre and tragic murder case involving a fraudulent Masonic ritual. Though Franklin was in no way implicated in the tragedy, beyond having been told in advance that the mock initiation was to take place, the *Mercury* attack focused on him.[45] On occasion, Bradford caught Franklin in what appears to have been a genuine lapse into partisanship in his capacity of clerk and printer to the Assembly.

One such case occurred in the winter of 1740. At the previous session the Assembly had presented a bill for raising money for public purposes and for repeal of an existing revenue measure. The Council and the governor felt that the Assembly bill would remove control of the streets, docks, wharves, and bridges from the mayor and commonality of Philadelphia. Presumably these facilities were managed for the benefit of all the inhabitants, and it was for this reason that the governor vetoed the bill. In Franklin's printing of the votes, however, he included the veto and the Assembly's protest against it, but he omitted the governor's message to the Assembly in which the reasons for his veto were set forth. On February 12 Andrew Bradford printed what was in effect an extra edition of the *Mercury*, introduced by a letter to himself from *"A.B., C.D., E.F., &c. &c. &c,"* which begged Bradford to print their complaint against his brother printer, though "People generally say there's no such thing as getting one Lawyer to prosecute another nor one Pickpocket to peach a Brother." Their complaint was couched in a letter to "Mr. Franklin," in which they accused him of suppressing the governor's message. They lashed him with his own weapon, a maxim: "You have had fair warning, *Ben,* you have been put in mind of the old Proverb, *Better late than never.*" Franklin had let the story out that he had dropped the message somewhere unspecified and lost it. "That Story indeed was like to have passed well enough, had not a very plain blunt Fellow declared publickly, that to his certain Knowledge it was all false." They enclosed a copy of the governor's "Reasons" so that Franklin could repair his minutes, and they concluded, "In this we do not say we heap Coals of Fire upon your Head, we only return you good for evil, and Heavens grant you may make a good Use of this kind Caution from your old Freinds, who wish you well tho' they can't at present give you a Place worth 60 or 70£. a Year." This letter is the first recorded accusation of political opportunism against Benjamin Franklin. It was not to be the last: that is a charge which persists to this day. It may be proof of that "old Saying, *Throw Dirt enough, and some will stick*," although the *Mercury* seems to have caught Franklin red-handed in this instance. In any event, it provides an interpretive footnote to Franklin's own account of his political career in the *Autobiography*.

Franklin was embroiled in one more protracted newspaper quarrel during his Philadelphia career, in which he capped a restrained and dignified defense of himself and his conduct of the post office with one of his most successful verse burlesques. The affair centered on the rivalry between Franklin and Bradford to publish the first American magazine in 1740–41, but the issues which arose during the controversy dated from 1737 when Franklin took over the postmastership. Franklin related the story accurately in his memoirs:

> Col. Spotswood, late Governor of Virginia, and then Post-Master, General, being dissatisfied with the Conduct of his Deputy at Philadelphia, respecting some Negligence in rendering, and Inexactitude of his Accounts, took from him the Commission and offered it to me. I accepted it readily, and found it of great Advantage; for tho' the Salary was small, it facilitated the Corespondence that improv'd my Newspaper, encreas'd the Number demanded, as well as the Advertisements to be inserted, so that it came to afford me a very considerable Income. My old Competitor's Newspaper declin'd proportionably, and I was satisfy'd without retaliating his

Refusal, while Postmaster, to permit my Papers being carried by the Riders. (*Autobiography,* p. 172)

Franklin did allow the *Mercury* free carriage until 1739. In October of that year, however, he received instructions from Colonel Spotswood to "commence Suit" against Bradford and no longer to "suffer to be carried by the Post any of his News-Papers." [46] The change in the Philadelphia post office was evidently accomplished without comment; however, as the *Autobiography* implies, it had an effect on both newspapers' circulation and advertising revenue. It was generally assumed by the public and the advertisers that control of the postriders assured the widest possible circulation, and so newspapers published by postmasters received the choicest advertising. Nonetheless Bradford bore it silently.

A year later, on November 6, 1740, the *American Weekly Mercury* printed a lengthy and ambitious "Plan of an Intended Magazine." The first such venture in the colonies, *The American Magazine, or A Monthly View of The Political State of the British Colonies,* would appear the following March if enough subscriptions at 12s. per year could be received. The next week the *Pennsylvania Gazette* published a similar prospectus. *The General Magazine, and Historical Chronicle, for all the British Plantations in America* could be expected in January. The same size as the projected *American Magazine,* it would cost only 9d. a copy. Lest anyone imagine that the two proposals were coincidental, Franklin cried foul in his advertisement.

> This MAGAZINE, in Imitation of those in England, was long since projected; a Correspondence is settled with Intelligent Men in most of the Colonies, and small Types are procured, for carrying it on in the best Manner. It would not, indeed, have been published quite so soon, were it not that a Person, to whom the Scheme was communicated in *Confidence,* has thought fit to advertise it in the last *Mercury,* without our Participation; and,

probably, with a View, by Starting before us, to discourage us from prosecuting our first Design, and reap the Advantage of it wholly to himself.[47]

The culprit was John Webbe, ironically the conveyancer and lawyer retained by Franklin to collect Bradford's post office indebtedness. Franklin had conceived the idea for an American magazine and had approached Webbe as a possible editor. Webbe evidently saw an opportunity to turn the project to his greater profit.

His duplicity patently exposed, Webbe nevertheless leaped to the attack. In the *Mercury* of November 20, Bradford printed his letter, aggressively titled "THE DETECTION." [48] "Tho' Nothing could be more imprudent in Mr. Franklin," it begins, "than to thrust me into his Advertisement, in any Shape whatsoever; yet he has not only thought fit to introduce me there, but has at the same Time accused me, of such Practices, which if I were guilty of, I should not deserve to breath in any Society." Webbe found Franklin's imprudence on this occasion characteristic of him: "As Mr. Franklin has now professedly applied his News Paper to the gratifying his own particular Malice by blackening the Reputation of a private Person; it is reasonable to believe that, without proper Animadversion on such a Proceedure, he will not stop at this single Instance of spitting his Malignity from his Press, but be incouraged to proceed in making use of it as an Engine to bespatter the Characters of every other Person he may happen to dislike." He echoed what was already a common theme in criticism of Benjamin Franklin, when he coupled this charge of malice with one of deviousness and cunning. The falsehoods in Franklin's advertisement were *"insinuated"* and thus "by far the most mischievous kind of Lying." Webbe could sooner forgive direct lying done with the audacity of a highwayman, but Franklin's indirect lying was like "the Slyness of a Pickpocket."

However, Webbe's explanation of the affair, though boldly

set forth, depended upon the shaving of fine distinctions. Franklin had mentioned his *"Desire"* of printing a magazine, if Webbe would compose one. "But surely his making the Proposal neither obliged me to the writing of one for him to print, nor restrained me from the printing of it at any other Press without his Leave or Participation." Webbe included some notes transcribed from Franklin's own handwriting which he interpreted as proof that Franklin's "long projected Scheme was never intended to be carried on by him in any other Capacity than that of a *meer* Printer." And beneath his letter Webbe promised "The Remainder of the *Detection* in the next."

"The Detection," however, was never renewed. The next week, in its place, the *Mercury* printed an essay by Webbe on the literary qualifications required for editing a magazine. He professed himself humbly willing to receive any just criticism of his work; he was not vainly confident of his literary gifts. Yet he felt moved to reply to the Gazetteer in self-defense, and had undertaken to respond not "to vindicate himself from being *a bad Writer* (for to that Accusation he has already pleaded GUILTY) but from the Charge of being a *bad Man."*

Franklin was managing the magazine controversy with splendid economy of wit and energy. He wrote not another word, but each week's *Pennsylvania Gazette* contained the original advertisement for the *General Magazine*—including the passage on Webbe's treachery. Webbe did not know whether to defend himself further or to let well enough alone. His confusion is obvious in his letter to the *Mercury* of December 4. "The Facts urged in my Vindication I endeavoured to set forth with all the Clearness I was capable of, without Artifice or a *studied* Perplexity; and, therefore, if there had been the *least* Misrepresentation, it could have been *most easily* detected. Facts *so stated,* and NOT DENIED, are, according to a *universal* Rule of judging, CONFESSED; and therefore Mr. Franklin's Silence is the *highest* Justification I can desire." [49] In a burst of magnanimity Webbe went on to announce that as long as Franklin remained silent and apparently subdued, he would suppress the remainder of "The Detection." But on the very heels of his supposed offer of truce, Webbe followed with another serious accusation against Franklin:

> This is a Kindness he could not reasonably expect at my Hands; Considering that he has since my first Letter, in Quality of Post-Master, taken upon him to deprive the *Mercury* of the Benefit of the Post, and will not permit it to travel with his *Gazette,* that charges me with the most infamous Practices. His Resentment against his Brother Printer is altogether unreasonable; for a Printer should be always acquitted from being a Party to any Writing when he discovers the Author, or when the Author subscribes his Name; except the other knows he publishes a Falsehood at the Time, which cannot be supposed to be the Case in Respect to what Mr. Bradford printed for me.

Webbe, the lawyer, seems almost to have been citing Franklin's own "Apology for Printers" as precedent in this justification of Bradford. In this case, however, a justification of Andrew Bradford was hardly to the point. It was true, as Webbe said, that the *Mercury* had been denied the post; b t nominally at least the loss of that privilege dated from t e arrival of Spotswood's letter more than a year before. In the *Gazette* of December 11, Franklin printed a signed explanation of these circumstances, including the text of the postmaster general's letter. Franklin's introductory paragraph said that he had ignored the first two "angry Papers" written against him in the *Mercury,* "as believing that both the Facts therein stated, and the extraordinary Reasonings upon them, might be safely enough left to themselves, without any Animadversion. . . . But the *last,* my Friends think 'tis necessary I should take some Notice of, as it contains an Accusation that has at least a Shew of Probability, being printed by a Person to whom it particularly relates, who could not but know whether it was true or false; and who, having still some Reputation to guard, it may be presum'd, could by no Means be prevail'd on to publish a Thing as Truth, which was contrary to his own Knowledge." [50] Franklin could not understand Bradford's publishing the story, but he could exonerate Bradford from the suspicion of having provided Webbe with the false information on which he based his attack on Franklin. "For this, in my Opinion, cannot possibly be: Inasmuch as that Person [Webbe] is thoroughly acquainted with the Affair, was employ'd as Attorney in the Action against Bradford, and had, at the very Time he was writing the Paragraph in Question, the Original Letter from Col. SPOTSWOOD, in his own Possession."

Webbe's rejoinder to this was swift and savage. Franklin's advertisement for the *General Magazine* was an ingenious invention, he thought, but this latest charge in the *Gazette* wonderfully supplied its place. The truth about the postal situation, Webbe explained, was that the *Mercury* had been bundled into unsealed packets and sent to the riders who distributed them on their routes. Though not strictly legal, the practice "was NO SECRET; and consequently could not be *unknown* to Mr. Franklin." Moreover, Webbe had understood "some Time before [Franklin] laid me under the Necessity of writing against him in my own Defence, that as he favoured Mr. Bradford by permitting the Postman to distribute his Papers, he had him therefore *under his Thumb;* and was confident, in Regard he could at any Time deprive him of that Privilege, that he would not, if he understood his own Interest, be prevailed upon to publish any Thing against him the Gazetteer." [51] Franklin had winked at the *Mercury's* being delivered by his riders until Webbe's letters began to appear. Then, said Webbe, the postman who usually carried the papers began to be "apprehensive it wou'd be displeasing to Mr. Franklin, were he to know he distributed them." From this Webbe inferred that Franklin "had already begun to put his

Threats against the *Mercury* in Execution." Furthermore, Webbe charged that Franklin realized, before he wrote his explanation in the *Gazette,* that Webbe's phrase, "depriving the *Mercury* of the Benefit of the Post," referred to Franklin's particular edict to his postman, not Spotswood's order of the previous year.

> He NOTWITHSTANDING, partly with a View, as I am apt to imagine, to convince the World of his great Address in Argument, undertook to prove, and did most *elaborately* and UN-DENIABLY prove (*what he was sure no Body would deny*) the Receipt of Mr. Spotswood's Orders. . . .
>
> Such an Absurdity would be pardonable, if it *only* arose from his natural Fondness of being thought a man of Sagacity. But because he could not in *one Respect* be said to deprive the *Mercury* of the Advantage of the Post, in as much as he had Orders so to do, that *Therefore* he did not in any *other Respect;* and from thence in express Terms *peremptorily* to charge me with writing and Mr. Bradford with publishing a *wilful* Falsehood, tho' the Gazetteer was thro'ly Sensible at the Time it was not one, is such *a flagrant* Evidence of his great CANDOUR and SINCERITY, as well as of a violent inclination to *defame,* that I think it may be safely left to it self without any farther Animadversion.

Once again an attack on Franklin took the form of an imputation of insincerity and deviousness. The intricacies of this controversy became yet more exquisite. Webbe went on to analyze the text of Franklin's defense, attempting to demonstrate the ways in which Franklin's rhetoric misrepresented the facts of the case. The Gazetteer had "instead of laying a Suspicion raised one, by going about to obviate Misrepresentations before he was called upon." It was hypocrisy, Webbe insisted, for Franklin to say that he was sorry to be obliged to mention that Bradford had been removed from the postmastership for negligence in his accounts. Franklin was under no obligation to mention that in the first place, and furthermore, "The Letter no where says so, and Mr. Bradford says he was removed by the *false* Representations and *private* Solicitations of the Gazetteer." Here, in what is advanced as a consideration of Franklin "in the Capacity of a Writer," and literally in parentheses, Webbe inserted the most serious charge yet leveled against Franklin.

> But the Post-Master General on the contrary, plainly declares, that for as much as on Inquiry he found, That the Sickness pleaded by Mr. Bradford was only pretended, he therefore thought that such an Imposition should not be passed over, without some Mark of his Resentment. If Mr. Bradford can prove, as he says he can, that his Sickness was not imaginary, no Body can be Suspected of giving that false Information of his State of Health to the Post-Master General but his Deputy here. It appears from the Scope of the Letter to which I refer, that the honourable Person who wrote it, designed it should be communicated to Mr. Bradford, which he declares never was done. Perhaps the Reason of concealing it from him, 'till after the Post-Master General's Death, was an Apprehension he might be convinced that the Order in it was obtained upon a Misrepresentation of Mr. Bradford, the Suspicion of which Mr. Franklin, tho' not charged with it, thought himself under a Necessity, even of going out of his Way, to clear himself from.

Webbe referred to the passage in Spotswood's letter in which the Postmaster General observed that Bradford "must *blush* upon a Trial, before his Towns-men," to have his letters produced, in which he had continually pleaded illness as the reason for not posting his accounts. "Whereas, upon Enquiry," Spotswood had continued, "I am well assured, that, for these two Years past, he has appeared abroad in as good State of Health, as ever he used to be." Webbe advanced himself as the person in the unique position of knowing both sides of the story. As Franklin's attorney, he had access to the letter which had been concealed from Bradford; as Bradford's associate, he had learned how Spotswood had been misinformed. Serious as was the charge, there was little evidence marshaled to prove it. Webbe did not offer proof that Bradford had been ill during the years in question; he only reported that Bradford said it could be proven. Nor could Webbe present copies of the letters Franklin had supposedly sent to Spotswood misrpresenting Bradford's condition. Moreover, Webbe did not categorically deny that Bradford had never been allowed to see Spotswood's letter; he only stated that Bradford "declares [it] never was done."

Poor Richard wrote, in 1740, "Many a Meal is lost for want of meat." It is almost as though he were commenting on Webbe's charges before they were published. Franklin did not reply to Webbe's letter of December 18. He must have considered these charges in the same light as he had the first two letters by Webbe, believing that they "might safely enough be left to themselves." Writing an account of the affair from Bradford's point of view, Anna Janney DeArmond suggests that Franklin's silence after "this not unconvincing statement," may imply an element of truth in the charges.[52] But even she does not advance the argument with much conviction. Neither Webbe nor Bradford himself renewed the controversy after this; perhaps, as the Yale editors suggest, each party to the conflict set to work in earnest to bring out the first magazine. It would seem to follow that had Webbe's accusations had real validity, they would not have been allowed to die; Bradford could have, and would have, spoken out in his own behalf.

Reading the exchange, one cannot fail to be struck with the sophistic tone of Webbe's letters, a fault he underscored for the reader by constantly charging Franklin with the same thing. Webbe could not and did not deny his original act of duplicity in taking Franklin's conception of a magazine to Bradford, and Franklin's advertisement for the *General Magazine* contained little more than a straightforward statement of the facts. Franklin managed his side of the controversy with dignity and restraint and—as is particularly important in quarrels of this sort—he kept the ball almost constantly in Webbe's court. He had answered the most plausible of Webbe's specific charges the best way he could, and he apparently regarded the rest with silent contempt. He could scarcely have replied directly to the implied charges against his moral character; however, it is tempting to read his bitterness into some of the sayings of Poor Richard, whose almanac must have been in preparation during the exchange with Bradford and Webbe.

> Best is the Tongue that feels the rein;
> He that talks much, must talk in vain;
> We from the wordy Torrent fly:
> Who listens to the chattering Pye? [53]

Poor Richard made proverbial reference to Webbe's kind of duplicity: "If you would keep your Secret from an enemy, tell it not to a friend." And he expressed similar sentiments in verse.

> *Monkeys* warm with envious spite,
> Their most obliging FRIENDS will bite;
> And, fond to copy human Ways,
> Practice new Mischiefs all their days.

Franklin may have been pondering his own conduct of the controversy when he wrote, "Let thy discontents be thy Secrets; if the world knows them, 'twill despise *thee* and increase *them*," and "Christianity commands us to pass by Injuries; Policy, to let them pass by us."

In the meantime, the race to publish the first colonial magazine drew close to its finish. On February 5 both the *Mercury* and the *Gazette* announced publication of their respective magazines for the "next week." Bradford's *American Magazine* won the race, appearing on February 13. Franklin's *General Magazine* came off the press only three days later. Having failed to prevent the publication of Bradford's magazine by his charge of piracy and then having lost the race to publish, Franklin vented his anger in ridicule. In the *Mercury* of February 19, Bradford had printed a long advertisement, written by Webbe for his magazine, which promised that each issue would

> contain something more than four Sheets, or an Equivalent to four of such Papers, as the *American Mercury* is printed on; so that there will be not less than fifty two Sheets published in one Year, which will comprehend double the Quantity of Matter (not reckoning the Advertisements) contained in a common News Paper during a like Course of Time. Price single, one Shilling; to Subscribers twelve Shillings per *ann*. Pennsylvania Currency. It seems unnecessary to add that every Body will be at Liberty as being a Thing of Course, to withdraw his Subscription when he pleases. As the principal Part of this Magazine is not a Transcript from printed Copy, but is a Work that requires a continual Study and Application, it cannot be afforded for less Money than is mentioned. But whether it be therefore worth that Money, the Reader *only* has the Right to judge. The News will be inserted in the next, which was omitted this Time, as not being thought proper to repeat, what had been so often told over in other publick Papers. Care is also promised for the Buyer's Sake, as well as from a Regard to the Reputation of the Country, to avoid reprinting any of the Rubbish or Sweepings of Printing-Houses.[54]

Franklin turned Webbe's ponderous advertisement into Irish dialect couplets, introduced by a correspondent who signed himself "Shelah," and who pretended to a knowledge of Webbe's national origin.

> To the Printer of the Pennsylvania *Gazette*
>
>   Your Adversary has always been shy of us his Country-Folks, and affected to be thought of some other Nation; but the Constraint with which he appears to write, *in Shoes,* and the great *Brogue* on his Pen at other Times, demonstrates him indisputably to be a TEAGUE.
>
> TEAGUE'S ADVERTISEMENT
>
> Arra Joy! my montly *Macasheen* shall contain Sheets four,
> Or an Equivalent, which is something more;
> So dat twelve Times four shall make fifty two,

Which is twice as much as fifty two Newsh-Papers do:
Prishe shingle *One Shilling:* But shubscribe for a Year,
You shall have it sheaper,* at de shame Prishe, Honey dear:
And if you will but shubscribe to take it de Year out,
You may leave off when you pleashe, before, no doubt.
'Tis true, my Book is dear; but de Reashon is plain,
The best Parts of it ish de Work of my own Brain:
How can odher Men's Writings be wort so much!
Arra! if you tink so, you're no vhery good Shudge.
De Newsh which I left out, becaush it was old,
And had been in odher Papers so often told,
I shall put into my nexsht (do 'tis shince told onesh more)
Becaush 'twill be newer dan it wash before.
For de dear Buyer's Shake, and de Land's Reputaish'
No Shweepings, but dose of my own Shcull shall have plaish;
And dose, you must tink, will be vhery fine: ⎫
For do dis Advertisement my Printer does Shign, ⎬
To tell you de Trute, de Shense is all mine. ⎭

Signed A. Bradford

* The Word *cheaper,* I own, is not express'd in the Original;
but it must have been intended to be understood; otherwise, what
Encouragement is there to taken by the Year, or where is the Induce-
ment to subscribe?

In reply to Franklin's derision, the *Mercury* of March 5 contained what Bradford's biographer calls "a dignified, though
somewhat pedantic, reply signed by Andrew Bradford." [55]
Bradford took full credit for his advertisement.

The Impropriety of charging that Advertisement on another
Person, whose Pen, as it is most politely expressed, is now said
to carry a Brogue on it; (tho' I am surprised that my Brother
Printer could so soon forget the Fondness he lately showed in being
thought the Author of a Scheme drawn up by that same Pen, which
he carried so far as actually to declare and publish to the whole
World, that he himself was the Author of it.) I say this Impropriety which he was guilty of, with his ridiculous Attempt to
mimick the Humour of *Teague,* and in broken Dutch too, as I am

informed, in Order, if his impotent Malice had permitted, to render the Irish completely ridiculous.

Bradford resented Franklin's having invoked national prejudices and observed archly "that his Majesty Subjects, however distinguished by Locality of Birth, are nevertheless all properly ranked under the general Denomination of Englishmen, as they are all equally, without the least Exception, intitled to the benefit of the Laws of England." His "Brother Printer" was therefore unjustified in making those distinctions, and Bradford steadfastly maintained "that those, who industriously endeavour to keep them up, have no other end in View in it than to Spirit up one Party to domineer over and oppress another Part of his Majesty's Subjects." I am inclined to disagree with Bradford's biographer and with Franklin's editors, who found Bradford's answer "heavy and humorless." Anna Janney DeArmond believes that the publicity of this exchange was good for both magazines, and though there was an edge of malice on both sides, it is possible that the *Mercury* piece was an attempt at mock-eloquence and so, humor. It is not very funny, but Franklin's Teague verses are not in very good taste either. Thoughtful readers must have sensed a reluctance on Franklin's part to enter into this fray in the first place. This was not the aggressive Gazetteer of a decade before, plunging into a battle of wits with a rival. Until Teague's advertisement Franklin had written only two brief animadversions, while item after scurrilous item was issued from Bradford's press. Franklin's own maturity and his public responsibilities as postmaster of Philadelphia are reflected in the restraint with which he conducted his defense.

The public provided its own judgment of the two new magazines. Bradford's *American Magazine* ceased publication after the third issue; Franklin's survived it by only three months. The six issues of the *General Magazine* reveal a classic pattern in Franklin's journalistic career: the adaptation of British literary and journalistic models for colonial consumption.

In this case, the British model was the *Gentleman's Magazine,*
which was ten years old in 1741. Edward Cave, founding editor of the *Gentleman's,* first used the term "magazine" in the
sense of a depository for news and the best features to be
found in the weekly papers and half-sheets of London and the
British Isles. When the *Gentleman's Magazine* first appeared
British papers were legion, and the public was delighted to
find the best of these selected and reprinted in a single publication. In contrast to its first American imitators, the *Gentleman's* enjoyed a long and distinguished run; it was published
until 1907 and numbered among its early contributors Richard
Savage, Mark Akenside, Christopher Smart, James Boswell,
Joseph Priestley, and Benjamin Franklin himself. During the
1730s the most popular feature of the *Gentleman's*—swelling
its circulation to an impressive 10,000 in 1738—was its reprinting of the Parliamentary debates.[56] After Parliament
decreed that the practice must stop, the *Gentleman's* printed
the same debates disguised as an appendix to Lemuel Gulliver's
"Account of the Famous Empire of Lilliput." The author of
this feature was Samuel Johnson. It was so successful that the
circulation rose another 50 percent.

Franklin saw the potential political impact of a magazine
in colonial terms. He hoped to disseminate political information that he felt should be known in America, and in the absence of an American parliament—and indeed an American
Johnson—he reprinted state papers, amounting to almost a
third of the space in the *General Magazine.* What he evidently hoped to achieve was a sense of community among the
several American colonies, the realization that they shared
common problems in their relations with the mother country.
To ascribe a revolutionary intent to Franklin in 1741 would
be wholly unwarranted. He did foresee, however, a time when
the colonies might present a solid front against the exercise of
"arbitrary Government and unlimited Power." He wrote almost nothing for the *General Magazine,* but the speeches and

documents he printed expressed colonial disaffection. An example is the exchange of messages between Governor George Clarke and the New York Assembly. Governor Clarke admonished the assemblymen to act with aggressive and unswerving loyalty to the Crown; "This, and only this, will remove, as to this Province, a Jealousy, which for some Years has obtained in *England,* that the Plantations are not without Thoughts of throwing off their Dependance on the Crown of *England.* I hope and believe no Man in this Province has any such Intention: But, neither my Hopes nor Belief will have the Weight of your Actions." The Assembly's reply contained an indignant rejoinder to the governor's suggestion, assuring him that no man in New York harbored such seditious thoughts, "for under what Government can we be better protected, or our Liberties and properties so well secured?" [57]

Next to colonial politics, colonial religion occupied the greatest share of the *General Magazine*'s attention. The Great Awakening was at its peak, and Franklin was much involved with the ministry of George Whitefield. Sermons and tracts for and against the Awakeners appeared in the magazine, and an occasional piece of revival poetry. Rather a horrible example of this sort of thing was quoted from the *New-England Weekly Journal* in the April issue:

> See Heaven-born TENNENT from Mount Sinai flies,
> With flaming Targets, light'ning in his Eyes!
> Hear him, with bless'd Experience, tell,
> The Law can do no more than doom to Hell!
> He rends the Cov'ring off th' infernal Pit,
> Lest tho'tless Souls, securely, drop in it. [58]

Franklin may have contributed one piece of his own verse—a little satirical piece on evangelistic technique—to the entire run of the *General Magazine*. [59] Magazine historian Frank Luther Mott believed so; the Yale editors have not seen fit to make the ascription. In any event, the *General Magazine* was

not Franklin's in the way the *American Magazine* was to be
Webbe's ("not a Transcript from Printed Copy, but . . . a
work that requires a continual Study and Application"). Evidently Franklin had not intended to edit the magazine himself,
and doubtless he was too busy to do it. Why it died is not
known; Franklin failed to memorialize the magazine or the
magazine controversy in the *Autobiography*. Certainly the
American newspapers were fewer and less full of interesting
material than the British. Then too, the *General Magazine*
was in direct competition with the larger, more elegant, and
more lively *Gentleman's Magazine*. Franklin must either have
misjudged the market, or come quickly to the conclusion that
whatever the potential impact of an American magazine on
colonial politics, the effort and expense involved in getting up
the *General Magazine* was simply too great. But both the
magazine and the controversy which attended its inception are
interesting, so clearly do they reflect Franklin's reputation,
attitudes, political position, and rhetorical ability at the beginning of the 1740s. Scarcely more than a decade before, he
had lashed out unmercifully when a "Brother Printer" stole
his idea for a newspaper. This time he elicited almost as vicious a response as he had from Samuel Keimer. But in the
magazine controversy he brought down the fury of his adversaries with a single, straightforward sentence—the statement
of Webbe's duplicity—persistently reprinted in the *Pennsylvania Gazette*. In one sense this was a remarkable achievement in controversial journalism; at the same time, Benjamin
Franklin in 1740 had little choice. He allowed himself perhaps
one lapse of taste in this affair—that is, of course, the Teague
verses. But the days of reckless, free-swinging controversy
were over for him; he was a man with too much to lose. He
had to preserve, untarnished if possible, his reputation, and
"Glass, China, and Reputation," as Poor Richard knew, "are
easily crack'd, and never well mended." [60] Franklin was caught
more than once in tight places; he may have had Andrew

Bradford under his thumb, as Webbe charged, but Bradford and the *Mercury* had him under their eye. It served no purpose for Franklin to provoke those who were but too ready to throw dirt; he knew that some would stick. The picture of Franklin reflected in the magazine controversy is the same one to be seen in *Poor Richard's Almanac* for that period and in a survey of his other controversial writings. He remained reckless enough to omit a governor's message from his transactions of the Pennsylvania Assembly, reckless enough to hurl a charge and a challenge at Webbe and Bradford, even though they might respond with damaging countercharges about his conduct of the post office. Franklin never lost that spirit of recklessness. But his mode of expressing it changed. As time went on, he was more and more frequently required to answer for himself, instead of inventing a mask or a voice to speak for him. In a way, then, he was already confronting the problem of creating his own voice—and face—in prose. On the success of that mask of himself, depended Franklin's reputation and his fortune.

After the failure of the *General Magazine* in the summer of 1741, Franklin laid aside journalistic adventures and journalistic controversy. The next several years seem a kind of lull in Franklin's biography. The *Gazette* and *Poor Richard's Almanac* continued to appear, but these were the least arresting years of Poor Richard. Franklin wrote about the desirability of a philosophical society, and the American Philosophical Society was the eventual result, though it did not actually get under way until after he left Pennsylvania. More importantly, this was the period in which Franklin became acquainted with the science of electricity. But in the background of these personal events was the protracted European war, one of whose engagements—the victory of Admiral Edward Vernon at Porto Bello in Panama—had been the subject of pieces in the *General Magazine*.

England was fighting a trade war of special importance to

the North American plantations. King George's War it was called in America after England declared war on France in 1744. The War of Jenkins' Ear was declared with Spain in 1739. If England could win, British-West Indian trade stood to expand at the expense of the French and Spanish. Furthermore, an English victory would mean the possibility of more favorable treaties with the Indians on the frontier. On the other hand, the fact that a state of war existed meant threats to the colonies from privateers of both France and Spain, and from Indians stirred up by the French and Spanish colonies ringing the seaboard. In Pennsylvania this war brought an end to the pacifist domination of provincial politics. The result was a political vacuum that was filled largely by nonsectarian moderates, led by Benjamin Franklin. He emerged as a potent political force in 1747.

If we examine briefly the deterioration of the situation in Pennsylvania during the war, the meaning of Franklin's participation at its climax will become clear. Since the beginning of the war with Spain, the pacifist Quaker party had been at odds with the government on the war issue. Though not alarmed for the safety of the province, the Assembly had agreed to provide £3,000 for the King's use. They further had no objections to the recruiting of volunteers among the freemen of Pennsylvania, but they boggled when the governor began enlisting servants at harvesttime. Soon over 250 white servants from both eastern and western counties had deserted their masters to fight in the West Indies, whereupon the Assembly resolved not to furnish the £3,000 after all. From about this time, Pennsylvania historian Theodore Thayer, dates the rise of the Gentleman's Party led by William Allen.[61] The elections of 1741 and 1742 were hotly and scurrilously contested, but though the Quaker party was beginning to split into pacifist and moderate factions and the Anglicans and Presbyterians of Allen's party made strong bids, a fundamentally pacifist Assembly was still seated in 1744. Its attitude was probably unrealistic, as Franklin and the moderates felt. To the governor's new demands for military appropriations it replied that all proposals would receive consideration, but that not too much could be expected from Pennsylvania, which, after all, was protected by friendly Indians to the west and the British navy on the seas.

As the French threat from the west developed into a clear and present danger the Assembly moderated slightly, but in the meantime word came from the Crown attorneys that Pennsylvania, though legally responsible for self-defense, was herself the only immediate judge of what measures were necessary to safeguard the province. During the final stages of King George's War, French privateers began appearing off the coast of British America. A French vessel went so far in July 1747 as to enter Delaware Bay, where it damaged some shipping and even sent a raiding party ashore near Newcastle. Rumors circulated that the French had knowledge of the navigation of the river and that six privateers would be sent to attack Philadelphia early the next spring. Pennsylvania was defenseless, having neither batteries nor militia. The Assembly refused to take the situation seriously, but a group of merchants raised a sum for fitting out a privateer.

Benjamin Franklin came forward at that moment with a more elaborate plan for defense. "I determined," he writes, "to try what might be done by a voluntary Association of the People" (*Autobiography*, p. 182). Franklin's plan sought the support of all moderate people in the province, who, he realized, were in the majority. His anonymous pamphlet, *Plain Truth: or, Serious Considerations on the Present State of the City of Philadelphia, and Province of Pennsylvania. By a Tradesman of Philadelphia,* appeared on November 17, 1747.[62] Among the political writings of Franklin's Philadelphia years it ranks alongside the "Half-hour's Conversation with a Friend." *Plain Truth* differed from the "Conversation," however, in the powerful effects it wrought in Pennsylvania.

The pamphlet is a catalogue of Franklin's rhetorical devices. He used proverbs to enforce his argument at several points: *"The English FEEL, but they do not SEE"* (according to Franklin, an Italian saying), *"When the Steed is stolen, you shut the Stable Door," "One Sword often keeps another in the Scabbard."* He called upon the classical authors Josephus and Sallust. He adapted the famous fable of the parts of the body to demonstrate the mutual dependency of all the citizens and Pennsylvania: "When the Feet are wounded, shall the Head say, *It is not me; I will not trouble myself to contrive Relief!"* And he related the anecdote of a man "who refused to pump in a sinking Ship, because one on board, whom he hated, would be saved by it as well as himself." This, he professed, he had found hard to believe until he saw a like dissension arise among his own neighbors. He incorporated a bit of imaginary dialogue to express the attitude of the Gentlemen's Party: *"What, say they, shall we lay out our Money to protect the Trade of Quakers? Shall we fight to defend Quakers? No; Let the Trade perish, and the City burn; let what will happen, we shall never lift a Finger to prevent it."* He illustrated the disunity of Pennsylvania in an elaborate simile. "At present," he wrote, "we are like the separate Filaments of Flax before the Thread is form'd, without Strength because without Connection; but UNION would make us strong and even formidable." He called history to witness the fortitude of the English Protestant, alluding to the siege of Londonderry by forces of James II in 1689.

Inevitably, Franklin chose a biblical text for the pamphlet, calling his readers' attention to Judges 18. *"And they came,* Verse 7, *to Laish, and saw the People that were therein, how they dwelt CARELESS, after the Manner of the Zidonians, QUIET and SECURE. . . . And they smote them with the Edge of the Sword, and burnt the City with* FIRE; *and there was no* DELIVERER, *because it was far from Zidon.* Not so far from Zidon, however, as Pennsylvania is from Britain; and yet we are, if possible, more *careless* than the People of Laish! As the Scriptures are given for our Reproof, Instruction and Warning, may we make a due Use of this Example, before it be too late!" After the manner of a New England jeremiad sermon, Franklin raised the possibility that Pennsylvania might fall victim to providential retribution: "It seems as if Heaven, justly displeas'd at our growing Wickedness, and determin'd to punish this once favour'd Land, had suffered our Chiefs to engage in these foolish and mischievous Contentions, for *little Posts* and *paltry Distinctions,* that our Hands might be bound up, our Understandings darkned and misled, and every Means of our Security neglected. . . . Where then shall we seek for Succour and Protection? The Government we are immediately under denies it to us; and if the Enemy comes, *we are far from* ZIDON, *and there is no Deliverer near.*" But whereas Increase or Cotton Mather would have counseled prayer and fasting, Franklin emphasized the secular situation and proposed earthly measures.

He appealed to the enlightened reason of his countrymen, analyzing at length the economic consequences of privateers in the Delaware Bay.

> Will not the first Effect of this be, an Enhauncing of the Price of all foreign Goods to the Tradesman and Farmer, who use or consume them? For the Rate of Insurance will increase in Proportion to the Hazard of Importing them; and in the same Proportion will the Price of those Goods increase. If the Price of the Tradesman's Work and the Farmer's Produce would encrease equally with the Price of foreign Commodities, the Damage would not be so great: But the direct contrary must happen. For the same Hazard, or Rate of Insurance, that raises the Price of what is imported, must be deducted out of, and lower the Price of what is exported. . . . And will not the Consequences be, A discouraging of many of the Vessels that us'd to come from other Places to purchase our Produce, and thereby a Turning of the Trade to Ports that can be entered with less Danger, and capable of furnish-

ing them with the same Commodities, as New-York, &c? A Lessening of Business to every Shopkeeper, together with Multitudes of bad Debts; the high Rate of Goods discouraging the Buyers, and the low Rates of their Labour and Produce rendering them unable to pay for what they had bought: Loss of Employment to the Tradesman, and bad Pay for what little he does: And lastly, Loss of many Inhabitants, who will retire to other Provinces not subject to the like Inconveniences; whence a Lowering of the Value of Lands, Lots, and Houses.

As Provincial Secretary Richard Peters saw, Franklin was making defense a class issue, meaning "to animate all the middling persons to undertake their own defense in opposition to the Quakers & the Gentlemen." [63] As Franklin put it, " 'Tis true, with very little Notice, the Rich may shift for themselves. The Means of speedy Flight are ready in their Hands; and with some previous Care to lodge Money and Effects in distant and secure Places, tho' they should lose much, yet enough may be left them, and to spare. But most unhappily circumstanced indeed are we, the middling People, the Tradesmen, Shopkeepers, and Farmers of this Province and City! We cannot all fly with our Families; and if we could, how shall we subsist?" Peters reported to the Penns in England that Franklin's plan fell "fowl of the Quakers & their opposers equally, as people from whom no good cou'd be expected." "Should we," Franklin asked, "address that wealthy and powerful Body of People, who have ever since the War governed our Elections, and filled almost every Seat in our Assembly." Here he meant the Quakers: "Should we remind them, that the Publick Money, raised *from All,* belongs *to All.* . . . Should we tell them, that tho' the Treasury be at present empty, it may soon be filled by the outstanding Publick Debts collected. . . . Should we conjure them by all the Ties of Neighbourhood, Friendship, Justice and Humanity, to consider these Things?" Franklin answered his long series of parallel rhetorical questions, "yet all would be in vain. . . .

Their religious Prepossessions are unchangeable, their Obstinacy invincible."

The Gentlemen, Franklin explained, were just as obstinate, but for no good religious reason. "And yet," he charged them, "you resolve not to perform this Duty, but act *contrary* to *your own* Consciences, because the Quakers act *according* to *theirs*." Caught in the middle was the middle class. "Thro' the Dissensions of our Leaders, thro' *mistaken Principles* of *Religion,* join'd with a Love of Worldy Power, on the one Hand; thro' *Pride, Envy* and *implacable Resentment* on the other; our Lives, our Families and little Fortunes, dear to us as any Great Man's can be to him, are to remain continually expos'd to Destruction."

Along with analysis, Franklin offered terror. He pictured the defenseless province under attack. "The Man that has a Wife and Children, will find them hanging on his Neck, beseeching him with Tears to quit the City, and save his Life, to guide and protect them in that Time of general Desolation and Ruin. All will run into Confusion, amidst Cries and Lamentations, and the Hurry and Disorder of Departers, carrying away their Effects." He invoked racial and sexual fears: "Confined to your Houses, you will have nothing to trust to but the Enemy's Mercy. Your best Fortune will be, to fall under the Power of Commanders of the King's Ships, able to controul the Mariners; and not into the Hands of *licentious Privateers.* Who can, without the utmost Horror, conceive the Miseries of the Latter! when your Persons, Fortunes, Wives and Daughters, shall be subject to the wanton and unbridled Rage, Rapine and Lust, of *Negroes, Molattoes,* and others, the vilest and most abandoned of Mankind." In a footnote Franklin reminded his readers that this was no flight of fancy, recalling the death of Captain Bernard Martin of the ship *Mary,* taken by a Spanish privateer. "Because he bravely defended himself and Vessel longer than they expected, for which every generous Enemy would have esteem'd him, did they, after he had struck and submitted, barbarously *stab* and *murder* him, tho' on his Knees begging Quarter!" But Franklin matched the emotional appeal of horror with a fervid paean to the potent warlike spirit of the Englishman. This passage he lifted almost intact from his commentary on the Burnet-Belcher controversy a score of years before: "Great Numbers of our People are of BRITISH RACE, and tho' the fierce fighting Animals of those happy Islands, are said to abate their native Fire and Intrepidity, when removed to a Foreign Clime, yet with the People 'tis not so; Our Neighbours of New-England afford the World a convincing Proof, that BRITONS, tho' a Hundred Years transplated, and to the remotest Part of the Earth, may yet retain, even to the third and fourth Descent, that *Zeal* for the *Publick Good,* that *military Prowess,* and that *undaunted Spirit,* which has in every Age distinguished their Nation."

In *Plain Truth* Franklin brought to bear every piece of ordnance in his rhetorical arsenal. And he recalled in his memoirs that the pamphlet "had a sudden and surprizing Effect." The text of the pamphlet had promised that "the Writer of it will, in a few Days, lay before [his Countrymen and Fellow Citizens] a Form of an ASSOCIATION for the Purposes herein mentioned." Franklin prepared the articles of the Association and arranged a large public meeting, supplying the hall with several copies of the instrument scattered about and enough pens and ink. "I harangu'd them a little on the Subject, read the Paper and explain'd it, and then distributed the Copies, which were eagerly signed, not the least Objection being made" (*Autobiography,* p. 183). At the end of the meeting, Franklin recalled, 1,200 signatures had been collected, and that number rose "to upwards of Ten Thousand," when copies were distributed about the countryside. A petition for financial aid from the Assembly was signed by 250 prominent citizens, sixty of them Quakers. When the Assembly refused to act, the Associators devised a lottery of £20,000 which was expected to

yield £3,000 for the Association. This lottery was so successful that they undertook a slightly larger one. Cannon were
procured and the Association fortified two batteries, a strong
one on William Allen's land at Wicaco and a smaller one of
eleven guns on William Atwood's wharf under Society Hill.
It was at the Wicaco battery that Franklin took his "Turn of
Duty . . . as a common Soldier."

The Penns' provincial secretary, Peters, was evidently relieved that at last something was being done to defend the
city. He tried to put the best possible face on the Association
in his letters to the Proprietors. He wrote that Franklin and
the other leaders had desired that he be informed of the
project at every step, since they had no intention of getting
around the Proprietors, but were moved only to safeguard
their own lives and property.[64] They believed, moreover, that
they were acting in the Proprietary interest; and they hoped
that the Penns might encourage them with gifts of cannon and
small arms. Though there might be "at the bottom of it a
personal antipathy to the Quakers, who brought the Country
into this dilemma," Peters assured the Proprietors that the
Associators "really desire to recommend themselves to the
Proprietaries."

At the beginning the Association seemed to have general
support from all but the rigidly pacifist elements among the
Quakers. Franklin wrote to Cadwallander Colden, his New
York colleague in natural philosophy, that "Tho' *Plain Truth*
bore somewhat hard on both Parties here, it has had the Happiness not to give much Offense to either." [65] From Peter's
letter to the Penns it appears that Franklin the politician
cleared the way for Franklin the controversialist. Peters said,
of course, that he was informed in advance of what Franklin
would do; but he also implies that elaborate negotiations went
on between Franklin's party and the Gentlemen, and that they
arrived at a scenario wherein the Allen party were to be at-
tacked in *Plain Truth,* then vindicate their conduct and join

in the common cause—all the papers being printed gratis in the *Pennsylvania Gazette*. In December, James Logan, the most prominent of the Quaker moderates, wrote Franklin to express his approbation "of thy new excellent project." Logan signed himself, "thy very loving friend." [66] But with the coming of spring, 1748, the era of good feeling was coming to an end. William Allen and the Gentlemen were having second thoughts. Pennsylvania historian Theodore Thayer believes that Allen's refusal to cooperate with Franklin proceeded from political considerations and growing personal jealousy. The popular leaders, and not the Gentlemen, were being elected officers of Association units. From his vantage point even Thomas Penn had to agree that "Such want of Spirit in People that have been finding fault with the Friends, is really surprizing and I am sure it would have been believed had a prophet foretold it." [67] The Allen party soon declared the plan illegal, insisting that the organization of militia and the appointment of officers belonged to the governor alone. Thomas Penn soon came around to the same opinion. He wrote a friend in March 1748: "I am sure the people of America are too often ready to act in defiance of the Government they live in, without associating themselves for that purpose." [68] In June he wrote Peters singling out Franklin among the leaders of the Association, and making a remarkably perceptive observation about him. "Mr. Franklin's doctrine that obedience to Governors is no more due them than protection to the people is not fit to be in the heads of the unthinking multitude. He is a dangerous man and I should be very glad if he inhabited any other country, as I believe him of a very uneasy spirit. However, as he is a sort of tribune of the people, he must be treated with regard." [69] By this time Peters too, under an avalanche of Penn's letters of disapproval, began to regard the Association as illegal. He was apprehensive of its leaders' intentions and fearful that it would advance the political interests of those hostile to the proprietary party.

With the war's end at about this time, however, the Association began to dwindle away. Franklin had gained province-wide fame and influence by his leadership. He had also made an enemy of his old friend and fellow Mason, William Allen, who now saw him, correctly, as a potential leader of the popular wing in Pennsylvania politics. But the fears of the Proprietor and the Gentlemen were temporarily laid to rest when Franklin and his friends made no moves to capitalize on their influence in the October elections. Evidently it was true, as Franklin claimed in his memoirs, that he was glad to have the Association's business completed in order to return to work on his project of establishing the Academy. The tone of relief is palpable in Penn's letter to Peters of August 31: "We are well pleased to find that the Association has had so good an Effect, that the persons associated have Commissions in the Common Form, and do not act but by Authority from the president and Council, as well as that they have been so ready to attend their Duty when in Times of danger; their readyness to defend their Country is very commendable, and it was with reluctance that we objected to any thing done by persons that in general might intend nothing more than to defend themselves under their legal Commanders." [70]

Thayer believes that Franklin pondered running for the Assembly in the autumn of 1748. Doubtless his opinion is based on Franklin's letter to Colden on the subject of his retirement. In the letter, dated September 29, he wrote, "I have refus'd engaging further in publick Affairs; The Share I had in the late Association, &c. having given me a little present Run of Popularity, there was a pretty general Intention of chusing me a Representative for the City at the next Election of Assemblymen; but I have desired all my Friends who spoke to me about it, to discourage it, declaring that I should not serve if chosen." [71] Franklin was elected to the Common Council of Philadelphia in 1748, but he resisted the draft—however strong—for nomination to the Assembly. His enemies had little to congratulate themselves about, however. Though he would not actually take a seat in the Assembly until 1751, he was in fact the key political figure and possibly the most powerful man in Pennsylvania.

The Association business marks a transition in Franklin's career. He began it as a journalist and rhetorician, with his inflammatory *Plain Truth*. He emerged from the affair as a full-fledged "tribune of the people." He retired from active control of the New-Printing Office in 1748, leaving it and the *Pennsylvania Gazette* in the hands of his partner, David Hall. (Ironically, in 1766, at the dissolution of Franklin's partnership with Hall, the *Gazette* became an organ of the Proprietary party.)[72] The two decades during which Franklin was active in the newspaper business in Philadelphia were the most important years of his growth, both as a writer and a man. His talent as a controversialist was tempered to take a keen edge. In England in the 1770s he would write a series of powerful and witty satires in defense of the American cause ("An Edict of the King of Prussia," "Rules by which a Great Empire May be Reduced to a Small One") which have been duly appreciated by other commentators, students, and patriots. In France during the Revolution he would compose the incisive, Swiftian "Sale of the Hessians" and in a serious propaganda effort, counterfeit a "Supplement to the Boston *Independent Chronicle*," which purported to describe actual atrocities of war committed by the British and the Indians incited by them. These were the works of Benjamin Franklin, master rhetorician. They were composed with that "marvelous Facility" that M. Simon so admired in the Roman authors, a facility born of constant application to "the Principles, the Difficulties, the Beauties, the Subleties, the Depths, the Riches" of his language. His lively years in the newspaper business had presented Franklin with varied demands; he was called upon to mimic old maids and ministers, coquettes and politicians. His pieces ran the tonal gamut from sweet reasonableness to fury.

When he boarded ship for England in June 1757 to begin his greatest career as servant to his country, his most dangerous weapon was his overpowering controversialist's prose.

Franklin had lost some of his Philadelphia controversies. He did not lose gracefully. And he was never to lose another fight. It was not so much that his years in Philadelphia taught him to avoid quarrels he could not win. Franklin never lost his convictions or all of his recklessness. He was no more reluctant to engage Britain's Parliament than he had been to take on the Mathers of Boston or the Synod of Philadelphia. But he had learned tactics and he had learned self-control. It is that seasoning of Franklin the writer and Franklin the man which renders an examination of the Philadelphia years so compelling.

When he retired in 1748, Benjamin Franklin surrendered all but one of his journalistic enterprises. He continued for another decade to compile *Poor Richard's Almanac*. Enlarged in 1748 to *Poor Richard Improved,* the almanac had just attained a new vitality; and, like Franklin's controversial journalism, it would be abandoned only at its triumphant climax, with the publication of "The Way to Wealth." The twenty-five issues of *Poor Richard* (1733–58) chronicle the same process of development that we have observed in this chapter. Moreover, the demands of the poor Richard persona prepared Franklin in a unique way for the writing of his *Autobiography*.

FOUR

Poor Richard's Almanac

Ben beats his Pate, and fancys wit will come;
But he may knock, there's no body at home.
Poor Richard, 1742

IN a number of respects *Poor Richard's Almanac* is unique among Benjamin Franklin's journalistic and literary endeavors. It was Franklin's longest sustained publication, stretching over the quarter century between 1733 and 1758; Franklin was actively engaged in publishing the *Gazette* only twenty years. Of all his nonscientific writings it was the most successful during his lifetime. The little almanac was itself a bestseller, and as Franklin recalled "came to be in such Demand that I reap'd considerable Profit from it, vending annually near ten Thousand" (*Autobiography,* p. 164). And the preface to the last number, comonly called "The Way to Wealth," became vastly popular, securing Franklin's fame as a moral teacher throughout the Western world. Within forty years of its original publication it was reprinted under various titles at least 145 times and translated into seven languages.[1] Unique too was the durability of Franklin's persona, Poor Richard Saunders. He was a character, we must suppose, created much as Alice Addertongue or Anthony Afterwit was created: in haste, against a deadline. But the correspondents to the newspaper died with their letters, while Richard

Saunders reappeared year after year; and he proved lively enough and flexible enough to do so. He did change but he was never entirely effaced. The changes that occurred in the tastes and attitudes of Richard Saunders reflect the development of Benjamin Franklin's mind during those years. The fact that Poor Richard, Philomath, was recognizable from year to year is Franklin's greatest achievement in characterization.

At the same time, Franklin's posterity has too often been unwilling to see him without the mask of Poor Richard. It might be plausibly argued that *Poor Richard's Almanac* has been more influential in shaping the symbolic figure of Benjamin Franklin than even the *Autobiography* itself. Clearly this involves dangerous distortions of an historical figure, as does any hasty identification of a literary character with his creator. Yet the case of Benjamin Franklin and Richard Saunders is the more complicated, inasmuch as most of the commentators responsible for the identification have actually read only "The Way to Wealth" and nothing else from *Poor Richard*. D. H. Lawrence's sketch provides a good example of this reasoning.

> I can remember, when I was a little boy, my father used to buy a scrubby yearly almanac with the sun and moon and stars on the cover. And it used to prophesy bloodshed and famine. But also crammed in the corners it had little anecdotes and humorisms, with a moral tag. And I used to have my little priggish laugh at the woman who counted her chickens before they were hatched and so forth, and I was convinced that honesty was the best policy, also a little priggishly. The author of these bits was Poor Richard, and Poor Richard was Benjamin Franklin, writing in Philadelphia well over a hundred years before.
>
> And probably I haven't got over those Poor Richard tags yet. I rankle still with them. They are thorns in young flesh.
>
> Because, although I still believe that honesty is the best policy, I dislike policy altogether.[2]

Rankled at the prudential maxims of Poor Richard, Lawrence found the same moral complacency in the *Autobiography*.

Doubtless he also found there a warrant for his assumption that the economic proverbs of "The Way to Wealth" fairly represented the wit and wisdom of *Poor Richard's Almanac* as a whole. When Franklin came to recall the almanac in his memoirs, he was obviously mindful of the success of "The Way to Wealth."

> And observing that [*Poor Richard*] was generally read, scarce any Neighbourhood in the Province being without it, I consider'd it as a proper Vehicle for conveying Instruction among the common People, who bought scarce any other Books. I therefore filled all the little Spaces that occurr'd between the Remarkable Days in the Calendar, with Proverbial Sentences, chiefly such as inculcated Industry and Frugality, as the Means of procuring Wealth and thereby securing Virtue, it being more difficult for a Man in Want to act always honestly, as (to use here one of those Proverbs) *it is hard for an empty Sack to stand upright.*

Franklin wrote this account of *Poor Richard* in 1788 near the beginning of the third installment of his memoirs. The discussion of the almanac is bracketed by his recollection of a plan for the establishment of an international party of virtue, "the Society of the *Free and Easy*," and an account of the newspaper in which Franklin remembered "as another Means of Communicating Instruction," where he had "frequently reprinted . . . Extracts from the Spectator and other moral Writers" (*Autobiography*, p. 165). Thus Franklin's explanation of his purpose in publishing *Poor Richard* is placed in the context of several projects designed to promote morality. This is slightly misleading, as an examination of the entire run of *Poor Richard* will show. Did Franklin's memory fail him here as it sometimes did during the composition of his memoirs? He remarks at the beginning of this installment that he was disappointed to have lost most of his papers during the war; very probably we have much easier access to *Poor Richard's Almanac* than did its author in 1788. It is more likely, however, that the context explains Franklin's emphasis here; and furthermore, it is true that during the last decade of *Poor Richard*'s run heavy emphasis rested on useful information. It was not quite accurate to say that Poor Richard's proverbs "chiefly . . . inculcated Industry and Frugality." It is Part 1 of the *Autobiography* which does that. Although the prudential maxims were a staple of Poor Richard's from the beginning, they could not be described as the predominant message of the almanac at any time—that is, until Franklin collected them in the summer of 1757.

The immense popularity of "The Way to Wealth" combined with the successful dramatization of the rewards of industry and frugality in Part 1 of the *Autobiography* are, then, principally responsible for the gross distortions of Benjamin Franklin's image. Serious historians and biographers who have sought to understand Franklin as a complex intellect rather than as an historical generalization have always recognized this distortion. A number of scholars in the last thirty years have directly challenged the easy identification of Franklin with Poor Richard. Harold A. Larrabee marked Franklin's 250th anniversary with a fine brief essay in which he pointed out that Franklin, as Father Abraham quoting Poor Richard "was a moralist discussing instrumental values and not final goods." [3] He concludes, "By leaving out Franklin's self-confessed youthful imprudences and making his advice appear to apply to the whole of anyone's career, many editors of his life story (especially for school children) have made him seem an impeccable, self-righteous, priggish preacher of material success through tireless commercialism." Larrabee at least began to perceive the damaging relationship between the *Autobiography* and "The Way to Wealth." A score of years earlier Carl Van Doren had decried the emphasis on "The Way to Wealth," insofar as it is taken for the "essence of [Franklin's] wisdom." "It is not that," wrote Van Doren, "and it gives only one aspect of the younger Franklin. Father Abraham at the auction is an old man talking about economy.

He has chosen from Poor Richard the sayings which specially prove his point, and left out the rest. Having the last word, he has had almost the only word." [4] In 1940 John F. Ross demonstrated that Poor Richard Saunders was a genuine literary creation, owing much to Franklin's reading of Swift.[5] And in 1963 David Levin wrote, "Some of us forget that Poor Richard is just as clearly Franklin's creation as is Mrs. Silence Dogood. . . . many of us forget that *The Way to Wealth* . . . is a humorous *tale* narrated by Poor Richard, who at first makes fun of himself and then reports the long speech made by another fictitious character named Father Abraham." [6]

All of this has been very helpful as a corrective of abuses. Yet the full value of this scholarship will have been realized only if it clears the air and reopens the discussion of *Poor Richard's Almanac* as a body of writings which sensitively reflect Franklin's development as a writer and as a man. This reevaluation of *Poor Richard* must be based upon a careful reading of all twenty-five almanacs. Carl Van Doren gave the almanac such a reading in the thirties and complained that "Nobody knows Poor Richard as he was in the racy years which made him known to his contemporaries." Based upon his examination of the almanac, John F. Ross asserted that by the mid-1740s Franklin had introduced a "didactic element" and that the original character of Poor Richard had begun to disappear, to "fade" to a point where Richard Saunders and Benjamin Franklin were no longer distinguishable from each other.[7] Both Van Doren and Ross point to the fact that the run of *Poor Richard's Almanac* may be divided into distinct phases, defined by changes in tone and apparent authorial intention. The limitations of Van Doren's work prevented his pursuing the subject of *Poor Richard* in detail, and though Ross offered an analysis of the almanac's "alteration," I am inclined to disagree with his conclusions. He sought to prove that the character of Poor Richard was simply a patchwork

of names and ideas who owed his early spirit to Swift's
Bickerstaff Papers. Ross argued, in effect, that when Franklin
left off borrowing from Swift he ceased playing the role of
Poor Richard altogether. Moreover, Ross found what he
took to be internal inconsistencies in the almanac from the beginning; for example the disparity between the character Poor
Richard revealed in his prefaces and the advice contained in
the maxims. " 'Early to bed, and early to rise' might make a
businessman healthy, wealthy, and wise—but it would be
ruinous for a star-gazer." [8] This may very well be, but Ross
conceived of Poor Richard Saunders as a flat and inflexible
character, whereas he may as easily be seen as a witty mathematician who could turn a neat proverb as well as predict the
weather. Ross's assertion that Richard Saunders gradually
became Benjamin Franklin may be met with the counterasser-
tion that Poor Richard represented major aspects of Franklin's
character all along and that character and creator both evolved
during the quarter century of the almanac—that the persona of
Poor Richard remained intact.

Poor Richard's Almanac changed from year to year, but as
the work of Ross and Van Doren implies, we may identify
certain distinct phases, marked by different dominant tones
and apparent differences in Franklin's conception of what his
almanac should provide its readers. There are three such
phases. During the first—roughly the first decade of publication—the emphasis falls heavily upon entertainment. The
rather brief second phase is morally didactic in tone. Poor
Richard adopts a bland benevolent air. The third and final
phase is that of *Poor Richard Improved* (1748–58), the expanded almanac which provided its readers with much useful
information on both the domestic and the natural sciences.
The development of Poor Richard's attitudes and purposes
was exactly parallel to that of Benjamin Franklin himself
during the twenty-five years. The spirit of the early Poor
Richard is entirely consistent with that of Franklin's other

publications during the mid-thirties. The mellowed moralism of the middle phase reflects a matured Franklin, who was nearing retirement at forty-two and had begun to publish his bawdry (such as "Advice to a Young Man on the Choice of a Mistress," 1745, and "The Speech of Miss Polly Baker," 1747) anonymously or not at all. The final period mirrors Franklin's growing public concern and responsibility: his interest in science, education, defense, and a provincial economy stifled by the want of currency. In this chapter we shall trace the development of *Poor Richard's Almanac,* from 1733 to 1747 first with reference to the author's annual prefaces. A survey of the maxims for the same period will reveal the same patterns of development. A final section of the chapter will discuss *Poor Richard Improved* and "The Way to Wealth."

Franklin entered the business of publishing his own almanac much as he had entered the newspaper business, in a contentious mood. The field was crowded and competitive, for a popular almanac was a valuable source of income for the colonial printer. The New Printing-Office had issued two annual almanacs since its founding. In 1729 Franklin and Meredith printed Thomas Godfrey's *Pennsylvania Almanack* for 1730. The next year they added John Jerman's well-known *American Almanack,* previously printed by Andrew Bradford. In the early autumn of 1732 both Jerman and Godfrey took their almanac copy to Bradford, leaving Franklin without an almanac to print. Jerman's reason for returning to his old printer is lost. The reason for Godfrey's desertion of the New Printing-Office is probaby not far to seek. Franklin tells, in the *Autobiography* (pp. 127–28), of the rupture between himself and the Godfrey family in about 1730, involving Mrs. Godfrey's unsuccessful attempt at matchmaking.[9] In any event, the loss of both Godfrey's and Jerman's almanacs to Franklin's competitors must have been a serious blow to the young printer. *Poor Richard* for 1733 was hastily compiled and in no sense original; it followed the established eighteenth-century pattern. The title seems to have been suggested by *Poor Robin's Almanack,* which James Franklin published at Newport, Rhode Island. Indeed, the name Richard Saunders was that of a real English astrologer and almanac-maker of the seventeenth century. Everything in *Poor Richard* was borrowed except the quality that would assure its commercial success, that is Franklin's wit and skill as a controversialist. He drew upon the techniques he had learned in the Boston office of the *New-England Courant* and polished in his campaign to put Samuel Keimer out of the newspaper business four years before. Franklin knew how to goad his competitors into filling their publications with free advertising for him. His Busy-Body papers had driven Keimer into a frenzy of Hudibrastic verses. Now his advertisement for *Poor Richard,* in the *Gazette* for late December, promised lively fare for purchasers of the new almanac.

> JUST PUBLISHED, for 1733: POOR RICHARD: AN ALMANACK containing the Lunations, Eclipses, Planets Motions and Aspects, Weather, Sun and Moon's rising and setting, Highwater, &c. besides many pleasant and witty Verses, Jests and Sayings, Author's Motive of Writing, Prediction of the Death of his friend Mr. Titan Leeds, Moon no Cuckold, Batchelor's Folly, Parson's Wine and Baker's Pudding, Short Visits, Kings and Bears, New Fashions, Game for Kisses, Katherine's Love, Different Sentiments, Signs of a Tempest, Death a Fisherman, Conjugal Debate, Men and Melons, H. the Prodigal, Breakfast in Bed, Oyster Lawsuit, &c. by RICHARD SAUNDERS, Philomat. Printed and sold by B. Franklin, Price 3*s.* 6*d.* per Dozen. Of whom also may be had Sheet Almanacks at 2*s.* 6*d.*[10]

The tantalizing references to Poor Richard's preface, verses, and proverbs scarcely point to a didactic intention on the author's part. Rather they accurately forecast the ribaldry and hoaxes of the early years.

In Poor Richard's first address to the reader, Franklin introduced his persona with characteristic economy. The star-gazer began by acknowledging that he might gain public favor by declaring that he was writing his almanac with nothing other than the public good in view; "but in this I should not be sincere; and Men are now a-days too wise to be deceiv'd by Pretences how specious soever. The plain Truth of the Matter is," he explained,

> I am excessive poor, and my Wife, good Woman, is, I tell her, excessive proud; she cannot bear, she says, to sit spinning in her Shift of Tow, while I do nothing but gaze at the Stars; and has threatened more than once to burn all my Books and Rattling-Traps (as she calls my Instruments) if I do not make some profitable Use of them for the good of my Family. The Printer has offer'd me some considerable share of the Profits, and I have thus begun to comply with my Dame's desire.[11]

Franklin gave Poor Richard Saunders circumstances as old as comedy itself. He was the destitute scholar with a termagant wife. The Saunders family might make only one public appearance a year, but the lines of their domestic conflict were clearly drawn. Franklin had an instinct for domestic comedy and an ear for the scoldings of the fishwife. The advantages of a fictional philomath should be obvious. Poor Richard could be anything Franklin wanted him to be, precisely *because* he was imaginary. Thomas Godfrey was just Thomas Godfrey, glazier and part-time mathematician. History might be interested in the fact that he glazed the windows in Independence Hall, and his contemporaries knew him as the man who invented Hadley's quadrant and received the recognition of the Royal Society for it. But his life was colorless when compared to that of Richard Saunders. No living man could match Poor Richard's poverty or his dreamy dedication to his books and rattling-traps. Few women indeed would sit spinning in a tow shift, and few could carp as colorfully as Bridget Saunders. The durability of the Poor Richard persona rests on just this, that he was a human commonplace with common, though exaggerated, human problems.

Poor Richard immediately made known his combative character as well. He first assailed perhaps his principal rival, Titan Leeds. The *Gazette*'s advertisement, with its "Prediction of the Death of his friend Mr. Titan Leeds," had adumbrated the first of several hoaxes to be perpetrated by Poor Richard. This one Franklin borrowed from Swift's "Predictions for 1708 by Isaac Bickerstaff, Esq." Poor Richard went on in his preface to say that even the economic motive would have been insufficient to induce him to publish an almanac of his own, for it would have "been overpower'd by my Regard for my good Friend and Fellow-Student, Mr. Titan Leeds, whose Interest I was extremely unwilling to hurt." It was with deep regret, Poor Richard said, that he had to announce the imminent death of Leeds, which of course, would remove that obstacle. He offered his astrological analysis and promised that Leeds would die October 17, 1733. He further asserted that Leed's own prediction of his death differed only in a matter of nine days. "This small difference between us we have disputed whenever we have met these 9 Years past; but at length he is inclinable to agree with my Judgment; Which of us is most exact, a little Time will now determine. As therefore these Provinces may not longer expect to see any of his Performances after this Year, I think myself free to take up the Task, and request a share of the publick Encouragement." Franklin was not only employing the outlines of Swift's hoax on Partridge; he was also using Swift's characteristic technique of providing sufficient corroborative detail to enhance the credibility of his story.

The hoax had been well planned by Swift and was as well executed by Franklin. The October date promised a climax at about the time the 1734 almanacs would be published. Perhaps apprehensive that he too might come under Poor Richard's attack, John Jerman returned with the copy for his 1734 almanac to the New Printing-Office. Titan Leeds, whose almanac was printed by Andrew Bradford, good-naturedly swallowed Poor Richard's bait. Franklin waited to read Leeds's reply before issuing *Poor Richard* so that he could spring the Swiftian trap.

He began his preface with an expression of gratitude to the public, whose "charitable Assistance last Year, in purchasing so large an Impression of my Almanacks, has made my Circumstances much more easy in the World." The Saunders's picturesque poverty had not been entirely alleviated, however.

> My Wife has been enabled to get a Pot of her own, and is no longer oblig'd to borrow one from a Neighbour; nor have we ever since been without something of our own to put in it. She has also got a pair of Shoes, two new Shifts, and a new warm Petticoat; and for my part, I have bought a second-hand Coat, so good, that I am now not asham'd to go to Town or be seen there. These Things have render'd her Temper so much more pacifick than it us'd to be, that I may say, I have slept more, and more quietly within this last Year, than in the three foregoing Years put together.[12]

Then Poor Richard turned to his prediction regarding the death of Leeds. Again supplying corroborative detail to support his deception, he said that he could not positively affirm whether his or Leeds's calculations of the time of death was correct, or in fact if Leeds were dead at all, "forasmuch as a Disorder in my own Family demanded my Presence, and would not permit me as I had intended, to be with him in his last Moments, to receive his last Embrace, to close his Eyes, and do the Duty of a Friend in performing the last Offices to the Departed." The stars are not infallible, Poor Richard admitted, and it is well known that "immediate particular Dispositions of Providence" may not set aside events dictated by the course of nature. But Saunders could report that there was "the strongest Probability" that his friend had expired on schedule, "for there appears in his Name, as I am assured, an Almanack for the Year 1734, in which I am treated in a very gross and unhandsome Manner; in which I am called *a false Predictor, an ignorant, a conceited Scribler, a Fool, and a*

Lyar." Poor Richard quoted Leeds's strongest epithets, rendering his hostility and the heat of the quarrel rather more intense than it actually was. Still, Poor Richard was sure that Leeds had been "too well bred to use any Man so indecently and so scurrilously."

> So that it is to be feared that Pamphlet may be only a Contrivance of somebody or other, who hopes perhaps to sell two or three Year's Almanacks still, by the sole Force and Virtue of Mr. Leeds's Name; but certainly, to put Words into the Mouth of a Gentleman and a Man of Letters, against his Friend, which the meanest and most scandalous of the People might be asham'd to utter even in a drunken Quarrel, is an unpardonable Injury to his Memory, and an Imposition upon the Publick.

Poor Richard's Almanac for these first few years is one of the most lighthearted and rollicking of Franklin's literary and journalistic performances. Though the device of a fictional philomath recommended itself by its several advantages to Franklin, concealment of himself was not one of them. The mask of Richard Saunders was one of Franklin's most transparent from the outset. There is much pure fun in the persona, and Van Doren was certainly correct when he surmised that, consciously or unconsciously, Franklin saw an almanac as the opportunity to play a new role, to fashion a new mask. Franklin, his readers, and even his rivals evidently enjoyed the annual masquerade. He often contrived to show his own face through the mask, winking as it were, and sharing an inside joke with his readers.

Leeds continued to take the controversy in good spirit, but his address to the reader in 1735 blundered further into the jaws of Franklin's trap. Poor Richard again waited to write his preface until Leeds had published, and then he sadly observed that though there was said to be a harmony among the stars " 'tis certain there is no Harmony among the Stargazers; but they are perpetually growling and snarling at one another like strange Curs, or like some Men at their Wives." Poor Richard has "receiv'd much Abuse from Titan Leeds deceas'd, (Titan Leeds when living would not have us'd me so!)," and it was here that he delivered the *coup de grâce* of the Swiftian joke. Leeds was undoubtedly "defunct and dead" for three reasons: first, because the stars are never disappointed except in the case of wise men; secondly, because the honor of astrology, of which he was a practitioner and his father before him, demanded it; and

> Thirdly, 'Tis plain to every one that reads his two last Almanacks (for 1734 and 35) that they are not written with that *Life* his Performances use to be written with; the Wit is low and flat, the little Hints dull and spiritless, nothing smart in them but Hudibras's Verses against Astrology at the Heads of the Months in the last, which no Astrologer but a *dead one* would have inserted, and no Man *living* would or could write such Stuff as the rest.

Leeds had, in fact, provided Franklin with another twist to the borrowed hoax in the syntax of his reply to Poor Richard. Saunders offered to convince Leeds "from his own Words" that he was dead;

> for in his Preface to his Almanack for 1734, he says, "Saunders adds another GROSS FALSHOOD in his Almanack, viz. that by my own Calculation I shall *survive* until the 26th of the said Month October 1733, which is as *untrue* as the former." Now if it be, as Leeds says, *untrue* and a *gross Falshood* that he surviv'd till the 26th of October 1733, then it is certainly *true* that he died *before* that Time: And if he died before that Time, he is dead now, to all Intents and Purposes, any thing he may say to the contrary notwithstanding.

Evidently *Poor Richard's Almanac* was firmly established in Pennsylvania by 1735. The *Gazette* for December 4, 1735, announced the next year's issue without the ballyhoo of the first three years:

> JUST PUBLISHED. John Jerman's and Poor Richard's ALMA-NACKS, for the Year 1736.

Jacob Taylor's, is now in the Press, and will speedily be published and sold by the Printer hereof.

In his preface for that year Poor Richard reflected sadly that the "general Approbation" of his readers had excited the envy and malice of his rivals. They sought to deprive him of the reputation he had gained by predicting Titan Leeds's death "by reporting that I my self was never alive. They say in short, *That there is no such a Man as I am;* and have spread this Notion so thoroughly in the Country, that I have been frequently told it to my Face by those that don't know me." Poor Richard professed to be perfectly satisfied of his own existence; how else could he appear to so many thousands each year—in print?

> I need not, indeed, have taken any Notice of so idle a Report, if it had not been for the sake of my Printer, to whom my Enemies are pleased to ascribe my Productions; and who it seems is as unwilling to father my Offspring, as I am to lose the Credit of it. Therefore to clear him entirely, as well as to vindicate my own Honour, I make this publick and serious Declaration, which I desire may be believed, to wit, *That what I have written heretofore, and do now write, neither was nor is written by any other Man or Men, Person or Persons whatsoever.* Those who are not satisfied with this, must needs be very unreasonable.[13]

This was just the sort of playful disclaimer that Franklin had made in the third of his Busy-Body papers, when he forbade "all Persons . . . on any Pretence to enquire who is the Author of this Paper, on Pain of his Displeasure." The game of masquerade is generally over when the face behind the mask is revealed. By his witty denials Poor Richard managed to sustain the illusion of a a fresh and funny disclosure. In his preface for 1737 he apologized for the inaccuracies of his weather forecasts; but he believed that the fault should be ascribed to the printer, who may have transposed or misplaced the predictions, "perhaps for the Conveniency of putting in his Holidays: And since, in spight of all I can say, People will give him great part of the Credit of making my Almanacks, 'tis but reasonable he should take some share of the Blame." [14]

Franklin's contemporary readers were not troubled, as his posterity has been, with the confused identification between Poor Richard and his creator. Yet the aggressiveness of Poor Richard's wit and the raciness of his observations were so typical of Franklin's publications during those early years that the almanac was unmistakably Franklin's work. For all their differences of station and character, their attitudes toward certain subjects run along roughly parallel lines. At certain points Poor Richard's observations provide subtle but valuable glimpses into Franklin's state of mind. In one such instance Poor Richard seems to supply the precise date for an episode Franklin described in his memoirs. In the *Autobiography* Franklin told how his rise to affluence affected his household. Describing his plain and frugal domestic life of the early years, he remembered that they "kept no idle Servants," their table was plain and simple, their furniture of the cheapest kind.

> For instance my Breakfast was a long time Bread and Milk, (no Tea) and I ate it out of a twopenny earthen Porringer with a Pewter Spoon. But mark how Luxury will enter Families, and make a Progress in Spite of Principle. Being call'd one Morning to Breakfast, I found it in a China Bowl with a Spoon of Silver. They had been bought for me without my Knowledge by my Wife, and had cost her the enormous Sum of three and twenty Shillings, for which she had no other Excuse or Apology to make, but that she thought *her* Husband deserv'd a Silver Spoon and China Bowl as well as any of his Neighbours.[15]

The context of this account in the *Autobiography* implies that it occurred during the time that Deborah Franklin carried a good deal of the responsibility for their stationery store and bookshop. This would place it between 1735 and 1739. The preface to *Poor Richard's Almanac* for 1738 relates a similar event in the Saunders family. Franklin varied the format of

this issue, replacing Poor Richard's usual address to the reader
with a letter composed by his famous wife, Bridget. She had
got hold of her husband's preface for the year and discovered
in it "some of his old Skitts at me." And so she prepared an
introduction of her own. Bridget seemed about as shrewish as
she had been described, and possibly as vain. She wrote, "And
now, forsooth! all the World must know, that Poor Dick's
Wife has lately taken a fancy to drink a little Tea now and
then. A mighty matter, truly, to make a Song of! 'Tis true, I
had a little Tea of a Present from the Printer last Year; and
what, must a body throw it away?" [16] Mistress Saunders's
reasoning is so similar to that of Deborah Franklin, recalled
in her husband's memoirs, that it would seem likely that the
china bowl and silver spoon appeared on Benjamin Franklin's
breakfast table one morning in 1737. I do not offer Bridget's
address as proof of the 1737 date, nor is it necessarily significant that luxury in the form of china and silver (a single
piece of each) overtook the Franklins at any particular time.
What this similarity between the *Autobiography* and *Poor
Richard* should demonstrate is that the almanac may yield
biographical insights of a kind hitherto unrecognized. While
affluence for Bridget Saunders meant her own pot and a bit of
tea from the printer, she in her preface and Poor Richard in
his reflect what must have been a feeling of high adventure in
amassing a fortune that the Franklins and the Saunders shared
during these years. And this attitude toward wealth *is* a matter of crucial importance in the interpretation of Franklin's
character. As we trace Poor Richard's ideas about affluence and
success throughout the history of the almanac, we shall see
that neither this early enthusiasm in rising fortunes nor Father
Abraham's prudential moralizing express the fullness of Franklin's ideas on the subject.

The preface to *Poor Richard*, 1739, is perhaps the most
typical of the almanac's early spirit. Franklin's robust scatol-
ogy is well represented. "Ignorant Men wonder how we As-

trologers foretell the Weather so exactly," he began, "Alas!
'tis as easy as pissing abed." The stargazer has only to scan the
heavens through his telescope:

> He spies perhaps VIRGO (or the Virgin); she turns her Head round
> as it were to see if any body observ'd her; then crouching down
> gently, with her Hands on her Knees, she looks wistfully for awhile
> right forward. He judges rightly what she's about: And having
> calculated the Distance and allow'd Time for its Falling, finds
> that next Spring we shall have a fine April shower.[17]

Furthermore, Poor Richard planted the seeds of a new controversy, this time with John Jerman, whose *American Almanack* for 1739 was published by Bradford. Saunders's "Brother
J--m-n" had consulted the stars to learn whether he should
feed his ailing horse a new-laid egg or a little broth. The stars,
he found "plainly gave their verdict for Broth, and the Horse
having sup'd his Broth;—Now, what do you think became of
that Horse? You shall know in my next." In this most leisurely
form of literary controversy, Franklin skillfully employed the
cliff-hanger. He began with this almanac an annual feature of
"True Prognostications"—frequently cryptic—which were
then to be unraveled the following year.

In this preface too, Poor Richard included the first of several reflections on his purposes in selecting the verses and
aphorisms for his almanac. These statements are of special
interest as, taken together, they show that Franklin's moral
seriousness underwent a gradual change during the years that
he published *Poor Richard*. "Besides the usual Things expected
in an Almanack," he began,

> I hope the profess'd Teachers of Mankind will excuse my scattering
> here and there some instructive Hints in Matters of Morality and
> Religion. And be not thou disturbed, O grave and sober Reader,
> if among the many serious Sentences in my Book, thou findest me
> trifling now and then, and talking idly. In all the Dishes I have
> hitherto cook'd for thee, there is solid Meat enough for thy Money.

There are Scraps from the Table of Wisdom, that will if well digested, yield strong Nourishment to thy Mind. But squeamish Stomachs cannot eat without Pickles; which, 'tis true are good for nothing else, but they provoke an Appetite. The Vain Youth that reads my Almanack for the sake of an idle Joke, will perhaps meet with a serious Reflection, that he may ever after be the better for.

As there is no hint that the morality Poor Richard most wishes to inculcate is the prudential, we must assume that industry and thrift were not uppermost in his (or Franklin's) mind at this time. An examination of the verses and maxims for the early almanacs will bear this out. The morality to which Poor Richard referred is general in nature; he professed to be more concerned that his readers be good than that they become rich. There is, however, an edge of sarcasm in this pronouncement, and perhaps withal a hint of moral ambivalence. Poor Richard has, in reality, taken a backhand swipe at the clergy, gently implying that others than "the profess'd Teachers of Mankind" may on occasion provide useful moral instruction. Poor Richard had used the clergy in this way before, as in his observations on "The Parson's Wine and the Baker's Pudding." And we are reminded of the sea-hens and black gowns episode as well as Franklin's antiestablishment defense of the Reverend Mr. Hemphill. If the presentation of events in the *Autobiography* is approximately chronological, it was probably about this time that Franklin made up his mind once and for all that he would no longer attend the Presbyterian meeting in Philadelphia. The story of Deborah's extravagance, which we have related to the 1738 preface, is followed, in Franklin's memoirs, by an account of his break with organized religion. Franklin says that he would have attended the services conducted by the Reverend Jedediah Andrews, had the minister preached Christian morality, "But his Discourses were chiefly either polemic Arguments, or Explications of the peculiar Doctrines of our Sect, and were all to me very dry, uninteresting and unedifying, since not a single moral Principle was inculcated or enforc'd" (*Autobiography*, p. 147). And so, though Benjamin Franklin had long had reservations about the clergy and had given them many "rubs" in the past, his specific quarrel with them in the late 1730s had to do with their failure, in his view, to discharge their social and ethical function. At the same time, Poor Richard scarcely adopts a tone of high moral seriousness. The burden of this statement is to defend his jokes and trifling against the objections of his grave and sober readers. To this purpose he chooses the jolly metaphor of meat and pickles. And so Poor Richard's rhetoric allowed him to chide the clergy for their weaknesses without promising to shoulder their burden himself. As we shall see, Poor Richard eventually turned his almanac conscientiously to a didactic purpose; but for the present both the manner and the matter of this statement indicate that delight was to prevail over instruction. The inclination to hearty humor and ribaldry was a part of Franklin's character throughout his life, but as he reached the age of discretion he apparently developed the ability to restrain his exuberant wit. Poor Richard himself expressed this attitude in 1742 when he wrote, "Strange! that a Man who has wit enough to write a Satyr; should have folly enough to publish it."

In this same 1739 preface Poor Richard again alluded wryly to his relationship with Franklin. Some people, he said, who had observed the great annual demand for the almanac had surmised that he must now be rich and could no longer style himself "Poor Dick." "But, the Case is this," he explained, "When I first begun to publish, the Printer made a fair Agreement with me for my Copies, by Virtue of which he runs away with the greatest Part of the Profit. However, much good may't do him; I do not grudge it him; he is a Man I have a great Regard for, and I wish his Profit ten times greater than it is."

The preface for 1739 is the most typical of the early exuberant Poor Richard. It is the climax of that phase, but it does not mark its end. Titan Leeds actually did die in 1738, it seems; for William and Andrew Bradford announced his death in the 1739 almanac bearing his name. They added, however, that he had provided them with calculations for seven years to come and that they would continue to issue his almanacs. Franklin forgot all about his story of John Jerman's horse. He printed instead a letter, mysteriously transmitted by the late Titan Leeds, in which Leeds assured his old friend Poor Richard that the latter had missed the exact time of his death by only "5 min. 53 sec. which must be allow'd to be no great matter in such Cases." Moreover, Leeds furnished Franklin with some predictions from beyond the grave:

> The People of this Infidel Age, perhaps, will hardly believe this Story. But you may give them these three Signs by which they shall be convinc'd of the Truth of it. About the middle of June next, J. J——n, Philomat, shall be openly reconciled to the Church of Rome, and give all his Goods and Chattles to the Chappel, being perverted by a certain *Country Schoolmaster*. On the 7th of September following my old Friend W. B——t shall be sober 9 Hours, to the Astonishment of all his Neighbours: And about the same time W.B. and A.B. will publish another Almanack in my Name, in spight of Truth and Common-Sense.[18]

The autumn of 1740 found Franklin embroiled in the controversy over the *General Magazine,* and no doubt he was devoting much time and energy to preparing the magazine for the press. In any case, the place of the usual "trifling Preface" in the 1741 almanac was filled by a chronology of important dates since the Glorious Revolution of 1688. This was the first time that another project took precedence over *Poor Richard's Almanac;* and it anticipates the transitional phase of the almanac's history during the mid-forties, when, according to Ross, "Franklin has definitely added the didactic element" and the character of Poor Richard "begins to fade." [19] However, Poor Richard returned with another long address to the reader in his almanac for 1742. Once more he expressed his gratitude for public favor, and once more he lamented his treatment at the hands of his rivals. But this time, beneath the conventionally playful surface of the complaint, there is a positively haunting undertone of wistfulness, a plea for privacy spoken with what sounds like genuine conviction:

> Both Authors and Printers were angry. Hard Names, and many, were bestow'd on me. They deny'd me to be the Author of my own Works; declar'd there never was any such Person; asserted that I was dead 60 Years ago; prognosticated my Death to happen with a Twelvemonth: with many other malicious Inconsistencies, the Effects of blind Passion, Envy at my Success; and a vain Hope of depriving me (dear Reader) of thy wonted Countenance and Favour.—*Who knows him?* they cry: *Where does he live?*—But what is that to them? If I delight in a private Life, have they any Right to drag me out of my Retirement? I have good Reasons for concealing the Place of my Abode.[20]

Neighbors and strangers too had hounded him, he said, for prophecies and advice on planting and husbandry. He had had enough of these "trifling Questions"; he no longer had the taste and leisure for them. "All that these angry Folks can say," he concluded, "will never provoke me to tell them where I live. I would eat my Nails first." Franklin is here repeating much the same formula as in the 1735 almanac when he argued at length the existence of Poor Richard Saunders, but here a brooding quality has replaced the levity. This is one of the most compelling passages in Franklin's writings. Not a retiring man, he habitually did conceal himself, both in print and in his civic projects—behind a literary mask or in the anonymity "of a *Number of Friends*." This policy had proven extremely effective, but it was more than merely a policy. Playing roles, masquerading, hiding—these were instinctual in Benjamin Franklin. Poor Richard's annoyed preface does not explain why he kept out of sight; it is a plea to be left alone with his private reasons.

In 1735 Poor Richard was inviting his rivals to play his

game of masquerade, to unmask him. He was sowing fertile ground for controversy. In the late summer of 1741 Poor Richard's creator had but recently closed the last and bitterest of his many Philadelphia newspaper controversies. The protracted quarrel that arose almost a year before—between Franklin, Bradford, and Webbe over the *General Magazine* and the postmastership—that quarrel had gained Franklin nothing. Both magazines had failed, and though Franklin retained the postmastership the publicity was all bad.[21] He knew well that allegations need not be proven to be damaging to a tradesman's reputation, and in 1741 Franklin was more than a tradesman and journalist. He had his position with the Assembly as well as in the Post Office to consider. Here as in the episode of Bridget Saunders's tea and Deborah Franklin's china bowl, Poor Richard was expressing Franklin's mood. Their attitudes were parallel, not their situations. Poor Richard was beset on all sides by the requests of his neighbors for predictions and advice; Franklin was beset by business of increasing complexity and by new and more determined enemies. Each of them was aggravated almost to the point of eating his nails.

In any event, this preface for 1742 marks the end of Poor Richard's first phase: combative, comic, ribald. While searching for a new voice, which he was to find for Poor Richard in the middle forties, Franklin affected to continue the quarrel with Jerman. In the same 1742 preface Poor Richard took umbrage at Jerman's calling him *"one of Baal's false Prophets,"* and went on to prove to his own satisfaction that Jerman's almanac contained ample evidence that he had converted to Catholicism as predicted. "Ah! Friend John," he concluded, "We must allow you to be a Poet, but you are certainly no Protestant. I could heartily wish your Religion were as good as your Verses."

Jerman's patience was apparently not so long as Leed's had been. Franklin had printed Jerman's almanacs in 1741 and

1742, including Jerman's rather good-humored rejoinder about the false prophet. But Jerman took his copy for 1743 to William Bradford,[22] from whose press he could issue an impatient response to Poor Richard's taunting. "The Reader may expect," he wrote, "a Reply from me to R—— S——rs alias B—— F——ns facetious Way of proving me *no Protestant.* I do hereby protest, that for *that* and such kind of Usage the *Printer* of that witty Performance shall not have the Benefit of my Almanack for this Year." [23] This may be the first time that Franklin was identified with Poor Richard in print. Jerman's tone reveals that the identification was common knowledge, although by that time it can scarcely have mattered. Franklin was no longer interested in games of hide-and-seek. The character of Poor Richard had entered a transitional phase. Franklin no longer cared to be identified with the almanac's earlier spirit. Nor had he evolved a voice for his persona which would neither embarrass himself nor seem entirely implausible as Poor Richard's. For three issues the character of Poor Richard wavered, perhaps as Ross suggests, on the brink of extinction. His preface for 1743 was not the contentious document Jerman's was. Franklin inserted an essay on winemaking from grapes of the province. It was introduced by Poor Richard, but this was clearly not the boisterous, combative Poor Richard of the early and middle thirties. Rather it looked ahead to the almanacs of the early fifties, in which useful information was a prominent feature. In 1744 Franklin introduced *Poor Richard* with a lackluster jibe at one of John Jerman's eclipse predictions. The address to the reader for 1745 was an essay on astronomy and an explanation of the symbols used by astrologers.

Most curious of all the prefaces to *Poor Richard,* however, was that of 1746, which marks the beginning of the second phase. Franklin introduced the almanac with a poem by Richard Saunders. John F. Ross describes these heroic couplets as "abstract" and "impersonal," and he asserts that they are as general as Pope's *Essay on Man*. Ross is accurate in purely descriptive terms, but he wishes to imply that Poor Richard Saunders has been completely effaced. The evidence does not support such an inference. The tone of these almanacs of the second period is all of a piece as an examination of the maxims will reveal. It is a different sort of Poor Richard who speaks to his readers, but it is a character whose development might have been forecast by the developments of the first three years. Evidently the Saunders have continued to prosper. Poor Richard's circumstances are now idyllic; he is no longer the idle star-gazer, but now seems to be a contented cottager. Bridget seems no longer the vain and acid termagant of a decade before but a cheerful though overworked housewife.

> Thanks to kind Readers and a careful Wife,
> With Plenty bless'd, I lead an easy Life;
> My Business Writing; hers to drain the Mead,
> Or crown the barren Hill with useful Shade;
> In the smooth Glebe to see the Plowshare worn,
> And fill the Granary with needful Corn.
> Press nectarous Cyder from my loaded Trees,
> Print the sweet Butter, turn the drying Cheese.[24]

Franklin's reading of James Thomson is clearly reflected in these lines. Of their reading Poor Richard writes:

> Some Books we read, tho' few there are that hit
> The happy Point where Wisdom joins with Wit;
> That set fair Virtue naked to our View,
> And teach us what is *decent,* what is *true.*

Poor Richard goes on to describe their temperate habits and benevolence toward the poor. Of politics he writes that they are "Free from the bitter Rage of Party Zeal/All those we love who seek the publick Weal," recalling the Busy-Body, who described himself as *"no Partyman, but a general Meddler."* The preface then closes in a tone of Popean moralism.

Cautious, if right; if wrong resolv'd to part
The Inmate Snake that folds about the Heart.
Observe the *Mean,* the *Motive* and the *End;*
Mending our selves, or striving still to mend.
Our Souls sincere, our Purpose fair and free,
Without Vain Glory or Hypocrisy:
Thankful if well; if ill, we kiss the Rod;
Resign with Hope, and put our Trust in GOD.

Ross is to be forgiven for finding this a less arresting performance than Poor Richard's evocation of the wistful Virgo and the April shower. Yet it is not without humor; Mrs. Saunders is still doing all of the work. She is now only more resigned to it, mellowed perhaps by plenty, perhaps by reading instructive authors.

Poor Richard was changed in 1746, but significantly he had not changed into the stereotype he has since become. The virtues he emphasized during this phase are moral more than economic. Throughout his career Poor Richard exhorted his readers to be good more often than he instructed them on how to become rich. Franklin remembered in his memoirs that even the economic maxims were ultimately a means of "securing Virtue, it being more difficult for a Man in Want to act always honestly." Poor Richard came back in 1747 with a preface which again stressed the moral purpose of the almanac.

Courteous Reader;

This is the 15th Time I have entertain'd thee with my annual Productions; I hope to thy Profit as well as mine. For besides the astronomical Calculations, and other Things usually contain'd in Almanacks, which have their daily Use indeed while the Year continues, but then become of no Value, I have constantly interspers'd *moral* Sentences, *prudent* Maxims, and *wise* Sayings, many of them containing *much good Sense* in *very few* Words, and therefore apt to leave *strong* and *lasting* Impressions on the Memory of young Persons, whereby they may receive Benefit as long as they live, when both Almanack and Almanack-maker have been long thrown by and forgotten. If I now and then insert a Joke or two, that seem to have little in them, my Apology is, that such may have their Use, since perhaps for their Sake light airy Minds peruse the rest, and so are struck by somewhat of more Weight and Moment.[25]

Although this was in substance the same apologia that Poor Richard had offered in 1739, a comparison of the two paragraphs reveals a marked change in emphasis and tone. In 1739 he had remarked, "I hope the profess'd Teachers of Mankind will excuse my scattering here and there some instructive Hints in Matters of Morality and Religion," implying—as he obviously felt—that he could do the job better than the derelict clergy did. At that time he had described his "trifling" and "talking idly" as the "Pickles" intended to "provoke an Appetite" for the "solid Meat" of the almanac. The jokes, he had said, were inserted to capture the attention of "Vain Youth" who "will perhaps meet with a serious Reflection, that he may ever after be the better for." Franklin had capped each paragraph with the same sentiment, but in 1747 the lighthearted quality imparted by the metaphors of food and appetite has been replaced by a straightforward statement of didactic purpose. Poor Richard's italics of such phrases as "*much good Sense* in *very few* Words" and "*strong* and *lasting* Impressions" lend emphasis to what appears to be the author's serious moral intent.

By the late forties Benjamin Franklin could allow himself the luxury of didacticism. He was to retire from business in 1748. Furthermore, *Poor Richard* had long since proven itself in the marketplace; Saunders no longer needed to try his wit against that of his rivals. And Poor Richard's raciness was no longer acceptable, for Poor Richard reflected upon Franklin's growing respectability. Yet Franklin only changed Poor Richard, only allowed him to grow as his creator had grown: older, wiser, mellower, more decorous. Franklin did not lose interest in the character or abandon him; indeed, if we may trust the older Franklin's memory at all, he *found* the character of Richard Saunders in the middle forties. He brought the almanac into line with his other projects for the improvement of his province. To teach through *Poor Richard* was no less than a luxury for Benjamin Franklin. He lived in an age and in a country which loved didactic literature, and to practice and if possible to inculcate virtue were always in his mature thoughts, as he reveals in the *Autobiography*.

From the preface of 1747, it was but a short step to the enlarged *Poor Richard Improved* of 1748, the third and last phase of the almanac's development. But we have examined the first two periods only in part; it is perhaps appropriate here to return to the beginning and examine the same pattern of development in Poor Richard's famous maxims.

The preface to *Poor Richard,* 1747, presents a striking contrast to the maxims of *Poor Richard,* 1733.[26] There is little purely moral advice among the latter, but much that blends moral and practical wisdom. In the early years, Poor Richard had much to say about dietary matters. "Eat to live, and not live to eat," he wrote, and "A fat kitchin, a lean Will," and "To lengthen thy Life, lessen thy Meals." He presented such specific caveats as "Cheese and salt meat, should be sparingly eat." And he delighted in putting men and food in proverbial juxtaposition: "Men and Melons are hard to know," and "Beware of meat twice boil'd, and an old Foe reconcil'd." The effect of this juxtaposition depends upon the order of the elements, and Franklin made the right decision in each instance. From the beginning Poor Richard catigated drunkenness. As our examination of the *Autobiography* will show, Franklin regarded toping as one of the two or three most dangerous habits to which a man might fall prey. By 1733 he had seen several young tradesmen whose careers had been blighted by drink, and he had seen an entire class of working men in London befuddled and impoverished by their beer. Poor Richard clamored admonitions: "Nothing more like a Fool, than a drunken

Man," "Take counsel in wine, but resolve afterwards in
water," and "He that drinks fast, pays slow." A couplet for
December greeted the holiday celebrant: "Time *eateth* all
things, could old Poets say;/The Times are chang'd, our
times *drink* all away." And there was consolation that month
for the suffering husband: "Never mind it, she'l be sober after
the Holidays."

Among Poor Richard's first comic maxims were the inevitable eighteenth-century reflections on the professions: law,
medicine, and the cloth.

> Never spare the Parson's wine, nor the Baker's pudding.
> He's a Fool that makes his Doctor his Heir.
> Beware of the young Doctor and the old Barber.
> God works wonders now and then;
> Behold! a Lawyer, an honest Man!

Saunders's cynicism about medicine was perhaps best stated
in this same almanac in the observation, "He's the best physician that knows the worthlessness of the most medicines."
Poor Richard's reflections on the clergy were generally no
more venomous than the "Parson's wine" quip, but his views
on the legal profession were pointed, and ironic verses appeared
annually above the court calendar at the back of the almanac.
In 1733 he presented a poem entitled, "The Benefit of going
to LAW."

> Two Beggars travelling along,
>   One blind, the other lame,
> Pick'd up an Oyster on the Way
>   To which they both laid claim:
> The matter rose so high, that they
>   Resolv'd to go to Law,
> As often richer Fools have done,
>   Who quarrel for a Straw.
> A Lawyer took it strait in hand,
>   Who knew his Business was,

To mind nor one nor t'other side,
   But make the best o' th' Cause;
As always in the Law's the Case:
   So he his Judgment gave,
And Lawyer-like he thus resolv'd
   What each of them should have:
      Blind Plaintiff, lame Defendant, share
      The Friendly Laws impartial Care,
      A Shell for him, a Shell for thee,
      The Middle is the Lawyer's Fee.

Poor Richard's earliest productions were full of sophomoric wisdom on the battle of the sexes. He reflected on the nature of the female, on marriage and cuckoldry. The verses for January presented one aspect of courtship.

Old Batchelor would have a Wife that's wise,
Fair, rich, and young, a Maiden for his Bed;
Not proud, nor churlish, but of faultless size;
A Country Housewife in the City bred.
He's a nice Fool, and long in vain hath staid;
He should bespeak her, there's none ready made.

The verses for April played on the name "Will' and concluded with the couplet, "For ne'er heard I of Woman good or ill/ But always loved best, her own sweet Will." And Poor Richard's advice to bachelors was "Ne'er take a Wife till thou hast a house (and a fire) to put her in." The verses for December sounded a typical theme of feminine vanity:

She that will eat her breakfast in her bed,
And spend the morn in dressing of her head,
And sit at dinner like a maiden bride,
And talk of nothing all day but of pride;
God in his mercy may do much to save her,
But what a case is he in that shall have her.

Poor Richard's cynicism on the subject of women and marriage was well grounded in his own experience. Some commen-

tators have been pleased to infer that Franklin's own marriage provided the grief that Poor Richard vented, but the
evidence does not force that conclusion. Thus it is perhaps better to let it alone. Poor Richard's jokes on the ladies were so
completely conventional and obviously sophomoric that they
lack genuine conviction born of agony. Equally conventional
was the tone in which Saunders extolled the "good woman."
"A house without a woman and Firelight, is like a body without soul or sprite," he wrote, without a hint of roasting anyone
in the fire. And he crooned "A good Wife lost is God's gift
lost." He even quoted William Strode's playful sestet on
idealized courtship as the verses for March.[27]

> My Love and I for Kisses play'd,
> She would keep stakes, I was content,
> But when I won she would be paid;
> This made me ask her what she meant:
> Quoth she, since you are in this wrangling vein,
> Here take your Kisses, give me mine again.

I have already surmised that *Poor Richard* for 1733 was
hastily compiled when Franklin found himself without an almanac to print and sell. The quality of the maxims was substantially improved in Poor Richard's second appearance.[28]
Probably Franklin lavished more time and effort on them,
while at the same time refining his technique in this unusual
literary form. Significantly, however, the major themes remained the same. Franklin showed more boldness on the subject of sex:

> You cannot pluck roses without fear of thorns,
> Nor enjoy a fair wife without danger of horns.

> Where there's Marriage without Love, there will be Love
> without Marriage.

> Happy's the Wooing, that's not long a doing.

> Neither a Fortress nor a Maidenhead will hold out long after
> they begin to parly.

The verses for June related a wry story of marital revelation:

> When Robin now three Days had married been,
>   And all his Friends and Neighbours gave him Joy;
> This Question of his Wife he asked then,
>   Why till her Marriage Day she prov'd so coy?
> Indeed (said he) 'twas well thou didst not yield,
>   For doubtless then my Purpose was to leave thee:
> *O Sir, I once before was so beguil'd,*
>   *And was resolv'd the next should not deceive me.*

Of the professions, Poor Richard observed, "Lawyers, Preachers, and Tomtits Eggs, there are more of them hatch'd than come to perfection," and "Many dishes many diseases/Many medicines few cures." He had the same sort of advice on matters of health: "Hot things, sharp things, sweet things, cold things/All rot the teeth, and make them look like old things." But he spiced his admonitions to temperance with ribald references.

> Be temperate in wine, in eating, girls, and sloth;
> Or the Gout will seize you and plague you both.

> Some of our Sparks to London town do go
> Fashions to see, and learn the World to know;
> Who at Return have nought but these to show,
> New Wig above, and new Disease below.

The famous prudential maxims are present in these early almanacs alongside Poor Richard's wit and ribaldry. In 1733 he had written, in addition to the proverb about a "fat kitchin" and a "lean will," "Distrust and caution are the parents of security." In 1734 he said, *"All* things are easy to Industry,/ *All* things difficult to *Sloth,"* "He that is rich need not live sparingly, and he that can live sparingly need not be rich," and "The thrifty maxim of the wary Dutch,/Is to save all the Money they can touch." The next year Poor Richard included his most famous proverb on industry, "Early to bed and early to rise, makes a man healthy, wealthy and wise." It is, of course, this maxim which John F. Ross fastened upon to demonstrate the inconsistency between the character of Poor Richard and his proverbs. Ross argues that it is misleading to attribute the proverbs of *Poor Richard's Almanac* to the comic astrologer; he observes that the maxims "are confined to the body of the almanac, with no particular reference to Richard; whereas the character is confined to the prefaces, with no indication of his proverbial wisdom." [29] In fact, the prefaces and the maxims represent no very substantial differences in style or purpose. During this first period of *Poor Richard,* the purpose of both was to entertain and amuse the public. If Poor Richard gave no hint, in his prefaces, of his proverbial "wisdom" he did supply evidence of his wit and aphoristic style. Merely because Saunders the raffish astrologer did not himself rise early, does not argue that he could not possibly have prescribed the regimen to others. Indeed, it is comically appropriate that he did so. In the proverbs as in the prefaces Poor Richard reflects a character parallel to that of his creator. The Franklin of Philadelphia in the early thirties was typified by the two strains of the indefatigable and frugal tradesman and the robust and irreverent wit. When he wrote "Eyes and Priests/Bear no Jests" and "Nothing but Money/Is sweeter than Honey" (1735) Poor Richard the maxim-monger reflected both Poor Richard the preface-writer and Benjamin Franklin of the New Printing-Office.

In *Poor Richard,* 1736, the earthy themes of sex and cuckoldry and the use of colorful language are at a peak of exuberance. "He that lives upon Hope," he wrote, "dies farting." [30]

> Let thy maidservant be faithful, strong, and homely.
> She that paints her Face, thinks of her Tail.
> Why does the blind man's wife paint herself?
> Force shites upon Reason's Back.
> Forwarn'd, forearm'd, unless in the case of Cuckolds, who are
> often forearm'd before warn'd.

The next year, however, found Poor Richard a sobered man. I have already cited autobiographical elements in the almanac, and I have asserted that at times the lives and careers of Franklin and Saunders almost converge. This is most movingly demonstrable in *Poor Richard, 1737.* In November 1736, Franklin's four-year-old son, Francis Folger, died of smallpox. On December 30 Franklin printed the following announcement in the *Gazette:*

> Understanding 'tis a current Report, that my Son Francis, who died lately of the Small Pox, had it by Inoculation; and being desired to satisfy the Publick in that Particular; inasmuch as some People are, by that Report (join'd with others of the like kind, and perhaps equally groundless) deter'd from having that Operation perform'd on their Children, I do hereby sincerely declare, that he was not inoculated, but receiv'd the Distemper in the common way of Infection: And I suppose the Report could only arise from its being my known Opinion, that Inoculation was a safe and beneficial Practice; and from my having said among my Acquaintance, that I intended to have my Child inoculated, as soon as he should have recovered sufficient Strength from a Flux with which he had been long afflicted.
>
> B. FRANKLIN

The almanac for the next year, which was undoubtedly being compiled during Frankie's protracted illness, contained verses poignantly relevant to Franklin's domestic tragedy.[31] The verses for January concerned inoculation.

> God offer'd to the Jews Salvation
> And 'twas refus'd by half the Nation:
> Thus, (tho' 'tis Life's great Preservation)
> Many oppose *Inoculation.*
>   We're told by one of the black Robe
> The Devil inoculated Job:
> Suppose 'tis true, what he does tell;
> Pray, Neighbours, *Did not Job do well?*

Though charged with wit and a wry thrust at the clergy, these were patently serious verses and recognizable as sentiments close to Franklin's heart at the time. Most personal of the verses were those for February on parental stoicism.

> The Thracian Infant, entring into Life,
> Both Parents mourn for, both receive with Grief:
> The Thracian Infant snatch'd by Death away,
> Both Parents to the Grave with Joy convey.
> This, Greece and Rome, you with Derision view;
> This is mere Thracian Ignorance to you:
> But if you weigh the Custom you despise,
> This Thracian Ignorance may teach the wise.

And elsewhere in the almanac Poor Richard remarked, "After crosses and losses men grow humbler and wiser." Thus did Franklin reflect on his own circumstances behind the persona of Poor Richard Saunders.

Indeed, the high spirited and racy quality of the early almanacs declines more perceptibly and from an earlier date in the proverbs than in the prefaces. This is perhaps easily understood, for flexible though he was, the character of Poor Richard imposed certain tonal requirements on the prefaces. We have seen how Franklin gradually modulated that character into his second phase, perhaps revealing some indecision along the way. The maxims reflected Poor Richard's wit, but as Ross observed, they did not reflect his mode of living. And so it is the maxims which may provide the more subtle indicator of Franklin's attitudes. In these almanacs of the late thirties the force of a greater number of proverbs is to promote thrift. There is a mellowed irony toward the vanity of human wishes. "Who has deceiv'd thee so oft as thy self?" Poor Richard asked in 1738, and "Is there any thing Men take more pains about than to render themselves unhappy?" [32] There is some economic advice: "He that would have a short Lent, let him borrow Money to be repaid at Easter" and "Buy what thou has no need of; and e're long thou shalt sell thy necessaries." But there is also the suggestion that some things besides honey may be sweeter than money. "Drive thy business," he says, "let not that drive thee." It is a moderate and sage Poor Richard who urges his readers to strive for virtue:

> Wink at small faults; remember thou hast great ones.
> Search others for their virtues, thy self for thy vices.
>   Each year one vicious habit rooted out,
>   In time might make the worst Man good throughout.
> Wish not so much to live long as to live well.

Poor Richard also had much to say of books and learning, and of their relation to wisdom.

> Read much, but not many Books.
> Write with the learned, pronounce with the vulgar.
> If thou has wit and learning, add to it Wisdom and Modesty.
> Reading makes a full Man, Meditation a profound Man, discourse a clear Man.

Despite its lively preface, *Poor Richard,* 1739, displays the trend toward moderation in the proverbs. There is a bit of the raciness of the preface in "Prythee isn't Miss Cloe's a comical Case?/She lends out her Tail, and she borrows her Face"; but in general the maxims run again to observations on human nature and exhortations to virtue: "Thirst after Desert, not Reward." In the almanacs of the early forties he began speaking of the disillusionments of wealth, and he pronounced on the burdens of business. The verses for August 1742, titled "The Busy-Man's Picture," reflect Franklin's experience as clearly as do those earlier ones on inoculation and parental grief.

> BUSINESS, thou Plague and Pleasure of my Life,
> Thou charming Mistress, thou vexatious Wife;
> Thou Enemy, thou Friend, to Joy, to Grief,
> Thou bring'st me all, and bring'st me no Relief,
> Thou bitter, sweet, thou pleasing, teasing Thing,
> Thou Bee, that with thy Honey wears a Sting;
> Some Respite, prithee do, yet do not give,
> I cannot with thee, nor without thee live.[33]

Franklin is known to have written little of the verse that appeared in *Poor Richard's Almanac,* but the temptation to ascribe this to him is great. The poem is slight, perhaps, but the couplets are balanced with assurance, and the aptness of the metaphors—the management of the paradoxes—carries the full force of conviction. In 1744 Poor Richard repeated with added strength his 1738 admonition to the tradesman: "Drive thy Business, or it will drive thee." And in the same almanac he observed, "He who multiplies Riches multiplies Cares." [34]

A benevolent moralism and a mellowed cynicism thus permeated the prefaces and maxims of *Poor Richard* during the forties. The verse preface for 1746 presented Poor Richard as a humble but contented countryman. Indeed, the ruling ideal of these years may have been stated in the maxim of 1734, recast for 1746: "A Plowman on his Legs is higher than a Gentleman on his Knees." [35] The idea dominates the almanac for 1747. [36] The verses for February extol humble virtue:

> See *Wealth* and *Pow'r!* Say, what can be more great?
> Nothing—but *Merit* in a low Estate.
> To Virtue's humblest Son let none prefer
> *Vice,* tho' a Croesus or a Conquerer.
> Shall Men, like Figures, pass for high or base,
> Slight, or important, only by their *Place?*
> Titles are Marks of honest Men, and Wise;
> The Fool, or Knave that wears a Title, lies.

The positive ideal is outlined in the verses for November.

> I envy none their Pageantry and Show;
> I envy none the Gilding of their Woe.
> Give me, indulgent Heav'n, with Mind serene,
> And guiltless Heart, to range the Sylvan Scene.
> No splendid Poverty, no smiling Care,
> No well bred Hate, or servile Grandeur there.
> The Sense is ravish'd, and the Soul is blest,

On every Thorn delightful Wisdom grows,
In every Rill a sweet Instruction flows.

Poor Richard propounds an ethic of benevolence when he writes, "There is no Man so bad, but he secretly respects the Good," and "A quiet Conscience sleeps in Thunder/But Rest and Guilt live far asunder." The theme of the good woman, present from the beginning alongside the more cynical view of the sex, is here expressed in the verses for May. Poor Richard appeals to the sense and sensibility of his young female readers.

Girls, mark my Words; and know, for Men of Sense
Your strongest Charms are native Innocence.
Shun all deceiving Arts; the Heart that's gain'd
By Craft alone, can ne'er be long retain'd.
Arts on the Mind, like Paint upon the Face,
Fright him, that's worth your Love, from your Embrace.
In simple Manners all the Secret lies.
Be kind and virtuous, you'll be blest and wise.

Even the customary verses on the law printed above the court calendar lack the broad and farcical humor of the early combative years. The satiric thrust at the profession is submerged in a wistful yearning for a world of prelapsarian beatitude:

From Earth to Heav'n when *Justice* fled,
The Laws decided in her Stead;
From Heav'n to Earth should she return,
Lawyers might beg, and Lawbooks burn.

The age of discretion had overtaken Poor Richard by 1747. His creator—the unacknowledged author of the sensational "Speech of Miss Polly Baker"—would, a year later, be called "a sort of tribune of the people" by a grudging Thomas Penn. The almanac lacked the incisive wit and rollicking good humor during this transitional phase, though there would be a marked resurgence of these qualities after 1748. Franklin had not resigned himself altogether to his second and greater career of public service, but he was weary of the press and entanglements of business. Poor Richard Saunders lived a sort of life Franklin probably aspired to when he planned his retirement. He moved his family from their house on (significantly) Market Street to a quieter section of town—in spirit, if not in fact, like the Saunders rural retreat. As Franklin remembered it, "I flatter'd myself that by the sufficient tho' moderate Fortune I had acquir'd, I had secur'd Leisure during the rest of my Life, for Philosophical Studies and Amusements . . . but the Publick now considering me as a Man of Leisure, laid hold of me for their Purposes." [37] *Poor Richard's Almanac* rather anticipated Franklin's resignation to a life of service, for he turned energetically to a career of informing and instructing his countrymen even before his creator had extricated himself from the hurly-burly of the printing business. The involvement in current provincial affairs reflected by *Poor Richard Improved* suggests that Franklin's recollection of his planned retirement was fond nostalgia. In any case, Poor Richard continued to reflect interests and concerns closest to those of Benjamin Franklin himself. The relationship between the mask of Poor Richard and the mind that fashioned it was intimate, but it was far more intricate than has been supposed. *Poor Richard's Almanac,* particularly during the first fifteen years, must be read as a subtle and sensitive reflector of Franklin's mind, not as a crude and candid equivalent.

If Poor Richard's initial intent (to titilate, amuse, sell) was clear, no less clear was his purpose in expanding the almanac in 1748 to *Poor Richard Improved.* He wanted to provide his readers more useful information. For fifteen years the format had remained the same: six pages of introductory matter and general information at the front, a page for each of the months, and six more pages of general information at the back.[38] In 1748 the pamphlet swelled to thirty-six pages, allowing each month two facing pages. The left-hand page was devoted to additional tables and literary material. Franklin's Yale editors have observed that there was a change in the nature of this material over the eleven years that Franklin prepared *Poor Richard Improved.*

> In the first few almanacs he dwelt mostly on historical events which had occurred during corresponding months of the previous years, and the lessons to be derived from them; later he introduced literary or scientific essays, some of which may have been original with him; most were obviously taken, at least in part, from other writers. Some of these essays occupy only a single page; others run through several months or even a whole year.[39]

Indeed, the editors assert that Poor Richard became "a sort of miniature general magazine, issued annually to delight and educate its readers."

Accordingly, Poor Richard greeted his readers in 1748 with an explanation of his enlarged publication. He had "taken the Liberty" to imitate the "well-known Method" of the late Jacob Taylor in giving two pages to each month. "Yet," he added, "I have not so far follow'd his Method, as not to continue my own where I thought it preferable; and thus my Book is increas'd to a Size beyond his, and contains much more Matter." At this point he inserted a tribute to Taylor in verse, rather bizarrely adapted from John Hughes's 1720 poem in honor of Sir Isaac Newton, "The Ecstasy." Beneath the verses he admonished his muse to "Souse down to Prose again . . . for Poetry's no more thy Element, than Air is that of the Flying-Fish; whose Flights, like thine, are therefore always short and heavy." Franklin preserved the mellow tone of self-deprecation typical of Richard Saunders, along with his modest assertion of the superiority of his book. Franklin may have seen *Poor Richard Improved* as a proper vehicle for instructing his countrymen, but Saunders remained fundamentally one of them—reading apparently "few Books" but the almanacs of his rivals, and pronouncing "with the vulgar." Poor Richard turned from his introductory remarks to introduce a long extract from Commander Christopher Middleton's report to the Royal Society on his unsuccessful expedition in search of the Northwest Passage. Franklin had extracted many wonderful curiosities from Middleton's account, and he couched them in his own lucid expository prose, largely uncolored by the character of Richard Saunders.

> The Hares, Rabbits, Foxes, and Partridges, in September and the beginning of October, change their Colour to a snowy White, and continue white till the following Spring.
>
> The Lakes and standing Waters, which are not above 10 or 12 Feet deep, are frozen to the Ground in Winter, and the Fishes therein all perish. Yet in Rivers near the Sea, and Lakes of a greater Depth than 10 or 12 Feet, Fishes are caught all the Winter by cutting Holes thro' the Ice, and therein putting Lines and Hooks. As soon as the fish are brought into the open Air, they instantly freeze stiff.

At the end of this passage, Franklin was careful to reassert the persona of Poor Richard, closing the preface with a bit of the philomath's fanciful prose.

> And now, my tender Reader, thou that shudderest when the Wind blows a little at N-West, and criest, *'Tis extrrrrream cohohold!* *'Tis terrrrrrible cohold!* what dost thou think of removing to that delightful Country? Or dost thou not rather chuse to stay in Pennsylvania, thanking God that *He has caused thy Lines to fall in pleasant Places.* I am Thy Friend to serve thee,
>
> R. SAUNDERS.

Poor Richard Saunders was not lost in the transition to *Poor Richard Improved.* If his new concern with scientific matters reflected Benjamin Franklin's preoccupation with natural philosphy during these years, he was merely doing as he had always done. The preoccupations of the character ran parallel to those of his creator. The mask was still useful in giving Franklin some distance from his medium of instruction. That distance was in some respects more important during these later years than it had been when Franklin employed it to keep himself above Poor Richard's battles with Leeds and Jerman. Now Poor Richard's comic quality made serious instruction more palatable. That Franklin was aware of this advantage, we shall see in his last two or three prefaces.

Poor Richard had presented an article on wine-making (1746), a cure for pleurisy propounded by Dr. Tennent (1740), and an article on "rattlesnake herb" (1737); nevertheless, the use of his personal preface for philosophical material was novel in 1748. Among the monthly curiosities Poor Richard included another scientific item. One of the notable events of January was the birth, in 1493, of "the famous Astronomer Copernicus." Copernicus had revived the Pythagorean theory of a heliocentric planetary system, Poor Richard reminded his readers. This theory, now the "generally receiv'd System of the World," had supplanted the Ptolemean system, which, in a homely metaphor, Poor Richard laughed to scorn.

> Mr. Whiston, a modern Astronomer, says, the Sun is 230,000 times bigger than the Earth, and 81 Millions of Miles distant from it: That vast Body must then have mov'd more than 480 Millions of Miles in 24 h. A prodigious Journey around this little Spot! How much more natural is Copernicus's Scheme! Ptolomy is compar'd to a whimsical Cook, who, instead of Turning his Meat in Roasting, should fix That, and contrive to have his whole Fire, Kitchen and all, whirling round it.

Poor Richard also included some deistic poetry of his own, including the verses for March. At the end of a sestet of rhyming tetrameters describing the sun, moon, fixed and mobile stars, he added an heroic couplet: "All these God's plastick Will from Nothing brought/Assign'd their Stations, and their Courses taught." March 20 was the twenty-first anniversary of Newton's death, Poor Richard noted; and he included two tributes by Thomson to the great physicist as well as Pope's famous couplet, "justly admired for its conciseness, strength, boldness, and sublimity": "Nature and nature's laws lay hid in light;/God said, *Let* NEWTON *be,* and all was light." In the very midst of these deistic verses, however, Poor Richard inserted a maxim on the meaning of the Christian revelation:

"The Heathens when they dy'd, went to Bed without a Candle." Later on, opposite the page for August, Franklin printed a timely discussion of *"Muschitoes, or Musketoes."* Perhaps inspired by recent microscopic studies of the mosquito, this item marveled that though the insect was so light that fifty hungry ones "scarce weigh a grain, yet each has all the parts necessary to life, motion, digestion, generation, &c. as veins, arteries, muscles, &c. each has in his little body room for the five senses. . . . How inconceivably small must their organs be! How inexpressibly fine the workmanship!" But Poor Richard typically added a Swiftian twist to the end of his description. "In a scarce summer," he wrote, "any citizen may provide Musketoes sufficient for his own family, by leaving tubs of rain-water uncover'd in his yard; for in such water they lay their eggs, which when hatch'd, become first little fish, afterwards put forth legs and wings, leave the water, and fly into your windows." How true to Poor Richard and yet how like Franklin that passage is, with the deist's celebration of God's great craftsmanship, the keen naturalist's description of the mosquito's life cycle, and the brief lesson cast in the Swiftian mode of satiric inversion which Franklin loved so well.

In the maxims, *Poor Richard Improved* retained the theme of contentment in one's station, so prevalent in the almanacs of the mid-1740s.

> Wealth and Content are not always Bed-fellows.
> Content makes poor men rich; Discontent makes rich Men poor.
> Having been poor is no shame, but being ashamed of it is.
> Too much plenty makes Mouth dainty.
> Who dainties love, shall Beggars prove.
>   *Industry's* bounteous Hand may *Plenty* bring,
>   But wanting *frugal Care,* 'twill soon take wing.
>
>   . . . .
>
>   Close Fraud and Wrong from griping *Av'rice* grow,
>   From rash *Profusion* desp'rate Acts and Woe.

A Man has no more *Goods* than he gets Good by.[40]

Closely related is the theme of general benevolence, present in previous issues, and expressed in a paragraph on the page opposite March 1749.

> The nose of a lady here, is not delighted with perfumes that she understands are in Arabia. Fine musick in China gives no pleasure to the nicest ear in Pennsilvania. Nor does the most exquisite dish serv'd up in Japan, regale a luxurious palate in any other country. But the benevolent mind of a virtuous man, is pleas'd, when it is inform'd of good and generous actions, in what part of the world soever they are done.

The almanac for 1750 displays the same themes. Of contentment Poor Richard writes, "A plain, clean, and decent Habit, proportioned to one's Circumstances, is one Mark of Wisdom," and "Discontented Minds and Fevers of the Body are not to be cured by changing Beds or Businesses." [41] As a sort of reprise on the item about mosquitos the previous year, Poor Richard presented a paragraph on bedbugs. The cure for these pests is scalding water poured or squirted "into the Joints, &c. of the Bedstead." The result of this treatment is expressed in proverbial style: "The old Ones are scalded to Death, and the Nits are spoilt, for a boil'd Egg never hatches." This is an interesting and characteristic example of what Charles W. Meister has called Franklin's "faith" in proverbial utterance. Meister writes that Franklin often "seemed willing to let a proverb carry practically the sole burden of proof of an argument he had advanced." [42] This faith in the proverb as a rhetorical device undoubtedly accounts for the extraordinary effort Franklin put into revising maxims for *Poor Richard*.

Poor Richard addressed his readers, in his issue for 1751, in a manner reminiscent of earlier years. The preface was a tongue-in-cheek defense of astrology, lamenting the fact that "Urania has been betrayed by her own Sons; those whom she had favour'd with the greatest Skill in her divine Art, the most eminent Astronomers among the Moderns, the Newtons, Halleys, and Whistons, have wantonly contemn'd and abus'd her, contrary to the Light of their own Consciences." [43] Otherwise the themes remain substantially the same. "Prosperity discovers Vice, Adversity Virtue," he writes, and "Many a Man would have been worse, if his Estate had been better." A long essay on microscopy occupies the right-hand pages for April through October and a line or two on that for November.

Parliament adopted the new-style calendar for Great Britain and her colonies in 1752, and poor Richard's preface for that year and part of the preface for the next explain the innovation. The hollowness of wealth is perhaps most concisely expressed in *Poor Richard Improved,* 1752: "Success has ruin'd many a Man." [44] As a concise and incisive comment on the human condition, this aphorism is matched only by Poor Richard's terse remark in 1749: "9 Men in 10 are suicides." [45] The almanac for 1754 is a good-natured performance, again somewhat in the earlier style. The preface sets out to prove that the first astrologers "were honest Husbandmen" as "so it seems are the last; for my Brethren Jerman and Moore, and myself, the only remaining Almanack-makers of this Country, are all of that Class." [46] The maxims are among the most charming and graceful of Poor Richard's career.

> The Bell calls others to Church, but itself never minds the Sermon.
> The Cat in Gloves catches no Mice.
> Some make Conscience of wearing a Hat in the Church, who make none of robbing the Altar.
> A child thinks 20 Shillings and 20 years can scarce ever be spent.
> Many Princes sin with David, but few repent with him.

Most of *Poor Richard Improved,* 1755, is devoted to a long account of Peru and the Andes, probably taken from an

English translation of Pierre Bouguer's *Relation Abregee du Voyage Fait au Perou*, a publication of the French Royal Academy, 1744. Of contentment Poor Richard writes,

> *Who is wise?* He that learns from every One.
> *Who is Powerful?* He that governs his Passions.
> *Who is rich?* He that is content.
> *Who is that?* Nobody.[47]

Of the prudential values Poor Richard comments, "God gives all Things to Industry," and "Diligence overcomes Difficulties, Sloth makes them." And he seems to be correcting his early proverb about money and honey with "When you taste Honey, remember Gall."

Poor Richard's address to his readers in 1756 is the last of three expressions of purpose of the almanac. Here, for the first time, he singles out prudential virtues as those he chiefly desires to inculcate. He has, he says, compiled his almanac "during now near two Revolutions of the Planet Jupiter," in hopes that it would provide useful information on the *"Day of the Month,* the *remarkable Days,* the *Changes of the Moon,* the *Sun and Moon's Rising and Setting, and* . . . the *Tides* and the *Weather."*

> But I hope this is not all the advantage thou hast reaped; for with a View to the Improvement of thy *Mind* and thy *Estate,* I have constantly interspers'd in every little Vacancy, *Moral Hints, Wise Sayings,* and *Maxims of Thrift,* tending to impress the Benefits arising from *Honesty, Sobriety, Industry* and *Frugality;* which if thou has duly observed, it is highly probable thou art *wiser* and *richer* many fold more than the Pence my Labours have cost thee. Howbeit, I shall not therefore raise my Price because thou art better able to pay; but being thankful for past Favours, shall endeavour to make my little Book more worthy thy Regard, by adding to those *Recipes* which were intended for the *Cure* of the *Mind,* some valuable Ones regarding the *Health* of the *Body.* They are recommended by the Skilful, and by successful Practice. I wish a blessing may

attend the Use of them, and to thee all Happiness, being Thy obliged Friend,

R. SAUNDERS [48]

Accordingly, Franklin did emphasize economy in the 1756
almanac. "A Correspondent" offered a proposal that Pennsylvania farmers use oxen instead of horses as draft animals.
Another essay, not unrelated to Father Abraham's speech two
years later, discussed the problem of scarce currency.

> You spend yearly at least *Two Hundred Thousand Pounds*, 'tis
> said, in European, East-Indian, and West-Indian Commodities:
> Supposing one Half of this Expense to be in *Things absolutely
> necessary,* the other Half may be call'd *Superfluities,* or at best,
> Conveniences, which however you might live without for one little
> Year, and not suffer exceedingly. Now to save this Half, observe
> these few Directions.
>
> 1. When you incline to have new Cloaths, look first well over
> the old Ones, and see if you cannot shift with them another Year,
> either by Scouring, Mending, or even Patching if necessary. Re-
> member a Patch on your Coat, and Money in your Pocket, is better
> and more creditable than a Writ on your Back, and no Money to
> take it off. [49]

Poor Richard provided three more "Directions," and concluded, "Thus at the Year's End, there will be *An Hundred
Thousand Pounds* more Money in your Country." This plea
and that of Father Abraham must be seen against the background of the perpetual shortage of currency in the colonies.
Poor Richard remarked here that he had recently visited a
friend in New Jersey, where Governor Belcher's request to the
Board of Trade for £70,000 in bills of credit to be made
legal tender had recently been rejected on the King's advice.
Some of the good humor evident in Poor Richard's relating
the speech of Father Abraham is present here, as he offers the
advice modestly. It costs nothing, he reminds his readers, "and
if you will not be angry with me for giving it, I promise you
not to be offended if you do not take it."

Poor Richard also included several recipes for the health of the body, as he had promised. Among these was "A RECEIPT for making *Dauphiny Soup,* which in Turkey is called *Touble,* and with which a great Number of Persons may be Plentifully fed at a very small Expense," and a method for preparing rice to the same purpose. Both of these recipes had appeared in the *London Magazine* of that year, and there is little doubt that Franklin inserted them for the use of the newly recruited Pennsylvania militia.[50] Poor Richard had come a long way from the days when his wife had neither a pot nor anything to go into it. Yet his tone of mild sententiousness and his gently humorous recognition of that quality in himself—these sustained the persona. True to the promise of his preface Poor Richard presented several items of pharmacology. One was a remedy of a glass of antimony "for the Dysentery or bloody Flux," another *"For the Ague or Intermitting Fever,"* and a third *"For the Dry-Gripes."*

This was the *Poor Richard* that Franklin remembered in the *Autobiography.* The almanac, which had begun as entertainment and then turned to moral instruction, was now a vehicle for Franklin's most practical advice to his fellow Pennsylvanians. Momentous events had occupied his retirement. He had been elected to the Philadelphia Common Council (1748), the Pennsylvania Assembly and Philadelphia Board of Alderman (1749). He had received honorary degrees from Harvard, Yale (1753), and William and Mary (1756); and he had been elected to the Royal Society in 1756, having received its Copley Medal in 1753. His theory of the identity of lightning and electricity had been verified by M. Dalibard in France (1752). In 1754 he had attended the Albany Congress, which adopted a plan of union for the colonies based largely on his proposals. Since 1753 he had served as Deputy Postmaster General of North America. In 1755 he had distinguished himself in the service of General Edward Braddock's elaborately disastrous expedition against the French and Indians. And later the same year he had taken the field himself, helping to organize Northampton County's defense against the Indians. The next year, assuming command in that county, he had built a line of three forts across the mountains. In February 1756, he had been commissioned colonel of the Philadelphia militia regiment. The summer of 1757 would see him embark on his first mission to England as provincial agent. James Parton wrote that Franklin "had given proof upon proof that he had the best head in Pennsylvania" by the time he was thirty.[51] To say this of the mid-1730s seems to verge on idolatry, but it can be said with confidence of the mid-fifties. And the character of *Poor Richard's Almanac* was in line with Franklin's public character. Franklin at fifty was young for a sage, but he had proven himself wise beyond his years.

Poor Richard undoubtedly expressed some of Franklin's weariness and frustration with public life in the last almanac, which Franklin composed on the voyage to England: "The first Mistake in publick Business, is the going into it," and "To serve the Publick faithfully, and at the same time please it entirely, is impracticable." [52] Franklin was employing Poor Richard as he had used his imaginary correspondents to the *Pennsylvania Gazette,* who wrote about slippery sidewalks and inadequate fire protection. In these last issues of *Poor Richard Improved* Franklin included a great deal of advice that was pertinent and practical—not abstract or moral, nor even especially entertaining. But *Poor Richard* had retained some of the liveliness of the early years; perhaps it was Franklin's renewed sense of purpose that infused new life into the pamphlet. In any case, Father Abraham's speech was not the only piece in the last almanacs that bore the stamp of Franklin's wit and inventiveness. In the issue for 1757, Poor Richard presented a Swiftian modest proposal which displays, with charm and wit, Franklin's ingenuity, his lucid scientific prose, and his themes of economy and proportion. Because the item is short and seldom reprinted, I present it in its entirety.

How to make a STRIKING SUNDIAL, by which not only a Man's own Family, but all his Neighbours for ten Miles round, may know what o'Clock it is, when the Sun shines, without seeing the Dial.

Chuse an open Place in your Yard or Garden, on which the Sun may shine all Day without any impediment from Trees or Buildings. On the Ground mark out your Hour Lines, as for a horizontal Dial, according to Art, taking Room enough for the Guns. On the Line for One o'Clock, place one Gun; on the Two o'Clock Line two Guns, and so of the rest. The Guns must all be charged with Powder, but Ball is unnecessary. Your Gnomon or Style must have twelve burning Glasses annex'd to it, and be so placed as that the Sun shining through the Glasses one after the other, shall cause the Focus or burning spot to fall on the Hour Line of One for Example, at one a Clock, and there kindle a Train of Gunpowder that shall fire one Gun. At Two a Clock, a Focus shall fall on the Hour Line of Two, and kindle another Train that shall discharge two Guns successively; and so of the rest.

Note, there must be 78 Guns in all. Thirty-two Pounders will be best for this Use; but 18 Pounders may do, and will cost less, as well as use less Powder, for nine Pounds of Powder will do for one Charge of each eighteen Pounder, whereas the Thirty-two Pounders would require for each Gun 16 Pounds.

Note also, That the chief Expense will be the Powder, for the Cannon once bought, will, with Care, last 100 Years.

Note moreover, That there will be a great Saving of Powder in cloudy Days.

Kind Reader, Methinks I hear thee say, *That is indeed a good Thing to know how the Time passes, but this Kind of Dial, notwithstanding the mentioned savings, would be very expensive; and the Cost greater than the Advantage.* Thou art wise, my Friend, to be so considerate beforehand; some Fools would not have found out so much, till they had made the Dial and try'd it. Let all such learn that many a private and many a publick Project, are like this *Striking Dial,* great Cost for little Profit.[53]

This was essentially the last time that Poor Richard and his creator would belong solely to the province of Pennsylvania. The preface Franklin composed for the next (and last) of his issues of the almanac and the voyage on which he composed it were to bring him a new sort of international celebrity. Indeed, it made both Franklin and Richard Saunders internationally famous. At the beginning of this chapter we reviewed the traditional lines of argument concerning *Poor Richard's Almanac*. It should be obvious, from the foregoing examination, that to generalize from Father Abraham to Poor Richard and thence to Benjamin Franklin is foolish and misleading. Yet, the "Speech of Father Abraham" must not be slighted in importance here, merely because its significance has been exaggerated elsewhere. That Franklin believed in industry and frugality is hardly open to question. Almost everyone does. Most moralists would deny that diligence and thrift are the highest human values; as Harold Larrabee pointed out, Father Abraham was talking about "instrumental values and not final goods." Now a careful reading of the passage in the *Autobiography* reveals that Benjamin Franklin knew the difference between instrumental values and final goods. It is hard, he observed, for an empty sack to stand upright. Hostile critics are frequently hasty readers. But in any event, a detailed analysis of *Poor Richard* has shown that more of his maxims treated of those higher values than inculcated prudential morality.

"The Way to Wealth" was perhaps a fortuitous literary and social accident. It was in one sense narrowly topical and in another almost universally applicable. Of its wide appeal Franklin himself wrote, "The Piece being universally approved was copied in all the Newspapers of the Continent, reprinted in Britain on a Broadside to be stuck up in Houses, two Translations were made of it in French, and great Numbers bought by the Clergy and Gentry to distribute gratis among their poor Parishioners and Tenants" (*Autobiography*,

p. 164). Franklin fairly—even modestly—represented, in this
passage, the extent of the document's distribution. He went
on, however, to touch upon its topicality—an important and
usually neglected aspect of the story. "In Pennsylvania," he
wrote, "as it discouraged useless Expense in foreign Superfluities, some thought it had its share of Influence in producing
that growing Plenty of Money which was observable for several Years after its Publication." Here was the ever-present
colonial problem: the subject of one of the first publications
bearing the imprint of the New Printing-Office in 1728, and
one of the prominent economic factors leading to the American Revolution. Even more specifically Father Abraham's
address was directed to the problem of new levies imposed in
Pennsylvania and other colonies to meet the expenses of the
Seven Years' War. Poor Richard wrote, "I stopt my Horse
lately where a great Number of People were collected at a
Vendue of Merchant Goods. The Hour of the Sale not being
come, they were conversing on the Badness of the Times, and
one of the Company call'd to a plain clean old Man, with
white Locks, *Pray, Father Abraham, what think you of the
Times? Won't these heavy Taxes quite ruin the Country?
How shall we be ever able to pay them? What would you
advise us to do?*" [54] Father Abraham's answer was the same
advice that Poor Richard's "Correspondent" had offered in
1756. Live "for little Year" without the superfluities; keep
£100,000 from flowing out of the provincial economy. The
lesson of the striking sundial was the same (though submerged in the humorous ingenuity of the fantastic device):
think of the long-range economic consequences of "advanta-
geous" projects. Poor Richard harped not only on his old
theme, but he returned to a favorite motif of the almanac—
going back to 1734: that is to say new clothes. In 1756 he
had recommended, "When you incline to have new Cloaths,
look first well over the old Ones, and see if you cannot shift
with them another Year." Poor Richard himself had in 1733

"bought a second-hand Coat, so good, that I am now not asham'd to go to Town or be seen there." Now, as he reflected upon Father Abraham's flattering knowledge of his almanac, Poor Richard derived a moral for himself. "I resolved to be the better for the Echo of it; and though I had at first determined to buy Stuff for a new Coat, I went away resolved to wear my old One a little longer." The repetition of this sort of motif from year to year contributes to sustaining the illusion of Poor Richard's character. So that while Poor Richard changed vastly over a quarter century, he always appeared in his good second-hand coat.

Yet, ironically, Poor Richard was the only auditor of Father Abraham's address who was moved to a prudent resolve. "Thus the old Gentleman ended his Harangue. The People heard it, and approved the Doctrine, and immediately practised the contrary, just as if it had been a common Sermon; for the Vendue opened, and they began to buy extravagently, notwithstanding his Cautions, and their own Fear of Taxes." In this instance the bell who had called others to church was the only one who did mind the sermon. This disarmingly humorous device was a staple of *Poor Richard's Almanac,* from the time Franklin set out to make it a vehicle for serious moral and practical instruction. As Poor Richard said of his advice in 1756, "if you will not be angry with me for giving it, I promise you not to be offended if you do not take it." These disclaimers of success preserve Poor Richard's modesty; he presents himself as a sort of Busy-Body, a *censor morum* conveying his remonstrances broadcast in the almanac. Yet he displays a sense of proportion that neither the Busy-Body nor Mrs. Silence Dogood possessed or needed. He pretends to know that people ignore wise sayings and good advice, but like the Ancient Mariner he is compelled to repeat them to anyone who will listen. What Benjamin Franklin knew or believed was that people will listen to reason if it is presented in a palatable form. The preacher of morality must eschew smugness and self-satisfaction. Poor Richard never demanded the admiration of his readers; he allowed them to see him in a faintly ridiculous light. And, perhaps a little paradoxically, this made him the more effective as a teacher. As Franklin observed in his memoirs, "a perfect Character might be attended with the Inconvenience of being envied and hated" (*Autobiography*, p. 156). Poor Richard's readers could learn from him because they were not obliged to hate him.

In the humble chimney corners of Pennsylvania, Poor Richard's comical circumstances and his eccentric humors were well known. Readers who had grown old with him knew that he never took himself seriously. But these qualities were lost upon the strangers into whose hands fell the reprints and translations. Most of the early reprintings of the speech adhered closely to Franklin's text, describing it as a preliminary address "prefixed to the Pennsylvania Almanack, entitled Poor Richard improved: for the Year 1758. Printed at Philadelphia"; but a little later in 1771, the prestigious *Gentleman's Magazine* printed a substantially altered version, the effect of which was to reduce the personal involvement of both Father Abraham and Poor Richard himself. Thus began the gradual blurring of distinctions which was to lead finally to the easy and damaging identification of Franklin with Father Abraham and his simplistic economics. In France, Poor Richard lost even his name. In French, *richard* has the meaning *a wealthy man,* so that *Pauvre Richard* would have seemed contradictory. French translators rechristened the work *La Science du Bonhomme Richard*; and Captain John Paul Jones bestowed the name upon his famous warship.[55]

It remains to say something about the achievement and the ultimate meaning of *Poor Richard's Almanac.* It was a humble book, three shillings, sixpence for the dozen; but Benjamin Franklin raised it to the level of literature. His contribution to the style of the English proverb has been well documented by Meister, Robert Newcomb, Richard F. Amacher, and others.[56] I have chosen to concentrate on the character of Richard Saunders, drawing upon his proverbial wisdom only as a reflection of that personality. For Richard Saunders was a richly living literary character, worthy of those two other illustrious journalists, Dickens and Twain. He made demands on his creator virtually unheard of in English literature. He appeared only once a year and then only briefly. Each year's almanac had somehow to bear the stamp of Richard Saunders's personality. And, year after year, *Poor Richard* bore the stamp of that same witty, eccentric mind. Certainly this consistency in the character of Poor Richard derived from the fact that from beginning to end he reflected specific aspects of Benjamin Franklin's mind. But Poor Richard's consistency was not what Emerson would call "a foolish consistency." Rather it was the dynamic consistency of all great literary characters. Poor Richard could change constantly while remaining always the same. He could grow with his creator without ever growing into Benjamin Franklin. John F. Ross concluded that "The final Richard speaks with the same voice which produced the Autobiography," [57] and this was a trenchant observation. Perhaps it suggests how much Franklin's *Autobiography* owes to *Poor Richard's Almanac*. For the *Autobiography* was no less a literary creation than *Poor Richard*. The speaker of the memoirs was a created literary mask and the "Benjamin Franklin" who appears in that narrative was, as David Levin has said, Franklin's finest literary character. In the final chapter we shall have much to say of the control Franklin exercised in his memoirs—that is, the ways in which he limited his own character and constructed accounts of other figures around himself, to the purpose of instructing his youthful readers. Suffice to say here, that in Poor Richard, Franklin evolved a mode of conveying instruction at once pointedly and agreeably. It involved a technique that Franklin claimed to have followed in his own dealings with others. "A benevolent Man," he asserted, "should allow

a few Faults in himself, to keep his Friends in Countenance"
(*Autobiography*, p. 156). Poor Richard used his faults and
eccentricities very well, and when Franklin came to write his
didactic life story he would draw upon the same resource.
There he adopted a tone of gentle irony toward the aspira-
tions and accomplishments of his youth, while making his
"youthful Errata" a prominent feature of the narrative.
Thereby he humanized himself without undercutting the essential point of the memoirs: that he succeeded by unswerving
application to certain fundamental principles. There he could
reflect whimsically on his old-man's vanity and garrulousness;
he could lament his weaknesses in method and organization,
his failure in mathematics, his struggles with pride. He could
even make guarded references to his sexual indiscretions. And
all of these things only reinforced the effectiveness of the lesson he sought to teach.

The retirement of Poor Richard Saunders at the very pin-
nacle of his success marked the end of what I have called
Franklin's literary apprenticeship. Some of his most amusing
and most hard-hitting political journalism was written in the
interval between 1758 and the Revolution, such famous pieces
as "Rules by Which a Great Empire May be Reduced to a
Small One" and "Edict by the King of Prussia" (1773) and
a bit later "The Sale of the Hessians" (1777). These classics and scores of minor letters and hoaxes have been widely
reprinted and justly admired by scholars and common readers
alike.[58] Doubtless many journalists of Franklin's posterity
have borrowed these formulas of satire which Franklin borrowed from Swift. But the point is, of course, that these were
the works of Franklin the master journalist, the master controversialist. The Franklin who had apprenticed himself forty
years before to Joseph Addison and John Bunyan and Jonathan Swift had learned all he would ever need to know about
writing. He would acquire only one further tool for his great
work of statesmanship and diplomacy—the French language.

With the final issues of *Poor Richard's Almanac* Franklin set into place the capstone of his art, though he would have called writing a craft—having set about to learn it as a craftsman does. Now he had a narrative posture—a mask or voice—suitable for his masterpiece. On July 7, 1757, when for the last time he signed himself "as ever, Thine to serve thee. RICHARD SAUNDERS," Franklin can scarcely have foreseen the services his pen would provide his countrymen. He may have had in mind one day to write an account of his youth; he had already written several imaginary autobiographical sketches. But even Lawrence's "sharp little man" who "knew what he was about" could not have envisioned the empires of self-reliance and self-help founded on his memoirs.

It has been the purpose of this investigation to reopen a book too hastily closed. *Poor Richard's Almanac* is a milestone on the way to Franklin's *Autobiography,* but we have seen that it is also much more. We have dwelt upon Richard's wit, but we have not exhausted it. The almanac is an odd literary form, but once the strangeness is overcome, *Poor Richard* makes good reading. In the hands of a writer of Franklin's talent, the almanac is literature. More than this, *Poor Richard* must be taken into account for the insights it provides into the development of Franklin's mind. This we have begun to do. At crucial moments in Franklin's life—the beginnings of his financial rise, the death of his only legitimate son, on the eve of retirement from business—Poor Richard seems to have spoken his creator's mind. The revelations may be all the more candid for their indirection; for we read not facts, figures, and dates, but feelings and attitudes. Franklin paused three times during the run of the almanac to reflect upon Poor Richard's purpose in publishing. Each statement of purpose weighed the values of delight and instruction, and each concluded that the pamphlet should both amuse and advise its readers. Yet each time Franklin adjusted the balance. His evolving attitude toward *Poor Richard's Almanac* suggested the development of Franklin's conception of his own role in the world. Broadly speaking these were the years of Franklin's maturation, and *Poor Richard's Almanac* chronicles the process. The pattern of maturation found in the almanac fits exactly the pattern suggested by Franklin's other publications during those years. And so, the one body of evidence tends to verify the other.

Finally, however, the present work will have been worthwhile if only it opens on a new line of investigation and even controversy concerning *Poor Richard*. It was Saunders himself who wrote in 1739, "Historians relate, not so much what is done, as what they would have believed." Historians and biographers cannot but bring their own preconceptions to the documentary remains of their subjects. The preconceptions of the simple, patriotic historians who canonized Benjamin Franklin and those of the debunkers that followed, wrought most harmfully upon Poor Dick Saunders. He has been made to support the two opposing views of Benjamin Franklin without ever having been allowed to speak in his own or Franklin's defense. Historians owe him a hearing. Whatever we decide about the ultimate significance of *Poor Richard's Almanac,* whatever we take to be its essential quality, whatever we conclude of Franklin from it, we must decide on the basis of a thorough knowledge of the almanac itself. At the least, we shall agree with the almanac's earliest known tribute, that of Poor Richard's fellow philomath, Jacob Taylor, written in 1745:

> They have a Right to write who understand
> The Skill profest, the Theme they have in Hand;
> All useful Arts in true Professors shine,
> And just Applause, Poor Richard, shall be thine;
> For equal Justice must return thy Due,
> Thy Words good Sense, thy Numbers pure and true.[59]

FIVE

The Autobiography
of Benjamin Franklin

Would you persuade, speak of Interest, not of Reason.
Poor Richard, 1734

IN 1782, while serving as executor of Mrs. Joseph Galloway's estate, the prominent Quaker merchant Abel James came upon a batch of Benjamin Franklin's papers.[1] Among these was the first installment of the *Autobiography,* twenty-three folio sheets apparently written during a two-week vacation eleven years before. In August 1771, Franklin had spent a pleasant fortnight at Twyford, the country estate of Jonathan Shipley, the liberal bishop of St. Asaph and a longtime friend of Franklin's. The bishop was the father of five young daughters, and tradition holds that the celebrated American visitor entertained the family each evening by reading a daily installment of his boyhood recollections. If indeed he wrote the twenty-three sheets in about two weeks, it is a testimony to the "marvelous Facility" that Franklin developed as a practicing journalist.

Perhaps the first American to read the manuscript, Abel James was perceptive enough to recognize the potential of the work "to promote a greater Spirit of Industry and early Attention to Business, Frugality and Temperance with the

American Youth." What James possibly failed to realize when he urged Franklin to complete his biography, was that the great inspirational work was already finished. The portion of the memoirs that James found among Mrs. Galloway's papers was artistically complete, a unified whole. Nothing that Franklin could append to the 1771 installment could add to its impact or enhance its effectiveness with the youth to whom it was directed. Franklin's British publisher, Benjamin Vaughan, agreed with James that the memoirs should be finished and offered to the public. Vaughan had read only Franklin's outline; the manuscript remained with James in Pennsylvania. It was Vaughan's idea to publish the memoirs as a companion to Franklin's projected *Art of Virtue,* for the wisdom that Franklin could share with the world. But foremost in Vaughan's mind was that Benjamin Franklin was a public man whose extraordinary life story must sooner or later be written. Far better, thought Vaughan, that Franklin write his own account of his career, than to leave it to "somebody else" who might manage it so as to do great harm. Vaughan's was of course no idle concern, for Franklin had his share of enemies; and eventually even his grandson, William Temple Franklin, would be suspected of skulduggery in his dilatory preparation of Franklin's collected works.

The biography that Franklin was urged to continue was not precisely the book he had begun. In 1771 he was already a celebrated scientist and savant. But in 1782 he was for Europeans the symbol of America: the American they knew best and the emblem of the energy, ingenuity, and courage of "a rising people." Vaughan believed that Franklin's life story might hasten the reestablishment of amicable Anglo-American relations. "Let Englishmen be made not only to respect, but even to love you," he wrote. "When they think well of individuals in your native country, they will go nearer to thinking well of your country; and when your countrymen see themselves well thought of by Englishmen, they will go nearer to thinking well of England. Extend your views even further; do not stop at those who speak the English tongue . . . think of bettering the whole race of men." As even Mark Twain admitted, Franklin "did a great many notable things for his country, and made her young name to be honored in many lands as the mother of such a son." And so, when Benjamin Franklin returned to his memoirs in 1784, the undertaking was seemingly of greater moment than it had been thirteen years before. He continued to follow the topic outline he had drawn up sometime during that period of composition in 1771, but he was writing for different reasons—writing, in fact, as a different man.

The Autobiography of Benjamin Franklin must, then, be seen and treated analytically as two books, governed by two sets of themes and narrative principles. I shall call Part 1 the first book; Parts 2, 3, and 4 comprise the second. Part 1 was written entirely at Twyford in 1771. The second book was written at three sittings. Part 2 was composed at Passy in France in 1784; in length it is less than a third of Part 1. Part 3, the longest section of the memoirs, was begun in the late summer of 1788. Franklin was back home and eighty-two years of age. He had served in various important capacities in the three years since his return to America, and having left the presidency of the Supreme Executive Council of Pennsylvania (a post roughly equivalent to the governorship) and having served as a delegate to the Constitutional Convention during the hot summer of 1787, he was at last retired. The very short fourth part was written in the winter of 1789–90 during his final illness. He died April 17, 1790.[2] The narrative was far from completion. Benjamin Vaughan had wanted Franklin's own account of his long public career, so that the events leading up to the American Revolution and the diplomatic history of the war might not be left to other hands to write. Obviously Benjamin Franklin's recollections of those years would have been of incalculable value. But Franklin lived in the present and for the future; even his eighty-four years did not leave him enough time for the past. The narrative takes his life only up to about 1758, with passing reference to events in 1759 and 1760.

Of the two books of Franklin's memoirs, the first is the more important. When we speak of Franklin's *Autobiography*, we generally refer to Part 1; it is the essential *Autobiography*. It provides a brief history of the Franklin family and an account of Franklin's boyhood and youth up to about the age of twenty-four. Most significantly, it narrates his rise from obscurity and poverty to a state of relative prosperity as a young tradesman with a going business, a frugal wife, and a circle of philosophical young friends. Franklin's fortune continued to grow after 1730; he was not a wealthy man at twenty-four. But he had found the way to wealth, and as he knew, *"after getting the first hundred Pound, it is more easy to get the second:* Money itself being of a prolific Nature" (*Autobiography*, p. 181). It is in this sense that Part 1 is complete and independent of the other three installments. It lays down the principles and dramatizes the process of achieving affluence in America. It is the sacred scripture of the American self-help tradition; it defines the American spirit. It is the text for the celebration and the condemnation of the national character. Part 1 is the narrative companion to Father Abraham's homily on industry and frugality; it is there that careless or hostile critics find their warrant for a charge of tireless commercialism and shallow materialism in Franklin's character. The remainder of the *Autobiography* scarcely convicts Benjamin Franklin on those charges. For he explains that he regarded the prudential values and their material rewards as the means ultimately of "securing Virtue, it being more difficult for a Man in Want to act always honestly." And he relates the story of his retirement at the age of forty-two with "a sufficient tho' moderate Fortune" (*Autobiography*, p. 196).

Part 1, or Book 1, dominates the reader's memory because it is unified and dramatic. I have fallen victim to its dominance more than once in the present study. For though the entire work has real literary merit, Part 1 is a rhetorical construct of subtle strength. That is to say, Franklin chose and arranged the incidents of his early life, placed emphasis on certain persons and neglected others, and indeed portrayed himself so as to inculcate a narrowly specific moral lesson. It is perhaps for this reason that questions respecting Franklin's candor are most frequently raised about Part 1. He does not seem to be telling the whole story. The reader may find himself wanting to know what it is Franklin is holding back, trying to hide. But we have come to realize that the question should be framed in the opposite way. Of a masterpiece of rhetoric it is appropriate to ask, why is certain information included? and why is it presented in this particular way? Questions of candor and veracity arise less frequently about the second book of Franklin's memoirs. His interpretation of events is sometimes open to question, but these later sections are more informal, less compact, seeming therefore to be more ingenuous. But in fact, the reader is simply dealing with two books representing different orders of structural complexity. Both are topical and roughly chronological in their arrangement; Book 1 has, in addition, the calculated rhetorical structure.

In this discussion I shall reverse the order of the two books, presuming to adopt a method recommended by Franklin himself in the essay, "On Literary Style." If the writer would inform, Franklin advises, "he must advance regularly from Things known to things unknown, distinctly without Confusion, and the lower he begins the better." The first book of Franklin's *Autobiography* is the more complex, as well as the more important of the two. Accordingly we shall examine it last.

2

Had Benjamin Franklin ignored the appeals of James and Vaughan and never returned to the writing of his memoirs, American letters would have been poorer for it. Part 1 carries almost all of the work's power and meaning, but the last three parts, Book 2, contain much of its charm. Some of Franklin's most incisive characterizations are to be found here: notably those of evangelist George Whitefield, Governor Robert Hunter Morris, and General Edward Braddock. Franklin's eyewitness account of the Great Awakening, the reminiscence of a sympathetic skeptic, is both accurate and amusing. Equally interesting is his analysis of the Pennsylvania Quakers in the mid-eighteenth century—a sect in turmoil and transition. In his discussion of his electrical experiments, Franklin reveals an instinctive grasp of the scientific method, a system but dimly understood by many of the influential philosophers of his age. Two little parables are included in the second book of the *Autobiography*. Franklin occasionally employed parables in his journalistic writings (one concludes the "Apology for Printers"), and the pair he inserted in his memoirs are among his finest.

Benjamin Vaughan, who had just published an edition of Franklin's scientific writings, had in mind to issue the *Autobiography* and *The Art of Virtue* as companion volumes. By 1788, when Franklin sat down for the third time to work on his memoirs, it was clear that he would never live to write his book on moral philosophy: "For it being connected in my Mind with a *great and extensive Project* that required the whole Man to execute, and which an unforeseen Succession of Employs prevented my attending to, it has hitherto remain'd unfinish'd" (*Autobiography*, p. 158). Accordingly he treated the subject repeatedly and at length in the course of his writing the last three parts. His notion of human morality was that while man was sadly imperfectible on earth, he could be improved by his own constant attention and sincere efforts. It was with this in mind that he had projected a book on the *Art* of virtue in the first place, "because it would have shown the *Means* and *Manner* of obtaining Virtue, which would have distinguish'd it from the mere Exhortation to be good." Unable to raise his planned system of practical morality, Franklin incorporated some of its principles into the narration of his own projects. Having presented in detail his ideas on the lighting and cleaning of streets, he offers an explanation: "Some may think these trifling Matters not worth minding or relating. But when they consider, that tho' Dust blown into the Eyes of a single Person or into a single Shop on a windy Day, is but of small Importance, yet the great Number of the Instances in a populous City, and its frequent Repetitions give it Weight and Consequence; perhaps they will not censure very severely those who bestow some of Attention to Affairs of this seemingly low Nature. Human Felicity is produc'd not so much by great Pieces of good Fortune that seldom happen, as by little Advantages that occur every Day" (*Autobiography*, p. 207). Thus, the second book of Franklin's *Autobiography* is a fabric woven of two threads: a narrative of Franklin's public career, and a treatise on the art of virtue.

Most of the relatively brief installment written at Passy in 1784 is given over to an account of Franklin's "bold and arduous Project of arriving at moral Perfection." Part 2 is a long footnote to Part 1. It does not advance the narrative in time but presents episodes coincident with those described in Part 1. But this is material thematically inappropriate to the narrative of Franklin's rise to affluence. To have incorporated an account of his youthful moral experiment into Part 1 would have blunted the impact of both stories by destroying the thematic unity of the narrative. Yet, because it was the foundation for Franklin's later speculations in ethics, the bold and arduous Project warranted special attention in the memoirs.

The implications of Franklin's experiment in moral self-improvement are far-reaching, and this passage in the *Autobiography* presents a delicate problem of tone—that is, of gauging accurately the writer's attitude toward his material. If it can be shown that Franklin is being ironic in his description of this Project—even very gently ironic—then he may be exonerated of total moral obtuseness.

The passage is as famous as it is troublesome.

> It was about this time that I conceiv'd the bold and arduous Project of arriving at moral Perfection. I wish'd to live without committing any Fault at any time; I would conquer all that either Natural Inclination, Custom, or Company might lead me into. As I knew, or thought I knew, what was right and wrong, I did not see why I might not *always* do the one and avoid the other. But I soon found I had undertaken a Task of more Difficulty than I had imagined. While my *Attention was taken up* in guarding against one Fault, I was often surpriz'd by another. Habit took the Advantage of Inattention. Inclination was sometimes too strong for Reason. I concluded at length, that the mere speculative Conviction that it was our Interest to be compleatly virtuous, was not sufficient to prevent our Slipping, and that the contrary Habits must be broken and good ones acquired and established, before we can have any Dependance on a steady uniform Rectitude of Conduct. For this purpose I therefore contriv'd the following Method. (*Autobiography,* p. 148)

Franklin's method was a table of thirteen virtues: Temperance, Silence, Order, Resolution, Frugality, Industry, Sincerity, Justice, Moderation, Cleanliness, Tranquility, Chastity, and Humility. Each virtue on the list was accompanied by an appropriate precept. Having failed in his attempt to practice all the virtues at once, Franklin determined to concentrate on them one at a time and to keep a ledger of his progress.

> I made a little Book in which I allotted a Page for each of the Virtues. I rul'd each Page with red Ink, so as to have seven Columns, one for each Day of the Week, marking each Column with a Letter

for the Day. I cross'd these Columns with thirteen red Lines, marking the Beginning of each Line with the first Letter of one of the Virtues, on which Line and in its proper Column I might mark by a little black Spot every Fault I found upon Examination to have been committed respecting that Virtue upon that Day.

I determined to give a Week's strict Attention to each of the Virtues successively. Thus is the first Week my great Guard was to avoid every the least Offence against Temperance, leaving the other Virtues to their ordinary Chance, only marking every Evening the Faults of the Day.

Concentrating on one virtue each week, Franklin could complete the list in thirteen weeks and so run through four courses in one year. The method was subject to further revisions. Franklin found it necessary to transfer his journal of transgressions to a book of ivory pages, for "by scraping out the Marks on the Paper of old Faults to make room for new Ones in a new Course [my little Book], became full of Holes." Franklin says that as his activities and interests multiplied he pursued his project with declining rigor: "After a while I went thro' one Course only in a Year, and afterwards only one in several Years, till at length I omitted them entirely." But he always carried his little ivory book with him.

Of his thirteen virtues, Order was the most vexing. Finding it impossible to become perfectly methodical, he says that he finally made up his mind to be content "with a faulty Character in that Respect." Here Franklin inserted one of the two parables included in the *Autobiography*.

Like the Man who in buying an Ax of a Smith my neighbour, desired to have the whole of its Surface as bright as the Edge; the Smith consented to grind it bright for him if he would turn the Wheel. He turn'd while the Smith press'd the broad Face of the Ax hard and heavily on the Stone, which made the Turning of it very fatiguing. The Man came every now and then from the Wheel to see how the Work went on; and at length would take his Ax as it was without farther Grinding. No, says the Smith, Turn on, turn on; we shall have it bright by and by; as yet 'tis only speckled. Yes, says the Man; but—*I think I like a speckled Ax best.* And I believe this may have been the Case with many who having for want of some such Means as I employ'd found the Difficulty of obtaining good, and breaking bad Habits, in other Points of Vice and Virtue, have given up the Struggle, and concluded that *a speckled Ax was best.* For something that pretended to be Reason was every now and then suggesting to me, that such extream Nicety as I exacted of my self might be a kind of Foppery in Morals, which if it were known would make me ridiculous; that a perfect Character might be attended with the Inconvenience of being envied and hated; and that a benevolent Man should allow a few Faults in himself, to keep his Friends in Countenance. (*Autobiography,* pp. 155–56)

D. H. Lawrence found the passage on Franklin's bold and arduous Project the single most offensive episode in the *Autobiography*: "The Perfectibility of Man! Ah heaven, what a dreary theme!" To Lawrence, Franklin's moral experiment bespoke the shallowness of his understanding of human nature. "The soul of man," explained Lawrence, "is a dark forest." The soul was the whole of man, a turbulent multiplicity, symbolized by the glowing red eyes of a wolf in the darkness. "Oh, but Benjamin fenced a little tract that he called the soul of man, and proceeded to get it into cultivation. . . . This is Benjamin's barbed wire fence. He made himself a list of virtues, which he trotted inside like a grey nag in a paddock." Lawrence's conception of the nature of man was antipodal to Franklin's. Both of them believed that morality had its foundation in human nature, but because they understood the nature of man so differently, their differences on the issue of ethics can never be resolved by outside arbitration. However, D. H. Lawrence committed an egregious fault in willfully misreading the text. He condemned Benjamin Franklin as a moral simpleton, but his free-swinging rhetoric swept aside the tonal subtleties of Franklin's prose. Robert F. Sayre, a cooler head, also ran into difficulty with the passage on the bold and arduous Project, although he was not angry about it. Sayre ob-

served correctly that the narrative voice of the Passy installment is typical of the little essays and bagatelles Franklin
composed for the amusement of his brilliant and accomplished
French admirers. But Sayre failed to find in the *Autobiography* the tone of self-parody which pervades all of those pieces:
"The Ephemera," "The Whistle," "The Dialogue between
Franklin and the Gout," and the celebrated letter to Mme.
Helvetius. "Franklin the writer," Sayre asserts, "never breaks
character in his story of this project or lifts his mask to expose
the man underneath."

> Thus Franklin collapses his philosopher's hubris in his "Quaker"
> simplicity. The two tendencies are beautifully reconciled, the frankly
> *naif* young Franklin commencing the project with his scheme to
> become perfect, the famous elder Franklin carrying the idea along as
> a worthy endeavor that all men should be interested in, and the
> sophisticated, consciously *naif* "Philosophical Quaker" finishing it
> in a discourse on pride and humility. The experience of fifty years
> before is thereby examined and recast in the mold of the present.
> The character of the young man is brought into line with the pose
> of the older man.[3]

Sayre is really saying that Franklin saw his bold and arduous
project differently from the perspective of a half century. Just
as he came to see that he had as a child paid too much for a
whistle, he saw as an older and very much wiser man that
his project of self-perfection was the chimera of ambitious inexperience. The point Sayre makes about the sophisticated
naïveté of the "Philosophical Quaker" eludes me. But it is
Franklin's retrospection which colors the passage and it was
Franklin's typical voice in his French compositions which supplied the tone of the episode.

David Levin first called attention to "the humorous self-
criticism with which Franklin introduces the account."[4] Levin
noted the irony in Franklin's descriptive phrase "the bold and
arduous Project." Franklin couches his entire account in comic
terms. Elevated metaphors of conquest, struggle, and guarding

recur. He describes the surprise onslaught of one fault "while my *Attention was taken up* in guarding against" another. It is true that he describes the project in such detail because he believes it to have been ultimately worthwhile, but some of the details—notably that of transferring his ledger to the ivory pages which could be washed clean of his many faults—seem to have been included for their humor more than their utility. The paper pages perforated with erasures are a comic symbol of the young Franklin's naïve boldness. The parable of the speckled ax is obviously humorous as is the rationalization Franklin took from it. It was perhaps not reason, only "something that pretended to be Reason" which warned Franklin against "Foppery in Morals." "So convenient a thing it is to be a *reasonable Creature,*" Franklin reminds us elsewhere. Franklin also tells the embarrassing story of how he happened to add Humility to the list of his virtues. "My List of Virtues contain'd at first but twelve: But a Quaker Friend having kindly inform'd me that I was generally thought proud; that my Pride show'd itself frequently in Conversation; that I was not content with being in the right when discussing any Point, but was overbearing and rather insolent; of which he convinc'd me by mentioning several Instances; I determined endeavouring to cure myself if I could of this Vice or Folly among the rest, and I added *Humility* to my List, giving an extensive Meaning to the Word." Franklin's "extensive Meaning" ("Imitate Jesus and Socrates") has incensed some of his critics, as has his admission that "I cannot boast of much Success in acquiring the *Reality* of this Virtue; but I had a good deal with regard to the *Appearance* of it." Lawrence cried, "The amusing part is the sort of humility it displays. 'Imitate Jesus and Socrates,' and mind you don't outshine either of these two. One can just imagine Socrates and Alcibiades roaring in their cups over Philadelphian Benjamin, and Jesus looking at him a little puzzled, and murmuring: 'Aren't you wise in your own conceit, Ben?'" But Franklin need not have

shared with posterity his discomfiture at the "several Instances" of his pride mentioned by the kindly Quaker. And his
concluding paragraph on the subject of pride and humility—
couched in the language of "humorous self-criticism"—is per-
spicacious and candid, if deficient in idealism. "In reality,"
Franklin writes, "there is perhaps no one of our natural Pas-
sions so hard to subdue as *Pride*. Disguise it, struggle with it,
beat it down, stifle it, mortify it as much as one pleases, it is
still alive, and will every now and then peep out and show
itself. You will see it perhaps often in this History. For even
if I could conceive that I had compleatly overcome it, I should
probably be proud of my Humility." John William Ward has
pointed out that in this passage "Franklin speaks like that
other and contrasting son of the Puritans, Jonathan Edwards,
on the nature of true virtue. Man, if he could achieve virtue,
would inevitably be proud of the achievement and so, at the
moment of success, fall back into sin." [5] Edwards and Franklin
differed only in tone, says Ward, "The insight is the same but
Franklin's skeptical and untroubled self-acceptance is far removed from Edwards' troubled and searching self-doubt."
Hostile readers prefer to label this self-acceptance smugness,
loathing on humanistic terms, perhaps, what Jonathan Edwards despised and feared as an orthodox Calvinist in the
hands of an angry God.

It may be, as David Levin has written, that we cannot
finally absolve Franklin "of all responsibility for the wide-
spread misunderstanding of his work." Levin asserts that
Franklin "invites difficulty by deliberately appearing to be more
simple than he is, by choosing the role of the inquisitive, experimental freeman. By daring to reduce metaphysical questions to the terms of practical experience, he sometimes seems
to dismiss them entirely, and he draws our attention away from
the books he has read." [6] If this is so, it means that Franklin's
long-practiced irony and his habit of masquerade had become
at last overrefined. His essay has suffered a similar fate to that

of Swift's "Modest Proposal" or Defoe's "Shortest Way with Dissenters": the irony missed, the humor lost, the reader put out of countenance. When he wrote of Alice Addertongue's account book of scandal, the satire was broad and funny. When he came to write of his own exercise in a similar mode, he adopted a voice and selected details so as to produce a delicate tone of gentle, nostalgic irony. The installment written at Passy is the most polished and graceful of the *Autobiography*'s four parts; the texture of the language is the finest here. D. H. Lawrence found Benjamin Franklin, the man he hated, most precisely delineated in this section, and I think his instincts were correct. Readers disposed to admire Franklin the man may very well encounter the essential Franklin in these pages. He tried to present himself here as he had Andrew Hamilton in "A Half-Hour's Conversation with a Friend"—as the philosophical gentleman at his leisure and in his best light. Franklin could not change the opinions of Hamilton's political enemies, nor can he win over readers of the *Autobiography* who will find his ethical position fundamentally mechanistic and inhuman (as is the case with Lawrence). But as David Levin has demonstrated, the reader is deluded who finds simplicity in Franklin's language or in his grasp of human nature.

The Passy installment of the memoirs presents an episode contemporaneous with the events of Part 1, the first book of Franklin's *Autobiography*. The bold and arduous Project formed Franklin's moral and spiritual life while his dedication to industry and frugality was establishing his modest fortune. The introduction of his art of virtue in the Passy section sounds the first of two major themes for the second book. The last two installments, both written in America, are largely a chronological narrative of Franklin's projects and promotions, beginning about 1733. Few of these episodes (or in one instance a group of episodes) are presented, however, without an accompanying moral application. Both Sayre and Levin imply that Franklin has managed, in this way, to present himself as the experimentalist and discoverer, inventing his moral calculus as he made his way through life. But it should be clear that Franklin was not trying to inculcate the experimental method of living in his readers, but rather to share with them the results of his experiments. As a scientist he knew that once a principle was discovered and verified it might be used but it need never be discovered again. The episodes of the second book, then, are particular instances illustrative of general principles. Most are short, scarcely longer than anecdotes; this was the form most congenial to Benjamin Franklin, the writer shaped by years of practical journalism. In form a typical episode resembles Franklin's letter to the *Gazette* in which the old man complained of slippery sidewalks. An example of this form is Franklin's account of his "first Promotion," to Clerk of the Pennsylvania Assembly in 1736.

> The Choice was made that Year without Opposition; but the Year following when I was again propos'd (the Choice, like that of the Members being annual) a new Member made a long Speech against me, in order to favour some other Candidate. I was however chosen; which was the more agreable to me, as besides the Pay for immediate Service as Clerk, the Place gave me a better Opportunity of keeping up an Interest among the Members, which secur'd to me the Business of Printing the Votes, Laws, Paper Money, and other occasional Jobbs for the Public, that on the whole were very profitable. I therefore did not like the Opposition of this new Member, who was a Gentleman of Fortune, and Education, with Talents that were likely to give him in time great Influence in the House, which indeed afterwards happened. I did not however aim at gaining his Favour by paying any servile Respect to him, but after some time took this other Method. Having heard that he had in his Library a certain very scarce and curious Book, I wrote a Note to him expressing my Desire of perusing that Book, and requesting he would do me the Favour of lending it to me for a few Days. He sent it immediately; and I return'd it in about a Week, with another Note expressing strongly my Sense of the Favour. When we next met in the House he spoke to me, (which

he had never done before) and with great Civility. And he ever afterwards manifested a Readiness to serve me on all Occasions, so that we became great Friends, and our Friendship continu'd to his Death. This is another Instance of the Truth of an old Maxim I had learnt, which says, *He that has once done you a Kindness will be more ready to do you another, than he whom you yourself have obliged.* And it shows how much more profitable it is prudently to remove, than to resent, return and continue inimical Proceedings. (*Autobiography,* pp. 171–72).

Franklin's account of the incident is particularly interesting. It leaves no sense that the episode had any real biographical or historical significance, yet it may have been a crucial moment in Franklin's political career. For the "new Member" was probably Isaac Norris, a wealthy Quaker merchant and a non-pacifist. Norris would become Franklin's close associate in the antiproprietary party, leader of that wing in the Assembly and Speaker of the House for fourteen years. Their alliance took them to Carlisle together for treaty negotiations with the Indians and to the Albany Congress of 1754. Had "inimical Proceedings" been continued between Norris and Franklin, the history of provincial Pennsylvania might have taken a decidedly different course. But Franklin's memoirs give not the slightest hint of this. In the context of the *Autobiography,* the incident is no more than an instance of the truth of an old maxim. An event of genuine historical importance is presented in a manner that conceals its importance—or ignores it—and instead the story is told for its moral and social application. This is an indication of the relative weight Franklin assigned to history and moral didacticism. The facts of his own life and the history of his times were expendable in a very old man's effort to leave the world even a sketchy outline of his art of virtue. As in so many of Franklin's moral fables the principle is driven home with a maxim.

Moving chronologically, Franklin next took up his promotion to the postmastership in 1737. I have quoted parts of this

passage in connection with the *General Magazine* controversy
and the charges and countercharges of malfeasance in the post
office. But again Franklin ignored all of that and offered Andrew Bradford's case as an admonition to young readers:
"Thus he [Bradford] suffer'd greatly from his Neglect in due
Accounting; and I mention it as a Lesson to those young Men
who may be employ'd in managing Affairs for others that they
should always render Accounts and make Remittances with
Great Clearness and Punctuality. The Character of observing
such a Conduct is the most powerful of all Recommendations
to new Employments and Increase of Business" (*Autobiography*, pp. 172–73).

Here as elsewhere Franklin presented his moral in terms of
policy and profit—language that promotes the gnashing of his
critics' teeth. Yet perhaps he employed that language rhetori-
cally, mindful of Poor Richard's maxim that an appeal to interest is more persuasive than an appeal to reason. Good
rhetoric, of course, only compounds the evil of bad morality;
and in Franklin's writings the profit-and-loss rhetoric becomes
perhaps inextricably bound up with the moral system. Thus,
as David Levin believes, Franklin's rhetorical strategy may
have played him false, concealing his finer moral intelligence.
However finely balanced the mechanism of Franklin's moral
sense, he did have a disconcerting habit of making his ends the
justification for his means—at least in his narration of the
events. As a rhetorician he was a manipulator of others' opinions. He was not merely the printer who transmitted a range
of opinions to his customers. And Benjamin Franklin was an
admirer of other successful manipulators.

It was this sort of professional admiration, evidently, that
first drew Franklin to the evangelist George Whitefield: "The
Multitudes of all Sects and Denominations that attended his
Sermons were enormous, and it was a matter of Speculation to
me who was one of the Number, to observe the extraordinary
Influence of his Oratory on his Hearers, and how much they

admir'd and respected him, notwithstanding his common Abuse of them, by assuring them they were naturally *half Beasts and half Devils*" (*Autobiography,* p. 175). Nevertheless, White- field's religion was vital and electrifying. Franklin liked his preaching as he had liked that of Samuel Hemphill, for it reawakened interest in religion and promoted useful civic proj- ects, such as the erecting of meetinghouses and the founding of orphanages. Franklin juxtaposed the vitality of the Great Awakening with the lethargy of Pennsylvania's Quaker politi- cal and religious establishment.

We have examined the early stages of the struggle by Frank- lin and his forces to wrest control of the province from the pacifist wing of the Quaker party. Recalling those years in his memoirs, Franklin set the Quakers down as a sect hopelessly entangled in a web of obsolete and inessential dogma. This, of course, was his complaint about the Presbyterians as well, and seemingly of all atrophied religious institutions. He found the Dunkers an exception to this rule, however, and wrote an account of his conversation with Michael Welfare, a founder of the sect. The Dunkers, Franklin was told, had declined to publish "the Articles of their Belief and the Rules of their Discipline," for fear of finding them too confining and impos- sible to amend at some later time. Franklin saw fit to cap this anecdote with his second parable: "This Modesty in a Sect is perhaps a singular Instance in the History of Mankind, every other Sect supposing itself in Possession of all Truth, and that those who differ are so far in the Wrong: Like a Man travelling in foggy Weather: Those at some Distance before him on the Road he sees wrapt up in the Fog, as well as those behind him, and also the People in the Fields on each side; but near him all appears clear. Tho' in truth he is as much in the Fog as any of them" (*Autobiography,* p. 191). Franklin bracketed his discussion of the Quakers with the story of George Whitefield and the parable of a man in the fog, giving a sense of thematic unity to a series of episodes. This is pos-

sibly the only occasion in the second book in which a sequence
of anecdotes is organized into a cycle whose meaning is clari-
fied by a moral tag appended to it. The larger structure imi-
tates the organization of the smaller units, such as those on
Isaac Norris's curious book and Andrew Bradford's dismissal
from the post office. The individual incidents in the Quaker
sequence are bare of their moral application, but the parable
of the man in a fog serves as the moral for the complete cycle.

As John F. Ross observed, Franklin's narrative voice
throughout the *Autobiography* sounds much like that of the
later Poor Richard. But in writing his memoirs Franklin found
occasions to imitate many other voices. He allowed many of
his dramatis personae to speak for themselves. And he explained the use he made of dialogue and from whom he learned
it. On his first trip to Philadelphia, Franklin helped to rescue
a drunken Dutchman who fell out of the boat in a storm.
Among the Dutchman's effects was a book which he asked
Franklin to dry for him. "It prov'd to be my old favourite
Author Bunyan's Pilgrim's Progress in Dutch, finely printed
on good Paper with Copper Cuts, a Dress better than I had
ever seen it wear in its own Language." Franklin then stops to
reflect upon Bunyan's contribution to English literature. "Honest John," he writes, "was the first that I know of who mix'd
Narration and Dialogue, a Method of Writing very engaging
to the Reader, who in the most interesting Parts finds himself
as it were brought into the Company, and present at the Discourse" (*Autobiography*, p. 72). Not infrequently Franklin
had used snippets of engaging dialogue in his journalistic pieces
to bring the reader into the company. The shopkeeper Patience
quoted a scolding mother, Anthony Afterwit echoed the
phraseology of his extravagant bride, and Celia Single repro-
duced an angry quarrel between a husband and wife. Franklin's
theory and practice of writing dialogue demanded a high order
of verisimilitude. The reader feels present at the discourse
only if the writer creates an illusion of reality, only if he suc-

cessfully reproduces the language and the tone of voice of the supposed speaker. Historically Franklin was an early prac- titioner of realistic dialogue in narrative prose, but his ear was good and though he used the device sparingly he had a keen sense of "the most interesting Parts" of a narrative, where speech could be employed to the greatest advantage.

He used dialects and other varieties of nonstandard speech to characterize the speaker. An early and possibly unfortunate example was "Teague's Advertisement" during the magazine controversy. In the *Autobiography* he tells of finding an old woman sweeping one morning before his London house. "She appeared very pale and feeble as just come out of a Fit of Sickness. I ask'd who employ'd her to sweep there. She said, 'Nobody; but I am very poor and in Distress, and I sweeps before Gentlefolkeses Doors, and hopes they will give me something'" (*Autobiography,* p. 205). There is poignance but no trace of humor in Franklin's imitation of the poor old woman's speech; she lives for the reader in all her distress and determination. Franklin liked to mimic the Quaker speech with its archaic personal pronouns. He managed to capture the gentleness of the Friends, and it is apparent that he admired their kindly spirit even though he disapproved of their politics. One of his Whitefield anecdotes depends for its humor on a punch line delivered in the Quaker manner. Franklin disagreed with Whitefield on the site for the evangelist's proposed or- phanage. Whitefield wanted to build it in Georgia where the orphans were, but Franklin thought it a better plan to locate the orphanage in Pennsylvania where there were carpenters and masons to build it. He reasoned, a little callously perhaps, that orphans were more readily transported than workmen and materials. Franklin went to hear Whitefield speak on the sub- ject, resolving to contribute nothing. But when the minister was finished preaching Franklin gave every penny he had with him. Nor was he the only skeptic so moved. "At this Sermon there was also one of our Club, who being of my Sentiments respecting the Building in Georgia, and suspecting a Collection might be intended, had by Precaution emptied his Pockets before he came from home; towards the Conclusion of the Discourse however, he felt a strong Desire to give, and apply'd to a Neighbour who stood near him to borrow some Money for the Purpose. The Application was unfortunately to perhaps the only Man in the Company who had the firmness not to be affected by the Preacher. His Answer was, *At any other time, Friend Hopkinson, I would lend to thee freely; but not now; for thee seems to be out of thy right Senses*" (*Autobiography*, pp. 177–78). The story would not be funny without the dialogue, and the impact of the dialogue depends on the surprise disclosure that the speaker is a Quaker.

Franklin's characterization of the ill-fated General Edward Braddock is based almost entirely upon Braddock's own words. This was a technique Franklin had used deftly since the time of Mrs. Dogood, and it was especially well adapted to presenting cautionary characters, who condemned themselves out of their own mouths. Such a figure is Franklin's Braddock, a military man modeled not after Richard Steele's sympathetic Captain Sentry, but cast in the tradition of the *Miles Gloriosus*, the boasting soldier who first appeared in Roman comedy. The story of Braddock and his campaign is a tragicomic fable about vainglory and a chapter in one of America's favorite myths: the legend of the brilliant ranks of disciplined British lobsterbacks defeated by the embattled farmers at Concord Bridge or General Andrew Jackson's sharpshooters at New Orleans. Franklin found General Braddock nonchalant and airily confident about his wilderness campaign against the French and Indians. " 'After taking Fort DuQuesne, says he, I am to proceed to Niagara; and having taken that, to Frontenac, if the Season will allow time; and I suppose it will; for Duquesne can hardly detain me above three or four Days; and then I can see nothing that can obstruct my March to Niagara' " (*Autobiography*, p. 223). Franklin was fearful that Braddock's strung-out line of march would render him vulnerable to ambush, and he told the general so. "He smil'd at my Ignorance, and reply'd, 'These Savages may indeed be a formidable Enemy to your raw American Militia; but upon the King's regular and disciplin'd Troops, Sir, it is impossible they should make any Impression.' I was conscious," Franklin concludes sardonically, "of an Impropriety in my Disputing with a military Man in Matters of his Profession, and said no more." When disaster struck Braddock it was not precisely as Franklin had feared. Braddock's advance guard blundered into an inferior force of French and Indians, but the latter quickly took the initiative and decimated Braddock's army, while sustaining only very light casualties. Two-thirds of the British force were killed or wounded; Franklin says that of eighty-six officers, sixty-three were casualties. Edward Braddock himself was mortally wounded. In contrast to his cocksure speeches before the campaign were the general's last words, as Franklin reported them: "Captain Orme, who was one of the General's Aid de Camps, and being grievously wounded was brought off with him, and continu'd with him to his Death, which happen'd in a few Days, told me, that he was totally silent, all the first Day, and at Night only said, *Who'd have thought it?* that he was silent again the following Days, only saying at last, *We shall better know how to deal with them another time;* and dy'd a few Minutes after." Reflecting upon "this whole Transaction," Franklin concluded that it "gave us Americans the first Suspicion that our exalted Ideas of the Prowess of British Regulars had not been well founded" (*Autobiography*, p. 226).

Franklin employed dialogue more than forty times in the *Autobiography*, the greatest number of instances being in Part 3, which contains the longest sections of straight narrative. Part 1, almost equal to Part 3 in length, contains only about half as many occurrences of dialogue. Most of the characters who speak in the *Autobiography* have only a sentence or two to say. As the creator of so many journalistic masks, however, Franklin was accustomed to establishing a character economically, in the first phrases of his letter to the gazetteer. The whine of Anthony Afterwit, the scolding of Bridget Saunders, the pluck of Polly Baker are immediately audible to the reader. The voices of the *Autobiography* carry the same conviction. Some of them were newly invented for Franklin's memoirs, but others—the Quaker voices, for example—had been in his journalistic repertoire for sixty years.

3

The second book of Franklin's *Autobiography* is a collection of splendid episodes and observations. Robert F. Sayre suggests the metaphor of pearls on a string, and no other description seems to serve as well. There is no single, paraphrasable moral lesson in this book, as there is in Part 1. Rather there are a multitude of moral observations and wise sayings. Franklin inveighs against careless accounting, the vanity of military men, love of disputation, rigidity in religious doctrines. There are of course literary choices made by the author in this book. Curious emphases are placed on certain anecdotes; the stories are arranged occasionally in such a way as to incline the reader in one direction or another. There is the process of winnowing out episodes considered to be of minor importance: the *General Magazine,* the Hamilton controversy, the births of Franklin's three children. We would like to know more about those children. William, the eldest, was illegitimate; neither his mother's name nor the date of his birth is known, though the first part of the *Autobiography* is cast in the form of a long letter to him. Franklin's daughter Sarah is never mentioned in the memoirs. His second son, Francis Folger, figures only briefly; Franklin recalls his death, and as he did in the *Gazette,* he recommends inoculation of children against the smallpox. We must look to *Poor Richard's Almanac* for a sense of the full impact of Frankie's death upon his father.

Franklin made definite literary choices in writing the last three parts of the *Autobiography*, but nothing in Book 2 resembles the elaborate and premeditated selection and ordering of events in the first installment. A number of critics in recent years have offered accounts of the structure of Part 1. Robert F. Sayre remarks that "Franklin's life was a plastic and unformed substance that could be pushed and prodded into whatever mold he chose to put it," [7] but to Sayre the *Autobiography* seems to be without form; it is "as shapeless as he was protean." David Levin and John William Ward believe that in a sense Franklin's writing distorts the true character of the man. Levin says that Franklin's "decision to portray himself as an inquisitive empiricist" and a variety of other stylistic matters "combine to make him seem philosophically more naïve, and practically more materialistic, than he is." And Ward cites "Franklin's great capacity to respond to the situation in which he found himself and to play the expected role." [8] In his illuminating essay, "An American Pilgrim's Progress," Charles Sanford attempts to show that Franklin borrowed his dramatic structure, as well as his notions about dialogue, from John Bunyan. Sanford traces the form of Franklin's memoirs to a pre-Columbian "rhetoric of spirit" which "functioned to give the otherwise sordid pursuit of material riches moral and spiritual sanction." Sanford believes that Franklin translated the spiritual allegory of a journey to the Celestial City into secular, commercial terms. "As a report on Franklin's spiritual progress in the new heaven on earth, the *Autobiography* in its basic dramatic form parallels Bunyan's great allegory. Franklin merely substituted . . . the secular story with a happy ending for a Christian story with a happy ending." [9]

These four scholars, Levin, Ward, Sanford, and Sayre, have done well to emphasize the essentially *literary* nature of Franklin's *Autobiography*. They have demonstrated that the book is an artifact, the product of a conscious shaping intellect. And they have shown that the Benjamin Franklin presented in the story is a genuine literary character. But none of these scholars has, I think, offered a satisfactory explanation of the *Autobiography*'s success as rhetoric. No one has fully explained why, as Abel James observed, "It almost insensibly leads the Youth into the Resolution of endeavouring to become as good and as eminent as the Journalist." Charles Sanford was on the right track when he pointed to a structural solution for the problem, but in calling the *Autobiography* a secularized *Pilgrim's Progress* he overly simplified Franklin's secularizing process. If the *Autobiography* is Bunyan secularized, it is Bunyan secularized beyond recognition. For in fact Franklin's dramatic problems were very different from "Honest John's." To the Christian allegorist, like Bunyan, "The Way to Wealth" was traditionally the road to Vanity Fair. However much the Protestant ethic operated in the lives of Protestant merchants and tradesmen, allegorists and autobiographers— including the American contemporaries of Franklin, John Woolman and Jonathan Edwards—eschewed the worldly life in their narratives. Bunyan might employ the journey, the landscape, the city metaphorically, but his real subject was the soul's solitary struggle with God and its own inclinations. Franklin describes a progress that is not solitary, nor really spiritual, but rather one which is social. The life Franklin describes was one of complex interrelationships, where a man's success depended heavily upon the actions and attitudes of other men: the confidence and custom of one's creditors and neighbors; the industry, frugality, and prudence of one's competitors. To the spiritual autobiographer none of this mattered. Bunyan's Christian might be the butt of his unknowing friends' jeers and taunts, but it was his business to trudge on his way. For nothing others could say or do could have the least effect on the matter of his personal salvation. Accordingly the spiritual autobiographer's relentless concentration was on self, and the critics of Franklin's *Autobiography* have placed their focus on his presentation of himself.

But as drama, or rhetoric, Franklin's first book does not work that way. He proclaims a didactic intention in the early paragraphs of this supposed letter to his son, William. He begins by observing that people like to have "any little Anecdotes" of their ancestors, and "imagining it may be equally agreeable to you to know the Circumstances of *my* Life . . . I sit down to write them for you" (*Autobiography*, p. 43). But he immediately adds: "To which I have besides some other Inducements. Having emerg'd from the Poverty and Obscurity in which I was born and bred, to a State of Affluence and some Degree of Reputation in the World, and having gone so far thro' Life with a considerable Share of Felicity, the conducing Means I made use of, which, with the Blessing of God, so well succeeded, my Posterity may like to know, as they may find some of them suitable to their own Situations, and therefore fit to be imitated." As autobiographer, then, Franklin confronted a problem he had often faced as a journalist: the problem of finding the proper dramatic vehicle for a piece of his advice. Here, however, he could not fall back on his favorite device of inventing a persona: "some Body to say it for you, when you don't care to appear yourself." But the technique he hit upon was very much like that, and it drew heavily upon his experience of creating journalistic masks; for here too he managed to divert attention from himself to persons whose predicaments were instructive. The essence of drama is conflict, as he knew. Thus, to scold his neighbors for their neglect of their icy sidewalks he invented an old man who was angry about falling down on the ice. To inveigh against calculating fathers who would marry their daughters without a dowry, he devised Anthony Afterwit, the young tradesman entrapped into stealing a wedding. Franklin knew that cautionary characters are more arresting to the reader than are exemplary ones.

He had always created personae whose purposes were thwarted, who were dogged by criticism, or who were misanthropically given to criticizing their neighbors. Silence Dogood, Martha Careful and Caelia Shortface, Patience, Poor Richard and Bridget Saunders all fit one another of these categories.

Part I of the *Autobiography* has as its structural principle a series of contrasting characters. Franklin places the story of his success into a context of failure. Failures are conspicuous among the supporting characters of this section of the memoirs: John Collins, James Ralph, Franklin's co-workers at the London printing house, Hugh Meredith, David Harry, and most deplorable of all, Samuel Keimer. The cautionary characters of the *Autobiography* are chosen or depicted so as to illustrate specific weaknesses of character which Franklin seems to have regarded as especially prejudicial and damaging to a young tradesman. Franklin concentrates on two major frailties of distinctly different kinds. One is drunkenness; the other is the failure to establish, prepare for, or practice diligently one's calling. In the first group of instances only the instrumental value of temperance is involved. However, Franklin's concept of vocation stems from a fundamental Protestant doctrine. Drunkenness ruins the tradesman's capacity for work, empties his pocketbook, and makes his creditors and his customers wary. Failure to find or to work hard at a calling manifests an inward rottenness. John Cotton, founding father of Massachusetts whose grandson and namesake was Cotton Mather, had written of the man who lives without a calling, "though thou hast two thousands to spend, yet if thou hast no calling, tending to publique good, thou art an uncleane beast." [10] Samuel Keimer and James Ralph are the "uncleane beasts" of Franklin's memoirs. John Collins and the London pressmen are the drunkards. Franklin's partner, Meredith, unites the two motifs of failure: he drank because he was working at the wrong calling. It is beside the point to accuse Franklin of distorting his relationship with Ralph or of ridiculing poor Keimer. They function in the narrative as personifications of weakness and error, just as Franklin makes his own youth an example of sober application.

In his choice and arrangement of examples Franklin employs the device he had recommended, of proceeding from simple to complex characters and situations. This pattern is observable in his treatment of drunkenness. Though himself the writer of drinking songs in his youth, Franklin had long considered temperance and sobriety cardinal virtues of the successful businessman. The *Autobiography* leaves the impression that drunkenness was the most prevalent and damaging vice that afflicted eighteenth-century tradesmen. Drink could swiftly ruin a promising career, as is demonstrated by the story of John Collins. Collins was the disputatious boyhood friend of Benjamin Franklin. It was after examining the texts of Benjamin's and Collins's arguments that Josiah Franklin advised his son to learn more about writing. Franklin encountered Collins again on his triumphant return to Boston in 1724 after seven months of success in Philadelphia, and Franklin remembers that when they were boys together Collins had more time for study than he had and "a wonderful Genius for Mathematical Learning." When Franklin last had seen him Collins had been "a sober as well as an industrious Lad; was much respected for his Learning by several of the Clergy and other Gentlemen, and seem'd to promise making a good Figure in Life" (*Autobiography,* p. 84). But in the interval Collins "had acquir'd a Habit of Sotting with Brandy" and was drunk daily. Collins resolved to return with Franklin to Pennsylvania, and his sotting was immediately costly as it prevented his going with Franklin to meet an influential man. "The then Governor of N York, Burnet . . . hearing from the Captain that a young Man, one of his Passengers, had a great many Books, desir'd he would bring me to see him. I waited upon him accordingly, and should have taken Collins with me but that he was not sober." In Philadelphia Collins toured the countinghouses offering them his mathematical ability; "but whether they discover'd his Dramming by his Breath, or by his Behaviour, tho' he had some Recommendations, he met with no Success in any Application." Collins lived on Franklin's generosity until an irreparable breach occurred between them. At length he shipped for Barbados to become a tutor. "He left me then, promising to remit me the first Money he should receive in order to discharge the Debt. But I never heard of him after" (*Autobiography*, p. 86).

At Watts's printinghouse in London Franklin earned the soubriquet of "the Water-American" for his campaign to reform the drinking habits of the English workmen. He proved that his nourishing breakfast of "hot Water-gruel, sprinkled with Pepper, crumb'd with Bread, and a bit of Butter in it" produced more and better work than their "muddling Breakfast of Beer and Bread and Cheese" (*Autobiography*, p. 101). The pressmen's beer was but one link in a chain of social ills. It kept them from doing good work and so kept their wages low. The six pints of beer a workman drank each day cost him four or five shillings per week, a substantial portion of his pay. "And thus," writes Franklin, "these poor Devils keep themselves always under." Franklin pictures the life of the English workman as wretched and futile enough to make his own possibly prudish abstinence seem to the reader the only reasonable behavior. "My constant Attendance . . . recommended me to the Master; and my uncommon Quickness at Composing, occasion'd my being put upon all Work of Dispatch which was generally better paid. So I went on now very agreably."

Franklin's first business partner is yet another example of a character weakened by drink, but, in Hugh Meredith, Franklin introduces other dimensions of the problem. He examines the causes of Meredith's drinking and its effects on customers and creditors, and so on Meredith's business. Hugh Meredith was born to farming but had apprenticed himself to Samuel Keimer. Franklin describes Meredith as having been "honest, sensible,

[he] had a great deal of solid Observation, was something of a Reader, but given to drink" (*Autobiography,* p. 108). Meredith's father hoped that through Franklin's influence his son might be reclaimed from liquor, and he proposed that the two young men go into business for themselves, promising to provide capital for the venture. Though the partnership was soon dissolved, it served to put Franklin on his feet in business. In the beginning the industry of both young men was admirable, but Meredith scarcely figures in the narrative after a short while. Noting "that I am apt to speak in the singular Number, though our Partnership still continu'd," Franklin explains that the entire management of the business lay upon him. "Meredith was no Compositor, a poor Pressman, and seldom sober" (*Autobiography,* p. 120). Financial problems developed. Meredith's father could not deliver the funds he had pledged, and Franklin's creditors demanded payment. Two of his friends came quietly to him offering to pay his debts; "but," he writes, "they did not like my continuing the Partnership with Meredith, who as they said was often seen drunk in the Streets, and playing at low Games in Alehouses, much to our Discredit." Meredith's drinking and frequenting taverns caused him to neglect his business and it drove business away from their shop. But in Meredith's case Franklin discloses the underlying cause of his failure as a printer and probably the cause of his drinking as well. Taking his leave of Franklin, Meredith explained, "I see this is a Business I am not fit for. I was bred a Farmer, and it was Folly in me to come to Town and put my Self at 30 Years of Age an Apprentice to learn a new Trade" (*Autobiography,* p. 123).

Meredith's failure is not the first instance in the *Autobiography* of a career blighted by neglect of calling. The story of James Ralph is an earlier and simpler example. Ralph was determined to make himself a poet, and it is the passage in which Franklin discusses his intention which hostile critics often cite to illustrate Franklin's low regard for poetry. However,

Franklin makes their mutual friend Charles Osborne the spokesman for his values here. "Osborne dissuaded [Ralph] . . . and advis'd him to think of nothing beyond the Business he was bred to; that in the mercantile way tho' he had no Stock, he might by his Diligence and Punctuality recommend himself to Employment as a Factor, and in time acquire wherewith to trade on his own Account" (*Autobiography,* p. 90). As Franklin tells the story, Ralph's courting of the Muse led him to abandon a family in Pennsylvania, live on Franklin's charity in London, take a tutoring position in the country using Franklin's name (so as to preserve his own unsullied for better literary days), and to write his unprofitable verses "till Pope cur'd him" in the *Dunciad*.[11] Franklin leaves Ralph's career on this note of aimlessness and futility, though in fact Ralph became by midcentury "one of the best political writers in England." [12] On the other hand, Franklin records the fact that Meredith returned to his true calling and so to ultimate success. "I gave him what he demanded and he went soon after to Carolina; from whence he sent me next Year two long Letters, containing the best Account that had been given of that Country, the Climate, Soil, Husbandry, &c. for in those Matters he was very judicious. I printed them in the Papers, and they gave grate Satisfaction to the Publick" (*Autobiography,* p. 123). Franklin's following up of Meredith's career is not merely a tribute to a friend who had helped launch his business. It illustrates, as does the career of James Ralph, the importance of diligence in a calling tending, as John Cotton put it, "to publique good."

In his recollections of Hugh Meredith, Franklin found a character compounded of strengths and weaknesses, virtues and vices. In the case of Samuel Keimer, he discovered a very paradigm of failure. Keimer was a fraud as a printer, indolent, and had, as Franklin says, "a good deal of the Knave in his Composition" (*Autobiography,* p. 79). It is not surprising that Keimer becomes the most fully developed supporting character

in the first book of the *Autobiography*. The decline of his fortunes, made inevitable by his comically knavish composition,
is played as the essential countermovement to Franklin's rise.
Indeed, Franklin is so careful to relate the two careers that
they might be plotted as a neat pair of curves.

Keimer was only half-prepared to practice his trade. Finding him newly set up in Philadelphia, the young Franklin "endeavour'd to put his Press (which he had not yet us'd, and of
which he understood nothing) in Order fit to be work'd with"
(*Autobiography*, p. 78). "Something of a Scholar," Keimer
wrote his indifferent verses in that famous slipshod fashion,
composing them "in the Types directly out of his Head."
Though he was just a boy, Franklin's brilliant promise attracted the attention of important people, and when the governor of the province approached the shop one day, it was
Franklin and not Keimer he had come to see. "I was not a
little surpriz'd," he recalls, "and Keimer star'd like a Pig
poison'd" (*Autobiography*, p. 80).

After eighteen months in London, Franklin returned to
Philadelphia and eventually to Keimer's employ. Franklin
soon realized that Keimer was willing to pay him good wages
only until he could train all of the apprentices, "and as soon
as I had instructed them . . . he should be able to do without
me" (*Autobiography*, p. 108). Though conscious of Keimer's
transparent scheme, Franklin stayed on knowing that he was
indispensable to the business. When Keimer contracted to print
paper money in New Jersey it was Franklin who contrived the
copperplate press and cut the devices. And again it was Franklin, rather than his boorish master, whom the prominent citizens of Burlington invited into their homes. Among the friends
he made there was the surveyor general, Isaac Decow, whose
own story of industry Franklin relates in the *Autobiography*
—along with Decow's prophetic opinion of the young Philadelphian. Decow, Franklin recalls, "was a shrewd sagacious old
Man, who told me that he began for himself when young by

wheeling Clay for the Brickmakers, learnt to write after he was of Age, carry'd the Chain for Surveyors, who taught him Surveying, and he had now by his Industry acquir'd a good Estate; and says he, I foresee, that you will soon work this Man out of his Business and make a Fortune in it at Philadelphia" (*Autobiography*, p. 113). It happened just as Decow said it would, for Franklin left Keimer no better able to conduct his business than he had ever been. While Keimer languished Franklin thrived. His superior product brought him profitable jobs, and his prominent friends provided him with some of the official printing of the province. Franklin recalls how he secured his credit as a tradesman by making certain to appear as industrious and frugal as he actually was. He "drest plainly," avoided the alehouses, and never went hunting or fishing. "And to show that I was not above my Business, I sometimes brought home the Paper I purchas'd at the Stores, thro' the Streets on a Wheelbarrow" (*Autobiography*, p. 126).

Summarizing the rewards of these exemplary business practices, Franklin contrasts his success with Keimer's inevitable and timely downfall. "Thus being esteem'd an industrious thriving young Man, and paying duly for what I bought, the Merchants who imported Stationary solicited my Custom, others proposed supplying me with Books, and I went on swimmingly. In the mean time Keimer's Credit and Business declining daily, he was at last forc'd to sell his Printing-house to satisfy his Creditors. He went to Barbadoes, and there lived some Years, in very poor Circumstances." Keimer, half-prepared for his trade, something of a voluptuary, "and a little Knavish withal," was driven from the field by industry, frugality, and prudence. Franklin closes this account of the rewards of industry and frugality with a story of prodigality.

[Keimer's] Apprentice David Harry, who I had instructed while I work'd with him, set up in his Place at Philadelphia, having bought his Materials. I was at first apprehensive of a powerful

Rival in Harry, as his Friends were very able, and he had a good deal of Interest. I therefore propos'd a Partnership to him; which he, fortunately for me, rejected with Scorn. He was very proud, dress'd like a Gentleman, liv'd expensively, took much Diversion and Pleasure abroad, ran in debt, and neglected his Business, upon which all Business left him; and finding nothing to do, he follow'd Keimer to Barbadoes, taking the Printinghouse with him. (*Autobiography*, p. 126)

In these passages Franklin summarizes three careers. He juxtaposes the conclusions of his rise and Keimer's decline. David Harry's venture is dismissed in a terse paragraph, which Franklin anticipates in the passage describing his own public display of industry and frugality. Franklin's detractors typically cite that passage as proof of his calculated manipulation of his public image. Franklin says, of course, that he was industrious and frugal first and then careful not to seem otherwise; the reader may choose to believe him or not, to despise him or not. In any case, the anecdote about pushing a wheelbarrow through the streets "to show that I was not above my Business," derives its full meaning from its context. David Harry was a young man with ability and influential friends. He failed because he appeared to put himself above his business. Here as in his account of Ralph, the London workmen, and throughout the narrative, Franklin presents the unhappy alternative to his "Way to Wealth." The reader's response to the choice is inevitable; he is "insensibly led" to Franklin's position.

It is this dramatic structure which makes the first book of the *Autobiography* the persuasive book that it is. It is for this reason that Franklin's memoirs succeed, while the exemplary biographies of Franklin based on the memoirs (those by Peter Parley, Parson Weems et al.) are cloyingly unconvincing. Mark Twain's parents *told* him about Benjamin Franklin; no wonder young Samuel Clemens rebelled. Franklin propounds a rigorous life style: an unappealing combination of hard work and self-denial. He promises a reward of "Affluence" or financial security—not of great wealth. But he does not dwell upon the pleasures of affluence, which has caused some of his critics to infer that he could not have known how to enjoy affluence or leisure. That is probably unfair. He was never allowed any leisure, but he implies he would have used it for his beloved experiments and observations in natural philosophy. But the point is that he employed a more persuasive device than the description of the good life. He presented instead the misery of self-inflicted failure and poverty. The *Autobiography* says, in effect, if a life of temperance and sobriety seems bleak and joyless, consider the life of the toper. If wearing the leather apron seems demeaning, consider the plight of the tradesman who dresses like a gentleman and cannot pay his tailor. A symbol of stagnancy, Barbados lies waiting to claim the sodden, the indolent, the prodigal.

Professor Sanford's engaging theory of Franklin's debt to Bunyan is devoted more to establishing the tradition than to demonstrating how the *Autobiography* sustains it. In fact, Franklin discarded as useless much of the rhetorical and metaphoric paraphernalia of the spiritual autobiographers and allegorists. He retained, however, their sharpness of focus: their adherence to a single aspect of life as their subject. Franklin states his purpose explicitly, and the dramatic structure of the book—his choice and arrangement of incidents—admirably serves that purpose. *The Autobiography of Benjamin Franklin* has had its social and economic implications, its impact on the American national character, because first of all it succeeds as all literature must, as a persuasive fable.

4

Benjamin Franklin the journalist became Benjamin Franklin the autobiographer with that grace and apparent ease that typified his performances throughout his life. He was, of course, a genius as Mark Twain observed. But he was a genius who believed in calling and was diligent in his; he kept his literary shop as he kept his printshop, so that one day they would keep him. His long and arduous apprenticeship as a writer laid the foundation for the work that would make his lasting literary reputation secure. He learned to construct fables and he learned to create characters; he learned to make his characters speak as though they were alive and real, and he learned to modulate his own voice so as to instruct his readers without seeming to do so. He learned to write quickly, accurately, and concisely, for his time at his writing desk was always short and the stakes were frequently high. We have looked closely at the manner in which he narrated his life, and we have examined a rather narrow aspect of the life he narrated. I find that I have liked and defend Franklin in this study. I can offer no excuse or apology for liking him; a great many people do. I have tried to defend him against the misreading of his works and of his intentions, where we are able to reconstruct the latter. Sometimes the distortion of his works and purposes has been willful, often merely careless. Franklin is an historical phenomenon. In its troubled search for its own identity, a young nation has found a plausible model in Franklin. Unlike those other great symbolic Americans: Washington, Jackson, Lincoln, Benjamin Franklin could not be regarded as an artifact, cast as it were in bronze by patriotic biographers and historians. Franklin was alive, real, to Nathaniel Hawthorne reflecting on the miniatures of him in the Louvre and to countless other readers of his memoirs. He was, to use biographer W. C. Bruce's phrase, "self-revealed."

I have tried to underscore the fact that Benjamin Franklin is not so much self-revealed as self-created, and by an examination of the documents central to the historical phenomenon (the *Autobiography* and *Poor Richard's Almanac*) to suggest the sort of distortions involved in the Franklin phenomenon. Readers have typically encountered two of Franklin's works,

"The Way to Wealth" and the *Autobiography*. Finding the latter apparently founded on the principles inculcated by the former, readers have been led to simple, reasonable, and damaging generalizations about their author. David Levin keenly observes that Franklin's autobiographic pose of homely simplicity tends to disarm the reader, to put him too much at ease. Ultimately his manner of presenting himself and what Levin calls "the fine simplicity of his exposition" are misleading. But Franklin had studied long and hard the techniques of disarming his readers, putting them at their ease; he had labored to achieve brevity and simplicity in his prose. He would sacrifice his vanity—in the form of his own voice—if he could find a voice, a pose which would carry his message more forcefully. A survey of Franklin's journalistic writings reveals how this attitude and his talent as a rhetorician evolved.

Notes
Index

Notes

CHAPTER ONE: Franklin's Journalism

1. *Studies in Classic American Literature* (New York, 1961), p. 9.

2. *Israel Potter,* in *The Works of Herman Melville* (New York, 1963), XI, 70.

3. James's letter and that of Benjamin Vaughan (see below in the text) are inserted, according to Franklin's directions, between Parts 1 and 2 of the *Autobiography.* See *The Autobiography of Benjamin Franklin,* ed. Leonard W. Labaree et al. (New Haven and London, 1964), pp. 133–40. All subsequent citations of the *Autobiography* in this book refer to the Yale edition.

4. Quoted by Mellon's son, the secretary of the treasury, in his tribute to Benjamin Franklin, "Franklin, the Father of Thrift in America," *The Amazing Benjamin Franklin,* ed. J. Henry Smythe, Jr. (New York, 1929), p. 40.

5. For a full and delightful account of all this, see Irvin G. Wyllie, *The Self-Made Man in America* (New Brunswick, N.J., 1954).

6. "The Late Benjamin Franklin," *Sketches New and Old, The Writings of Mark Twain* (New York and London, 1917), XIX, 214–15.

7. *The Great Gatsby* (New York, 1925). See David Levin, "The Autobiography of Benjamin Franklin: The Puritan Experimenter in Life and Art," *Yale Review,* 53 (December 1963), 258–75. Levin alludes to *The Great Gatsby,* p. 275.

8. "Benjamin Franklin," reprinted in *Benjamin Franklin and the American Character,* Charles L. Sanford, ed. (Boston, 1955), p. 53, from Angoff's *A Literary History of the American People* (New York, 1931).

9. *Shelburne Essays,* Fourth Series (New York, 1907), p. 152.

10. Hawthorne, *French and Italian Notebooks,* ed. George Parsons Lathrop (Boston and New York, 1883), p. 28.

11. Cairns, *A History of American Literature* (New York, 1912), p. 97.

12. Richard E. Amacher, *Benjamin Franklin* (New Haven, 1962), p. 47.

13. See Frank Luther Mott, *American Journalism* (New York, 1950), pp.

21–22. For a more detailed treatment, see Elizabeth C. Cook, *Literary Influences in Colonial Newspapers, 1704–1750* (New York, 1912), pp. 31–56.

14. Walter Graham, *English Literary Periodicals* (New York, 1930), pp. 69–70.

15. See *The Spectator,* ed. Donald F. Bond (Oxford, 1965), I, xxxviii. Quoted from Defoe's *Review,* October 4, 1711.

16. Graham, *English Literary Periodicals,* p. 55.

17. *Autobiography,* p. 88. Franklin recalled rationalizing his eating of fresh cod, notwithstanding his vegetarianism.

18. *American Weekly Mercury* (Philadelphia), No. 1050 (February 12, 1740). Actually an extra or *Postscript* to the *Mercury,* printed by Franklin's competitor, Andrew Bradford. The criticism was of Franklin's conduct in printing the proceedings of the Pennsylvania Assembly.

19. *The Papers of Benjamin Franklin,* ed. Leonard W. Labaree (New Haven, 1959–), I, 328. Hereinafter referred to as *Papers.* The essay, first prepared for Franklin's Junto, was then published in the *Pennsylvania Gazette,* August 2, 1733.

20. *Autobiography,* p. 66. Line 574 of the *Essay on Criticism.*

21. The three quoted rules are from "On Literary Style," *Papers,* I, 329–30.

22. *Proposals Relating to the Education of Youth* is reprinted in *Papers,* III, 395–421.

23. "Idea of the English School" is reprinted in *Papers,* IV, 101–8.

24. Letter to William Strahan, February 12, 1745. *Papers,* III, 14.

25. *Papers,* II, 333. From *Poor Richard,* 1742.

26. Ward, "Who Was Benjamin Franklin?" *The American Scholar,* 32 (Autumn 1963), 553.

27. *Papers,* II, 220. From *Poor Richard,* 1739.

CHAPTER TWO: Silence Dogood of Boston

1. Miller, *The New England Mind: From Colony to Province* (New York, 1953), p. 334.

2. *Ibid.,* p. 344.

3. Quotations from the *New-England Courant* are transcribed from the facsimile edition, Perry Miller, ed. (Boston, 1956).

4. Quoted in Miller, *The New England Mind,* pp. 337–38.

5. Quotations from the Dogood Papers have been transcribed from the facsimiles of the *New England Courant.* These transcriptions have been read against those in *Papers,* I, 8–45. I have not noted variant readings, but have, in those instances, followed the *Courant.*

6. Horner, "Franklin's 'Dogood Papers' Re-Examined," *Studies in Philology,* 37 (1940), 521.

7. *Ibid.,* p. 501.

8. The third volume of the *Spectator* included papers number 170–251.

9. *The Spectator,* ed. Donald F. Bond, II, 204–5.

10. See Miller, *The New England Mind,* p. 343, and Horner, " 'Dogood Papers' Re-Examined," p. 515.

11. The *Spectator,* ed. Donald F. Bond, II, 367.

12. Ibid., pp. 356–57, 438. No. 220 was written by Steele.

13. See *Papers,* I, 31, n. 2.

14. See Horner, " 'Dogood Papers' Re-Examined," pp. 511–12.

15. See *Papers,* I, 43, n. 3.

16. Quoted ibid., p. 45, n. 7.

CHAPTER THREE: The Philadelphia Years

1. Joseph Breintnall was a charter member of Franklin's Junto, a Quaker merchant, something of a writer and naturalist.

2. *Papers,* I, 112.

3. According to Anna Janney DeArmond, Bradford's biographer. See *Andrew Bradford, Colonial Journalist* (Newark, Delaware, 1949), p. 45.

4. *Papers,* I, 115.

5. Ibid., p. 121.

6. Ibid., p. 122.

7. Ibid., p. 127.

8. The writer, signing himself "Morisini," concluded with a particularly knavish triplet:

> From barking Cur the Mastiff flies,
> But when behind, he bites his Thighs,
> He turns—and pisses out his Eyes.

9. Or Eurcrites and Putibolus. The compositor was inconsistent.

10. *Papers,* I, 184.

11. For the entire sequence, see ibid., pp. 221–26.

12. October 15, 1730. See ibid., pp. 177–81.

13. According to the Yale editors, who inserted the piece in deference to tradition. See ibid., p. 182.

14. Ibid., p. 238. Cf. *Autobiography,* pp. 127–28.

15. *Papers,* I, 242.

16. Ibid., p. 247.

17. This exchange appears ibid., II, 128–29.

18. "The Speech of Miss Polly Baker" and a brief summary of its history appears ibid., III, 120–25. For a complete treatment of the subject see Max Hall, *Benjamin Franklin and Polly Baker: The History of a Literary Deception* (Chapel Hill, N.C., 1960).

19. *Papers,* I, 250.

20. Ibid., p. 318. Frosting a shoe meant attaching a pointed piece of iron to its heel for walking on the ice.

21. Ibid., p. 188.

22. Ibid., II, 12–15. B.F.'s own account is in the *Autobiography,* pp. 174–75.

For the political and social background of this, as well as a complete account of the volunteer fire department subsequently founded in the city, see Harold E. Gillingham, "Philadelphia's First Fire Defenses," *Pennsylvania Magazine of History and Biography*, 56 (October 1932), 360–62.

23. The "Apology for Printers" appears in *Papers*, I, 194–95.

24. *American Weekly Mercury*, January 6, 1735. Quoted by DeArmond, *Andrew Bradford*, p. 98.

25. Quoted by Elizabeth C. Cook, *Literary Influences in Colonial Newspapers, 1704–1750*, pp. 86–87.

26. Quoted by Guy Soulliard Klett, *Presbyterians in Colonial Pennsylvania* (Philadelphia, 1937), p. 43. In the last sentence some transcriptions read "scent" for "scout."

27. The "Dialogue Between Two Presbyterians" appears in *Papers*, II, 27–33.

28. See *Papers*, II, 29, n. 7. Theophilus Grew was a successful private teacher of mathematics to whom B.F. sent his son, William, in 1738.

29. For details of their response and more about the Synod's action, see Richard Webster, *History of the Presbyterian Church in America* (Philadelphia, 1857).

30. See *Papers*, II, 37.

31. Ibid., p. 66.

32. Ibid., p. 94.

33. Quoted from Richard Webster by Klett, *Presbyterians in Colonial Pennsylvania*, p. 144.

34. *Papers*, II, 259.

35. From the *Gazette* of July 24, 1740. Ibid., p. 261.

36. N[icolas] B. W[ainwright], "Nicolas Scull's 'Junto Verses,'" *Pennsylvania Magazine of History and Biography*, 73 (January 1949), 82.

37. *Autobiography*, p. 124. Franklin was in error on this point, however: Andrew Bradford printed the currency voted in 1729. Franklin got the contract for £40,000 authorized in 1731. The pamphlet entitled *The Nature and Necessity of a Paper-Currency* appears in *Papers*, I, 141–57.

38. *Papers*, I, 160.

39. Ibid., p. 176.

40. Unlike the Royal colony of Massachusetts, the Province of Pennsylvania was a proprietary colony, owned by the descendents of William Penn, who named the governors and attempted to administer the colony as a profit-making operation.

41. See DeArmond, *Andrew Bradford*, pp. 87 ff.

42. So says Anna Janney DeArmond.

43. The "Conversation" appears in *Papers*, I, 333–38.

44. *Papers*, I, 181.

45. For details of the affair see Julius F. Sachse, *Benjamin Franklin as a Freemason* (Philadelphia, 1906), and *Papers*, II, 198–202. For a reflection on the events and the newspaper controversy see my essay, "The Bizarre Death of

Daniel Rees and the Continuity of Franklin Criticism," *Early American Literature,* 4 (1969), 73–85.

46. *Papers,* II, 236. The manuscript of the letter has not survived; the editors have published it as reprinted in the *Gazette* on December 11, 1740.

47. *Papers,* II, 264.

48. *American Weekly Mercury,* No. 1091. Reprinted ibid., pp. 265–69.

49. *American Weekly Mercury,* No. 1092. Reprinted in *Papers,* II, 273–74.

50. *Papers,* II, 275.

51. *American Weekly Mercury,* No. 1094. Reprinted ibid., pp. 277–78.

52. DeArmond, *Andrew Bradford,* p. 232.

53. *Papers,* II, 293.

54. Reprinted ibid., p. 304.

55. DeArmond, *Andrew Bradford,* p. 233. His reply appeared in the *American Weekly Mercury,* No. 1105. Part of it is reprinted in *Papers,* II, 305–6, n. 9.

56. See James Playsted Wood, *Magazines in the United States* (New York, 1956), p. 8.

57. *The General Magazine* (facsimile), Lyon N. Richardson, ed. (New York, 1938), pp. 252, 256. The speech and the Assembly's reply appeared in the April issue and were dated April 15, 1741.

58. *The General Magazine,* p. 281.

59. Frank Luther Mott, *A History of American Magazines 1741–1850* (New York, 1930), p. 76.

60. *Poor Richard,* 1750. *Papers,* III, 454.

61. In this account of the political controversies of 1744–48, I am relying heavily upon Thayer's *Pennsylvania Politics and the Growth of Democracy* (Harrisburg, Pa., 1953), pp. 12–24.

62. *Plain Truth* is reprinted in *Papers,* III, 180–204.

63. Quoted in Thayer, *Pennsylvania Politics,* p. 21. See also *Papers,* III, 215–16.

64. Peters's letter is reprinted in *Papers,* III, 214–18.

65. *Papers,* III, 213. The letter is dated November 27, 1747.

66. Logan's letter also appears in *Papers,* III, 219.

67. Quoted in Thayer, *Pennsylvania Politics,* p. 22.

68. Penn's letter is reprinted in part in *Papers,* III, 186.

69. Quoted in Thayer, *Pennsylvania Politics,* p. 23. The letter is dated June 19, 1748. See also *Papers,* III, 186n.

70. An excerpt from Penn's letter appears in *Papers,* III, 188.

71. *Papers,* III, 318.

72. See Carl and Jessica Bridenbaugh, *Rebels and Gentlemen: Philadelphia in the Age of Franklin* (New York, 1942), p. 74.

CHAPTER FOUR: *Poor Richard's Almanac*

1. See *Autobiography,* p. 164n.

2. *Studies in Classic American Literature,* p. 14.

3. Harold A. Larrabee, "Poor Richard in an Age of Plenty," *Harper's Magazine*, 212 (January 1956), 64–68.

4. Carl Van Doren, *Benjamin Franklin* (New York, 1938), p. 109.

5. See "The Character of Poor Richard: Its Source and Alteration," *PMLA*, 55 (September 1940), 785–94.

6. "The Autobiography of Benjamin Franklin: The Puritan Experimenter," pp. 258–59.

7. See Ross, "The Character of Poor Richard," p. 792.

8. Ibid., p. 793.

9. See my discussion of the Anthony Afterwit letter in the text above.

10. *Papers*, I, 280.

11. Ibid., p. 311.

12. Ibid., pp. 349–50.

13. Ibid., II, 136.

14. Ibid., p. 163.

15. *Autobiography*, p. 145. See the footnote for the editors' rationale for their estimate of the date of this incident.

16. *Papers*, II, 191.

17. Ibid., pp. 217–18.

18. Ibid., pp. 246–47. The last of these predictions was indeed true; the Bradfords' did publish Leeds's *American Almanack* for 1740. The second prediction was probably directed at William Birkett, the compiler of *Poor Will's Almanack*. And Jerman replied to the prediction concerning him in the preface to his almanac for 1741, which Franklin printed: "And as for the false Prophesy concerning me, that Poor Richard put in his Almanack the last Year, I do hereby declare and protest, That it is altogether false and Untrue; which is evidently known to all that know me, and plainly shews, that he is one of Baal's false Prophets."

19. Ross, "The Character of Poor Richard," p. 792.

20. *Papers*, II, 332.

21. See my detailed discussion of the *General Magazine* affair in the text above.

22. Of New York, father of Philadelphia printer, Andrew Bradford.

23. Reprinted in *Papers*, II, 332, n. 2.

24. Ibid., III, 60.

25. Ibid., p. 100.

26. For these maxims see ibid., I, 311–18.

27. William Strode (1602–45). Identified by Wilfred P. Mustard in his letter "Poor Richard's Poetry," *Nation*, March 22, 1906, p. 239. Claude M. Simpson has informed me that the verses for December and March go back at least to 1640. Clearly Franklin composed little of Poor Richard's poetry.

28. See *Papers*, I, 351–78.

29. Ross, "The Character of Poor Richard," p. 793.

30. See *Papers*, II, 136–44 for the almanac for 1736. This may have been a

misprint. Recast for Father Abraham's speech in 1758, it read, "He that lives on hope will die fasting" (See *Papers,* VII, 342). The Yale editors do not reject the possibility that as they say, "The 'old' Father Abraham of 1757 may have been more discreet than the young Richard Saunders of 1735" (342, n. 18).

31. See *Papers,* II, 166–71.

32. The maxims for 1738 appear ibid., pp. 192–97.

33. *Papers,* II, 336.

34. Ibid., p. 399.

35. Ibid., III, 63. In 1734 the maxim read, "An innocent *Plowman* is more worthy than a vicious *Prince.*"

36. The maxims for 1747 appear ibid., pp. 101–6.

37. *Autobiography,* p. 196.

38. See *Papers,* III, 243–44.

39. Ibid., p. 244. See the note. One long essay occupied all of the available space in the almanacs for both 1753 and 1754.

40. The maxims for 1749 appear in *Papers,* III, 335–50.

41. The maxims for 1750 appear ibid., pp. 441–56.

42. Meister, "Franklin as a Proverb Stylist," *American Literature,* 24 (1952–53), 162.

43. *Papers,* IV, 84.

44. Ibid., p. 252.

45. Ibid., III, 346.

46. Ibid., V, 181.

47. Ibid., p. 473.

48. Ibid., VI, 315–16.

49. Ibid., IV, 323.

50. See ibid., pp. 332 ff and 332, n. 5.

51. *The Life and Times of Benjamin Franklin* (Boston, 1864), I, 329.

52. *Papers,* VII, 353, 355.

53. Ibid., pp. 75–76.

54. Ibid., p. 340.

55. See ibid., pp. 326–40. The Yale editors present an exhaustive account of the bibliographic history of "The Way to Wealth" through the eighteenth century.

56. See Newcomb's "The Sources of Benjamin Franklin's Sayings of Poor Richard," Diss., University of Maryland, 1957. Also Newcomb's essays: "Benjamin Franklin and Montaigne," *Modern Language Notes,* 72 (November 1957), 489–91; "Poor Richard's Debt to Lord Halifax," *PMLA,* 70 (June 1955), 535–39.

57. Ross, "The Character of Poor Richard," p. 794.

58. See especially Verner W. Crane, ed. *Benjamin Franklin's Letters to the Press, 1758–1775* (Chapel Hill, N.C., 1950).

59. Franklin proudly reprinted this tribute from Taylor's almanac in the *Pennsylvania Gazette* (September 17, 1747). See *Papers,* III, 237.

CHAPTER FIVE: *The Autobiography of Benjamin Franklin*

1. The story begins in 1776 when Franklin embarked for France as one of the American commissioners to Versailles. He packed a collection of his papers in a trunk, which was stored at the country home of his old friend, Joseph Galloway. During the war Galloway switched his allegiance to the British side, and sometime in 1777–78 the house was raided and the papers destroyed or scattered. Mrs. Galloway had remained in Philadelphia during the occupation; perhaps the manuscript of Franklin's memoirs had been removed from the trunk and kept in her possession. In any event, this is how it fell into James's hands. For a brief summary of the composition of Franklin's memoirs, see *Autobiography,* pp. 22–26.

2. In his important book, *The Examined Self: Benjamin Franklin, Henry Adams, Henry James* (Princeton, 1964), Robert F. Sayre posits a three-part structure for the *Autobiography,* corresponding to Franklin's three periods of composition: Twyford, Passy, Philadelphia. While this allows him to make some useful observations about the prose style of the Passy installment, it seems to me that Sayre is forced to make excessively nice distinctions between the French and Pennsylvania materials. He writes, "We can begin by noting . . . that the two later parts have one important thing in common: both are accounts of projects" (p. 26). Sayre's "two later parts" have essentially the same subject and purpose, so that I prefer to consider them one.

3. Sayre, *The Examined Self,* p. 31.

4. Levin, "The Autobiography of Benjamin Franklin: The Puritan Experimenter," p. 272.

5. Ward, "Who Was Benjamin Franklin?" p. 549.

6. Levin, "The Autobiography of Benjamin Franklin: The Puritan Experimenter," pp. 272–73.

7. Sayre, *The Examined Self,* p. 20.

8. Ward, "Who Was Benjamin Franklin?" p. 548.

9. Sanford's essay appeared in the *American Quarterly,* 4 (Winter 1955), 297–310; reprinted in *Benjamin Franklin and the American Character,* Charles L. Sanford, ed., pp. 64–73.

10. From Cotton's *The Way of Life* (1641) quoted in Miller, *The New England Mind,* p. 41.

11. Pope "cur'd" Ralph in the second edition of the *Dunciad:* "Silence, ye Wolves, while Ralph to Cynthia howls/And makes the Night Hideous—Answer him ye Owls!"

12. As Franklin himself says in the third installment of the memoirs, written in 1788. Labaree et al. record that not only did Ralph and Franklin renew their friendship in 1757, Ralph helped Franklin with his propaganda activities. (See *Autobiography,* p. 248, 295.)

Index